WITHDRAWN

HARVARD LIBRARY

WITHDRAWN

Architecture, Artifacts, and Arts in the Harmony Society of George Rapp
The Material Culture
of a Nineteenth-Century American Utopian Community

ARCHITECTURE, ARTIFACTS, AND ARTS IN THE HARMONY SOCIETY OF GEORGE RAPP
The Material Culture
of a Nineteenth-Century American Utopian Community

Paul Douglas

With a Foreword by
Donald Pitzer

The Edwin Mellen Press
Lewiston•Queenston•Lampeter

HX
656
.H2
D68
2008

Library of Congress Cataloging-in-Publication Data

Douglas, Paul.
  Architecture, artifacts, and arts in the Harmony Society of George Rapp : the material culture of a nineteenth-century American utopian community / Paul Douglas ; with a foreword by Donald E. Pitzer.
      p. cm.
  Includes bibliographical references and index.
  ISBN-13: 978-0-7734-4877-3
  ISBN-10: 0-7734-4877-2
  1. Harmony Society--History. 2. Collective settlements--United States--History--19th century. 3. Material culture--United States--History--19th century. I. Title.

  HX656.H2D68 2008
  974.8'92--dc22
                                        2008048034
hors série.

A CIP catalog record for this book is available from the British Library.

Front cover: "The Goddess in the Garden", a life-sized carved figure of *Harmonie*, a symbol of the Society, that graces George Rapp's garden Pavilion in Economy

Copyright © 2008 Paul Douglas

All rights reserved. For information contact

        The Edwin Mellen Press   The Edwin Mellen Press
        Box 450   Box 67
        Lewiston, New York   Queenston, Ontario
        USA 14092-0450   CANADA L0S 1L0

The Edwin Mellen Press, Ltd.
Lampeter, Ceredigion, Wales
UNITED KINGDOM SA48 8LT

Printed in the United States of America

For Matthew and Justin

Contents

List of Illustrations vii
Foreword by Donald Pitzer ix
Acknowledgements xiii
Introduction 1
Chapter 1: The Harmony Society: An Historical Survey 15
Chapter 2: The Town Planning of the Harmony Society 39
Chapter 3: Harmonist Buildings 67
Chapter 4: Harmonist Furniture 127
Chapter 5: Arts and Artifacts 145
Chapter 6: The Harmony Society: Reflections on the Material Culture 175
Appendix – Periodicals Subscribed to by the Harmonists 183
Bibliography 185
Index 199

List of Illustrations

1. Inscription on the back of a stair riser in No. 2 dormitory

2. New Harmony as envisioned in a drawing by Stedman Whitwell

3. Map of 17th century Iptingen, Germany

4. Map of Harmony, Pennsylvania

5. Medieval style buildings at the Ephrata Cloister

6. Log house at Harmony, Pennsylvania, ca. 1805

7. Floor plans of a typical Rhine Valley dwelling

8. Dormitory No. 2 at New Harmony, Indiana

9. The George Rapp House from the rear

10. Lintel details at Harmony, Pennsylvania

11. The classical pediment of the Frederick Rapp House in Harmony

12. Clock face from the church at Harmony

13. The 1822 church at New Harmony

14. The 1822 church from a drawing by David Dale Owen

15. The Grotto at Economy

16. The Granary at New Harmony

17. Birds eye view of Economy

18. Wine cellar at Economy

19. The 1829 cotton factory at Economy

20. Harmonist table and *stuhl*

21. Trunk with rounded top at New Harmony

22. Cupboard (dish or wine) at Economy

23. Single bed at Economy

24. George Rapp's bed at Economy

25. Trustees Room in the Rapp House

26. Harmonist clothing in the 1870s

27. Rose motif from the grave stone of John Rapp at Harmony

28. Newell post with the rose motif in the George Rapp House

29. Fire engine at New Harmony

30. Water pump at Economy

31. The Baker House at Economy

32. Feast Hall at Economy

33. Feast Hall Interior

34. Granary at Economy

35. Rapp House at Economy

36. Church at Economy

37. Interior of Grotto

38. Map of New Harmony by Eusebius Böhm

39. Drawing of factory machinery at Economy

40. Pelican on slipware plate at Economy

41. Silk tribute piece for George Rapp

Foreword

Next to the Shakers, the Harmony Society of George Rapp was one of the best-known and economically successful communal utopian movements in 19th Century America. Yet, unlike the Shakers, the material culture of Rapp's Harmonists has not gained wide public or scholarly notice, this despite the fact that the 1,600 Germans who followed their millennial prophet to the United States after 1803 planned and built three architecturally fascinating towns – towns with churches, gardens, mills, factories, stores, schools, dwellings, and dormitories. Thousands of visitors each year visit the museums, interpretative centers, and restored buildings in these villages: Harmony, Pennsylvania, where Rapp's Harmonists lived from 1804 to 1814; New Harmony, Indiana, their home from 1814 to 1824; and Economy (now Ambridge), Pennsylvania, where they persisted until 1905.

Published accounts have largely neglected the importance and implications of the Harmony Society's built environment. Most histories have focused on the Harmonists' religious beliefs, communal organization, and financial success. These works emphasize the Harmonists' Radical Pietism, pacifism, celibacy, and millennialism. They detail the harmony and disharmony produced by Rapp's charismatic, authoritarian leadership. And they explain their capitalistic achievements, trading their produce and products in twenty-two states and ten foreign countries and pioneering in the railroad, steel, and oil industries as well as in silk production.

Paul Douglas's book addresses this material culture vacuum left by such previous works. His research, begun in the 1960s, is presented here as the first effort designed exclusively to explain the nature and significance of Harmonist town planning, architecture, furniture, and cultural interest in the arts. It puts the Harmony Society story in the context of cultural and communal history. It gives readers a graphic, illustrated description of the architectural styles and features that influenced Harmonist leaders. It also provides a comparative analysis with the material culture of other major historic communal groups. In addition to the Shakers, these groups include the Seventh-day Baptists of Ephrata, Pennsylvania; Separatists of Zoar, Ohio; Perfectionists of Oneida, New York; Inspirationists of Amana, Iowa; Janssonists of Bishop Hill, Illinois; and the communities of the secular Owenites and Fourierists.

Douglas convincingly argues that Harmonist leaders had to keep their communal villages progressive and experimental to insure that members not be lured away by the worldly attractions of American society. One way was to shed gradually the medieval architectural influence of their German past and to embrace the Renaissance style with its Classical elements as well as certain Georgian designs. This placed the Harmony Society architecturally midway between the medieval structures of the Ephrata Cloister and the futuristic towns planned by Robert Owen and Charles Fourier.

The influence of Harmonist religious beliefs and practices upon their material culture is clearly pointed out. As millennialists, they fastened upon the golden rose allusion that Martin Luther used in referring to the New Jerusalem in his translation of Micah 4:8. They made the rose their symbol for the coming kingdom of God, placed it on several structures, and used it as their trademark. This rose greeted members on the pediment of the main door as they entered their brick cruciform church in New Harmony. Lilies, pelicans, and the Virgin Sophia appear as mystical elements on Harmonist buildings and artifacts. Their celibacy affected the nature of housing in Economy. Those still having children were housed on the outskirts of town. Ever practical, the Harmonists adjusted their architecture to suit new circumstances. They first constructed dormitory-like community houses in New Harmony, mostly to lodge the growing number of maturing young people of both sexes. No such lodgings were built later in Economy. Douglas reasons that perhaps the communal father discovered that his young disciples living together and influencing each other might become disruptive to the community. At Economy Rapp scattered them into households throughout the village. Perhaps surprisingly, we also learn that despite the Harmony Society's commitment to the equality of primitive Christian community of goods, preferential treatment was commonplace. It occurred from the dimensions and appointments of Father Rapp's house right down to how close your house was to his and to the differing sizes of custom made beds.

By exploring Harmony Society appreciation, acquisition, and creations in the arts, painting, sculpture, and music, Douglas explodes the myth of the unsophisticated German peasant that has hounded the Harmonists' path. George Rapp's house in Economy was decorated with expensive religious and secular paintings still there today. A large statue of a female figure representing Harmony still graces Rapp's garden Pavilion, and is "The Goddess in the Garden" to whom Douglas refers. Music was composed, commissioned, played, and published by the Harmony Society on its own press. The Harmonist library was well stocked with an array of books, magazines, and newspapers. Their schools instructed both girls and boys in a broad liberal arts curriculum until age fourteen. Then girls were apprenticed in household duties and boys in the trades.

Thus, Douglas achieves his objective to reveal new insights into the Harmonists themselves through their material culture. In his words, they "were not isolated visionaries, blind to the cultures of the past and to those surrounding them." Instead they were "aware of and took from these cultures in the planning of their villages and in the style of their structures." Second, "the Harmonists did not eschew the 'worldly' arts as antithetical to their communal purpose" . . . [but] used these 'worldly' styles in their furnishings . . . ." Third, the Harmonists "were progressive and experimental, capable of changing to meet the social, cultural, intellectual, and physical needs of the members . . . ."

Although the Harmony Society ended in 1905 and its considerable assets reverted to the state of Pennsylvania in 1916, its three towns continue as living villages. Readers still can see many of the buildings, furnishings, and artifacts Douglas describes. The most recent information on Harmonist-related events and developments in each of the Harmony Society towns can be found on their websites: Harmony at www.harmony-pa.us; New Harmony at www.usi.edu/hnh; and Old Economy Village at www.oldeconomyvillage.org .

The harmony and peace reflected in the Harmonists' villages, art, music, and philosophy speaks to the needs of our 21st Century. In 1824, George Rapp, in his *Thoughts on the Destiny of Man*, described New Harmony in idealistic terms as a place "where those who occupy its peaceful dwellings, are so closely united by the endearing ties of friendship, confidence and love, that one heart beats in all, and their common industry provides for all. . . . one lives in the breast of another, and forgets himself; all their undertakings are influenced by a social spirit, glowing with noble energy, and generous feeling, and pressing forward to the haven of their mutual prosperity."(p. 66)

May Paul Douglas's book move us in this direction.

Donald E. Pitzer
Professor Emeritus of History
Director Emeritus, Center for Communal Studies
University of Southern Indiana
Evansville, Indiana

Acknowledgements

I would like to thank Dr. Donald Pitzer, one of America's foremost scholars of communal societies, for his sage advice and suggestions regarding my approach to the Harmony Society. Dr. Joe White of the University of Pittsburgh provided valuable insights on the Harmonist period in Harmony, Pennsylvania, and being in Frederick Rapp's house, which is now owned by Joe, gave me a sense of the continuity of Harmonist history. I would also like to thank Sarah Buffington at Old Economy Village and Amanda Bryden at Historic New Harmony for their help in showing me the collections, archives and settings of their communities. Finally, Dan Reibel, the former curator at Old Economy, led me through attics and cellars in his attempt to help me understand the lives of the Harmonists. I would also like to thank the Office of Research Grants at Towson University for providing funding for my research.

Introduction

Some years ago when I was a student in a graduate course in American social and cultural history I volunteered to do a short paper on the importance of communes in American history. After reading what was said in the text used in the class, Alice Felt Tyler's Freedom's Ferment, and several other articles and books, I came to the conclusion that the communards had an interesting philosophy but that it was difficult to tell what their surroundings and daily lives were like. And so during a period of two years I visited a number of the remaining communes or historical sites to take photographs and get a sense of what living in a commune might be like. I was surprised by what I found. Rather than the sterile environments I expected, many of the villages were attractive and impressive. The Shakers' round stone barn at Hancock, Massachusetts, and their Trustees House with a double spiral stairway at Pleasant Hill, Kentucky, were examples of striking architecture. Other village objects that opened my eyes to the complexity of communal living were the large gambrel roofed church at Bishop Hill, Illinois; the impressive garden at Zoar, Ohio; the curved roof Shaker meeting house at Mt. Lebanon, New York, visited by Charles Dickens; and the factory building at Amana, Iowa. Knowing of my interest in communal societies, my in-laws gave my wife and me a beautiful walnut dining room table and chairs made to order at Amana. It was after these visits that I realized that the material culture of communal societies provided insights into community history, lifestyle, and dynamics, and that a study of the arts, architecture, and objects would give a different sense of the reality of the communal experience, one that written documents could not.

This study examines the material culture of the Harmony Society, a group of German Pietists who came to the United States in 1803 and ultimately built three villages: Harmony, Pennsylvania; New Harmony, Indiana; and Economy, Pennsylvania. The examination of the material culture at these villages gives insights into the changing attitudes of the Society. Since the Harmonists twice abandoned their American village and moved the entire community to a new location, their villages provide a model for determining how the Society adapted to place and time. Because of the process of abandoning and re-creating their built environment, changes in the philosophy of the community are more evident in its material culture than they would be if the Society had remained in the same village throughout its existence. As this study shows, the Society's evolving interactions with the outside world in both economic and artistic areas were reflected in its material culture. And as the group leaders struggled with the issue of maintaining celibacy, they experimented with different living conditions to accommodate those in the community who may have been questioning the celibate way of life.

The Harmonists were just one of hundreds of communes established in America in the eighteenth and nineteenth century. Some lasted for a few years, others for a few decades, and several, including the Shakers and the Harmonists, lasted for over a century. In Arthur Bestor's groundbreaking study of American communes, he puts the number of communal societies prior to 1860 at 130.[1] In a more recent study, Donald Pitzer includes not only the traditional groups that maintained a communal structure throughout their history but also those groups such as the Inspirationists at Amana who abandoned their communism in the 1930s but continued as members of the Inspirationist religious movement and private residents in the communities of their seven original villages. In an appendix, Pitzer lists nearly 1400 "communal utopias" founded in America up to 1965, including such groups as Benedictines, Branch Davidians, and Hutterites,[2] and since 1965 thousands of intentional communities have been created by the

---

[1] Arthur Bestor, Backwoods Utopias. (Philadelphia: University of Pennsylvania Press, 1970. Reprint of 1950 edition), 285.
[2] Donald Pitzer, America's Communal Utopias (Chapel Hill: The University of North Carolina Press, 1997), 449-494.

youth, ecology, and co-housing movements as described by Timothy Miller in The 60's Communes.

Among those communities with a lifespan measured in decades is the Ephrata Cloister in Lancaster County, Pennsylvania, founded in 1732 by the German Pietist Johann Conrad Beissel. Although the Ephratans are best known for their "cultural accomplishments in calligraphy, manuscript illumination . . . and choral music, [and the sisters] attained great proficiency in drafting, rubricating, and illustrating *Fraktur,*"[3] the Cloister attempted to emulate the monastic ideal of living simply and built their Chapel and *Saron* (sisters' house) in the medieval Germanic architectural style. While the Ephratans did interact with the outside world in producing and distributing books from the Ephrata press and in establishing commercial connections in Philadelphia to sell their products, if anything characterizes their philosoph y of interacting with the world only as much as was necessary to maintain their monastic lifestyle it is the style of the chapel and sisters' house that reinforced the belief that the modern world was to be used only as a means to maintain the purity of their existence.

The first communitarian group to have a national and even international reputation was the Shakers, who immigrated from England in 1774 led by "Mother" Ann Lee. As Arthur Bestor has observed,

> the missionary journey that Ann Lee and the elders of her church made through Massachusetts and Connecticut in the years 1781-83 was a momentous event in the history of communitarianism. American converts quickly outnumbered the original immigrants, for the first time in the history of such sects.[4]

After Ann Lee's death in 1784 she was succeeded by an English follower, James Whittaker, one of the eight original Shakers. When he died two Americans, Joseph Meacham and Lucy Wright, took over the leadership positions. The

---

[3] Donald Durnbaugh, "Communitarian Societies in America," in Pitzer, America's Communal Utopias (Chapel Hill: The University of North Carolina Press, 1997), 25.
[4] Arthur Bestor, Backwoods Utopias (Philadelphia: University of Pennsylvania Press, 1970. Reprint of 1950 edition), 31.

Shakers expanded rapidly in eighteenth-and nineteenth-century America, creating New England communities at Watervliet and New Lebanon, New York; Hancock, Tyringham, Shirley, and Harvard, Massachusetts; Enfield, Connecticut; Alfred and Sabbathday Lake, Maine; and Enfield and Canterbury, New Hampshire. By the beginning of the nineteenth century the Shakers expanded to the west, creating communities in Ohio and Kentucky, and in West Union, Indiana, their furthest west settlement. In the nineteenth century the Shakers built nineteen communities; at their peak in 1850 total membership reached almost 4,000. As Priscilla Brewer has observed, "during a history that has already spanned more than 200 years, at least 20,000 Americans have lived part of their lives as Shakers."[5] While the Shakers isolated themselves from the outside world to a certain extent, they were practical enough to understand that they needed external income if they were to survive and prosper, and so they successfully sold seeds and furniture in order to get hard cash from the outside world. During their glory years the Shakers built comfortable villages with a simple architecture and furniture that mirrored their philosophy of living simple lives.

Another successful utopian experiment was the Community of True Inspiration at Amana, Iowa. These Germans, who established their first settlement, Ebenezer, near Buffalo, New York, moved to Iowa in 1855 and built seven villages contiguous with one another. They continued to prosper until the great depression in the late 1920s, and in 1932 "Amana made its 'Great Change' from the communal system to a joint-stock corporation with the power to operate the businesses of the old community and to regulate any new private enterprises that might be established."[6] While no longer communistic today, the Inspirationists of Amana still sell handsome furniture as a way of sustaining their heritage. What Donald Pitzer calls "developmental communalism" has allowed

---

[5] "The Shakers of Mother Ann Lee," in Pitzer, America's Communal Utopias, 37.
[6] Jonathan Andelson, "The Community of True Inspiration from Germany to the Amana Colonies," in Pitzer, America's Communal Utopias, 197.

them to continue to exist as a religious movement and a reasonably prosperous community with a sense of communal history.

Not far from Amana was the Swedish inspired community of Bishop Hill, Illinois, which had a relatively short lifespan of fifteen years (1846-1861). At Bishop Hill over twenty buildings were erected, including the "Big Brick," a ninety-six room, four-story high dormitory.[7] The brick and stucco Steeple Building was designed in the classical revival style with Palladian facades. A large church with a gambrel roof seated some 1,000 people, although the number in the community was perhaps half that number. Both the impressive Steeple Building and the church still stand and are open to the public, the former once having a huge cooking pot displayed near its front door as a reminder of the communal meals that were prepared for the members.

In upstate New York, the reformer John Humphrey Noyes established and ran the Community of Perfectionists in Oneida. Relations between the sexes were quite unlike those between the celibate Shakers. Noyes advocated a system of "complex marriage" in which any man or woman in the community could cohabit with another member; Noyes also suggested that the young of one gender and the old of another should be allowed to have sexual relationships. Even more progressive, the system of "stirpiculture," a kind of eugenics, was practiced. According to this system certain men and women should be allowed to mate so that they could create perfect children. As a result, there were some twenty "stirps" born in the community. The Perfectionists enjoyed a high level of cultural sophistication, with a library and a theater for dramatic performances and concerts. As described in 1874 by Charles Nordhoff, who visited numerous communes in the nineteenth century, the women at Oneida did not wear traditional dresses, but a dress

> consisting of a bodice, loose trousers, and a short skirt falling to just above the knee. Their hair is cut just below the ears, and I noticed that the

---

[7] The "Big Brick" is no longer standing, but there is a painting of it done by Bishop Hill artist Olaf Krans.

younger women usually gave it a curl. The dress is no doubt extremely convenient; it admits of walking in mud or snow, and allows freedom of exercise; and it is entirely modest.[8]

By the 1870s the Perfectionists had some 283 members at Oneida and nearby Wallingford, and they supported themselves with many economic ventures, including sawmilling, blacksmithing, and silk production. But their most lucrative source of business income was from the production of steel traps, many of which were sold to the Hudson's Bay Company. When the Perfectionists dissolved the society in 1881 community holdings were estimated to be $600,000, and the remaining members adapted to their new circumstances by creating a joint stock company to manufacture the famous Oneida dinnerware that is still marketed today.

Other communities included the Zoarites of Ohio, who, like the Harmonists, came from Württemberg and were dissenters from the established Lutheran Church. The "Separatists" of Zoar, or Zoarites as they came to be called, established their village in 1818 and prospered under the leadership of Joseph Bimeler. After his death in 1853 the commitment of the members began to wane, and in 1898 the community was dissolved.

Among these communitarian groups, the Harmony Society was unique in creating three new villages (and selling two) in nineteenth century America. Unlike the Shakers who built a number of new villages while keeping the old ones, the Harmonists built and then sold two villages before settling on a third community north of Pittsburgh. Fortunately, much of the material culture of the Harmonists remains since the towns were not destroyed when the group left; instead, each town, including all of the buildings, was sold in its entirety to a new owner.

Before I visited the restored Harmonist towns, my readings in the history of communitarian societies had given me the impression that the Harmonists, like

---

[8] Charles Nordhoff, The Communistic Societies of the United States, from Personal Visit and Observation. (New York: Dover Publications, 1966. Reprint of 1875 edition), 282.

other Pietistic groups in the nineteenth century, led essentially dull lives in sterile surroundings. While many of the observations of travelers during the nineteenth century noted how efficient the Harmonist communities were, others indicated that while the Harmonists were efficient and practical they lacked the educational, cultural and artistic benefits available in the outside world. When William Newnham Blane described New Harmony, Indiana, in 1822 he said that the members were "a somewhat improved order of industrious monks and nuns, except they are very unwilling to have anything known about themselves. . . ."[9] He went on to say that the

> people, under the present system, are a set of well-fed, well-clothed, hard working vassals. They are very grave and serious. During the whole time I was at Harmony I never saw one of them laugh; indeed, they appeared to me to enjoy only a sort of melancholy contentment, which makes a decided difference between them and inhabitants of the other parts of the country, who without fanaticism or celibacy, find themselves well off and comfortable.[10]

An editorial in the Philadelphia National Gazette and Literary Register in 1820 responded to a positive description of New Harmony by a German visitor by saying that the advantages of life in mainstream America surpass those of life in the Harmony Society, which the editorialist compared to

> a fraternity whose desires and operations are limited to animal economy; who are chiefly intent upon the acquisition of acres and the increase of stock, and live in fat contented ignorance, strangers to the grandest creations and exercises of the mind, to the most animating emotions of the soul, and to the comprehensive wonder-working sympathies that arise from a large and diversified sphere of beneficence.[11]

John Woods, a neighbor of the Harmonists in Indiana, visited New Harmony in 1820 and observed that "they are a most industrious people; but the greater part

---

[9] Karl J. R. Arndt, A Documentary History of the Indiana Decade of the Harmony Society: 1820-1824 (Indianapolis: Indiana Historical Society, 1978) 2: 526.
[10] Ibid, 527.
[11] Ibid, 852.

of them are not very enlightened."[12] And another visitor to New Harmony, Thomas Hulme, said that

> this congregation of far-seeing, ingenious, crafty, and bold, and of ignorant, simple, superstitious, and obedient, Germans, has shown what may be done. But their example, I believe, will generally only tend to confirm this free people in their suspicion that labour is concomitant to slavery or ignorance.[13]

The famous J. A. Roebling, builder of the Brooklyn Bridge listened to a sermon by George Rapp in 1831 and said that "Old Rapp...on Sundays preaches unreasonable stuff to them [members of the Society], keeps them in stupidity and does not allow them to marry" and predicts (accurately, in fact) that "a crisis threatens the entire unnatural Rappish establishment soon."[14]

However, my examination of the Harmony villages led me to agree with those travelers who found the Society to be an admirable expression of the communitarian impulse. A century after the Harmonists disbanded, the remaining material culture at Economy reveals that the Harmonists lived in aesthetically pleasant surroundings, enjoyed a comfortable standard of living, and had opportunities for cultural and intellectual improvement.

With the exception of studies of the Shakers, it was not until the 1960s, a period when numerous communes were established by counterculturists, that authors of popular histories began to see the importance of the communitarian tradition in American history, although the record is spotty.[15] In Allan Nevins' and Henry Steele Commager's America, The Story of a Free People (1943) there is no mention of communes, nor is there anything about the role of communitarian societies in Samuel Eliot Morison's best selling The Oxford History of the American People (1965). Robert Kelly's The Shaping of the American Past

---

[12] Ibid, 32.
[13] Journal of a Tour in the Western Countries of America, September 30, 1818-August 8, 1819, Reprinted in Reuben Gold Thwaits, Early Western Travels, (Cleveland, 1904-1907) II, 55.
[14] Karl J. R. Arndt, Economy on the Ohio, 1826-1834 (Worcester: The Harmony Society Press, 1984), 627.
[15] For a discussion of the literature of communitarian societies, see Pitzer's "Bibliographical Essay," in America's Communal Utopias, 495-505.

(1978), a popular high school history text book, says nothing about the subject, nor, surprisingly, does Howard Zinn in his left-leaning A People's History of the United States (1980). Even as late as 1997 Paul Johnson's A History of the American People dismisses the Harmonists by saying that "they practiced auricular confession, among other things, and proved highly successful farmers and traders. But as they strictly opposed marriage and procreation they eventually ceased to exist."[16] The point is that for the most part the history of communes has been relegated to books on that particular topic, not general histories of America, and in that sense communitarian history has been marginalized in the types of books aimed at students and mainstream readers rather than academic specialists.

By studying the material culture of the Harmony Society I demonstrate several points that historians have not. First, the Harmonists were not isolated visionaries, blind to the cultures of the past and to those surrounding them, but were instead aware of and took from these cultures in the planning of their villages and in the style of their structures. Second, the Harmonists did not eschew the "worldly" arts as antithetical to their communal purpose. In his study of the artistic expression of Pietistic socialist communities Donald Drew Egbert contends that the Pietistic groups "frowned upon worldly fashion" and rejected "nearly all arts except those immediately useful and necessary either for simple everyday existence, such as architecture and the household arts, or for communal worship in some very simple Protestant and evangelical way."[17] As I show, however, the Harmonists used these "worldly" styles in their furnishings and owned both religious and secular paintings. Third, the Harmonists were not primarily conservative peasants with a reactionary conception of an ideal community pegged at a certain level of time. Instead, they were progressive and experimental, capable of changing to meet the social, cultural, intellectual, and physical needs of the members and of competing successfully with the outside world in financial matters. Not only did they sell their products to others, but they

---

[16] Ibid, 301.
[17] Donald Drew Egbert, Socialism and American Art, (Princeton University Press, 1967), 7.

bought items such as steam engines and steam boats from the outside in order to be progressive and competitive. Far from being a static community, the Harmony Society was fluid and flexible, except for George Rapp's rigidity regarding celibacy and his refusal to grant compensation to those who left the community for their time and contributions. It is this combination of the traditional and the innovative, the isolation from the outside world and the engagement with it, that made the Harmony Society such a complex group.

In this work I make generalizations about the Society as a result of my examination of the material culture. John Ruskin has said that "great nations write their autobiographies in three manuscripts, the book of their deeds; the book of their words; and the book of their art. Not one of these books can be understood unless we read the two others, but of the three, the only trustworthy one is the last." While Ruskin tended to emphasize the fine arts in his studies, I will discuss such "trustworthy" examples of material culture as town planning, domestic and public architecture, and household objects. My basic assumption is that the material culture often reveals attitudes and practices in the community that were not always consciously espoused or publicly announced. That is, since much of the material culture of the Harmonists was not a self-conscious expression of a particular philosophical tenet, it tends to reveal attitudes held by members as assumed beliefs. Jules Prown has observed,

> because underlying cultural assumptions and beliefs are taken for granted or repressed, they are not visible in what a society says, or does, or makes – its self-conscious expressions. They are, however, detectable in the way things are said, or done, or made – that is, in their style.[18]

Furthermore, according to Prown,

> By undertaking cultural interpretation through artifacts, we engage the other culture in the first instance not with our minds, the seat of our cultural biases, but with our senses. . . . To identify with people from the past or from other places empathetically through the senses is clearly a different way of engaging them abstractly through the reading of written

---

[18] "The Truth of Material Culture: History or Fiction?" in Stephen Lubar, History from Things, (Washington: Smithsonian Institution Press, 1993), 4.

words. Instead of our minds making intellectual contact with their minds, our senses make affective contact with their sensory experience.[19]

An example of this "affective contact" might be the recent experience I had in walking around the interior of one of the Society's dormitories at New Harmony, Indiana. There, on the back of an exposed stair riser, is an inscription made by one of the members of the community, and no doubt a resident of the dormitory, expressing his feeling about leaving the community as the Harmonists prepared to abandon New Harmony after a ten year period there and traveling to Pennsylvania to create a third village (Figure 1). There, still clearly visible after more than 180 years, is the statement "In the 24th of May, 1824 we have departed. Lord, with thy great help and goodness, in body and soul protect us. L Scheel." While the written records can tell us that this was "Lorenz Ludwig Scheel, born June 10, 1703. Arrived April 1807. Signed agreements February 15, 1816 and January 1, 1921. Withdrew March 25, 1826, Contributed $570.40; donation received $88,"[20] the inscription on the stairway gives us a sense of the nostalgia and anticipation of a man who was leaving a home that he had known for ten years to start a new life in a new village. While the written record may give us the facts, the material culture often allows us to glimpse the real people who were making the history of the Harmony Society.

The most detailed analysis of the material culture in this study is that of Economy, where the Society built the final expression of what they felt was the perfect community. Although much of the material culture at Harmony and New Harmony was removed when the community relocated, buildings remain at all three communities today and there are numerous artifacts at Old Economy, a museum village owned and administered by the Commonwealth of Pennsylvania. While an examination of the material culture of the Harmonists is a fruitful way to understand their world, it can also be misleading. For example, when the

---

[19] Ibid, 17.
[20] Karl J. R. Arndt, George Rapp's Disciples, Pioneers and Heirs: A Register of Harmonists in America (Evansville: University of Southern Indiana Press, 1992), 179.

Harmonists sold their second village to the social reformer and mill owner of New Lanark, Scotland, Robert Owen, they purposely removed objects in one of the Harmonist dormitories so that the new owners did not know that there were kitchen facilities there. In this case I rely on written records more than material objects. And, as I suggest in my chapter on the objects found at Harmony Society museums today, it is sometimes difficult to determine which of these objects were original to the community and which were put there in the twentieth century by restorationists and curators after the community had dissolved. One must recognize what has been called "the fecklessness of data survival," which refers to the phenomenon of selection by which some objects survive while others do not and by which, in the case of the Harmonists, some objects are used in museum displays as representing the Society while others are ignored or have been lost.

Although I base my conclusions as much as possible on the material evidence, this evidence can go only so far in explaining much of the history and philosophy of the Harmonists. As a result, I often depend on the extensive scholarship of Karl J. R. Arndt, whose "documentary histories" of the Harmonists are models of the effective use of primary documents to understand history.

Several times in this study I refer to the Shakers and often compare Shaker buildings and artifacts with those of the Harmonists. The reason for this is that there is an extensive body of scholarly studies on Shaker buildings and furniture, especially by Edward Deming and Faith Andrews, whose groundbreaking books first brought the qualities of Shaker style to public attention, and subsequently by other scholars who have extolled the virtues of the simple Shaker furniture as an expression of Shaker philosophy.

So much have Shaker furniture and music been studied that the Shakers have become iconic communards who modeled their buildings and their furniture on their philosophical tenets. Indeed, the Andrews referred to the furniture of the Shakers as "religion in wood."

The Harmonists, on the other hand, are not as famous. There are no furniture companies who have a line of Harmonist furniture as there are for the Shakers, no musical composition that has captured the interest of audiences as has Aaron Copeland's Appalachian Spring symphony which uses the Shaker song "Simple Gifts" as a refrain, and no Ken Burns' award winning documentary. As recently as the 1970s the remaining Shaker sisters who still wore their traditional dress occasionally met tourists at their villages, or addressed scholars at conferences to explain their way of life. I remember meeting the charming Eldress Gertrude Soule, one of the last of the Shaker leaders, at a conference in the 1970s in Cleveland.[21] When the Harmonists came to an end, however, there were no quaintly dressed members as nostalgic reminders of what the community had been. Instead the last two trustees, John and Susie Duss, the former a worldly man who gave concerts in New York City, eventually moved with his wife and some of the Harmonist objects to Florida when they retired. It was not until the 1930s when the Commonwealth of Pennsylvania provided funding to create a museum village at Economy that there was a revival in interest in the Harmonists.

Since the Harmonists went into a state of decline and finally dissolved at the beginning of the twentieth century they have been for the most part forgotten. Unlike the Shakers, they have no place in the cultural imagination of Americans. This study attempts to change this perception by showing how unique the Harmonists were not in rejecting the outside world but in often adapting to it, emulating it, and successfully competing with it in economic matters.

I approach the material culture not as a trained architect, archeologist, or town planner but as a cultural anthropologist attempting to find the social, religious, and economic implications revealed in Harmonist material culture. In my attempt to provide a new perspective on the Harmony Society I propose certain theses that I hope will lead to further reinterpretation and reevaluation by other scholars. I

---

[21] As of 2008, there were seven Shaker sisters and brothers at Sabbathday Lake, Maine.

also hope this study will stimulate scholars to examine the material culture of other communal societies.

One final note: Throughout this study I have used the terms "commune," "communal society," and "communitarians" interchangeably to reflect the current practice. The Harmony Society was, of course, "communistic," but I have avoided the term because of the negative connotations that persist from events in the Soviet Union and China in the twentieth century.

Chapter 1

The Harmony Society: An Historical Survey

Twenty-five miles north of Pittsburgh on the east bank of the Ohio River and surrounded by huge industrial plants and the sprawling, working-class town of Ambridge, Pennsylvania, lies an orderly little block of buildings, vineyards and gardens that were once parts of a thriving communitarian village. Called Economy by its inhabitants, this village was the third and last community built by the Harmonists, a group of German Pietists who came to America in the first decade of the nineteenth century. From 1805 to 1905 these practical (and mystical) Germans were living proof of the possibility of a successful communal society in an essentially capitalistic environment.

Several nineteenth century economic reformers, including Friedrich List, Hezekiah Niles, Matthew Carey, George Flower, Charles Nordhoff, William Hinds, and John Humphrey Noyes, cited the Harmonist village as a concrete example of economic prosperity and social harmony existing side-by-side. In 1820, for example, the American economist Matthew Carey, who was concerned about the destructive tendencies of American dependence upon foreign manufacturers, asserted that the Harmony Society was unique in combining agriculture and manufacturing successfully. "To this delightful picture of the blessed effects of judicious distribution of industry," he wrote in The New Olive Branch, "the statesman ought to direct his eyes steadily." The Harmony Society, he continued,

> holds out a most instructive lesson on the true policy to promote human happiness, and to advance the wealth, power, and the resources of nations.

...The Harmonists were true practical political economists. They did not, like so large a portion of the rest of the people of the United States lavish their wealth on the manufacture of a distant hemisphere, nor buy abroad cheap those articles which they could produce at home. In the sound and strong language of Mr. Jefferson, they "placed the manufacturer beside the agriculturist"; and they have reaped the copious harvest which such a policy cannot fail to secure.[1]

Although Thomas Jefferson himself was never fully reconciled to the existence of manufacturing in America, it seems likely that he would have approved of the Harmonist merging of manufacturing and agriculture. Not only would the manufacturing decrease the community's dependence upon Europe, his reasoning might have gone, but the agricultural interests would have prevented the growth of an environment dominated by machines. Perhaps a symbolic blending of the interrelatedness between manufacturing and agriculture is the Harmonists' shipping almost 1000 sheep to New Harmony where they would provide the wool that was processed in a factory that was driven by a steam engine.

While Jefferson did not advocate communism on the national scale, he was aware of the existence of the Harmony Society and other communistic groups in the United States, and wrote that

> on the principle of a communion of property, small societies may exist in habits of virtue, order, industry, and peace, and consequently in a state of as much happiness as Heaven has been pleased to deal out to imperfect humanity, I can readily conceive, and indeed have seen its proofs in various small societies which have been constituted on that principle.[2]

Through the intercession of some Baltimore friends, George Rapp actually did meet with Thomas Jefferson in July of 1804 so that he could present an unsuccessful petition to the President asking for special consideration for purchasing a large tract of land in Ohio. After the meeting Jefferson wrote Albert

---

[1] Matthew Carey, Essays on Political Economy (Philadelphia: American Antiquarian Society, 1822), 346.
[2] Andrew Lipscomb, ed., The Writings of Thomas Jefferson (Washington: The Thomas Jefferson Memorial Association, 1903) XV: 399.

Gallatin saying that Rapp's group could not wait until Congress convened since they did not have much money and that they were proceeding to lands on the Muskingum River "where they wish to have 40,000 acres at the usual price, but with longer indulgence as to the time of payment. I told them I would immediately write to you to consider what we could do for them."[3]

Even during the period when Economy's manufacturing interests overshadowed its agricultural production, the village was more similar to Jefferson's Monticello than it was to Birmingham, England, having none of the poverty, crime and overcrowded conditions that existed there, but incorporating such elements as steam machinery and large scale manufacturing that were characteristic of English manufacturing towns. At Economy the Harmonists managed to create a community that was based on the manufacture of woolen and cotton goods in steam-machine operated factories while maintaining a pleasant and comfortable environment for the inhabitants. The Harmonist leaders saw no reason why agriculture had to be the base for a successful community or why the use of steam machinery and large scale manufacturing should be excluded as it was in the more conservative Shaker communities and the commune at Ephrata, Pennsylvania, based on a medieval model of an agricultural village.

Economy was conceived as both a garden in the wilderness and an efficient and well run machine. According to George Rapp, the leader of the community, the Harmonist village was a "temple of God erected in a green and tranquil, and delightful valley, that those who are susceptible of light may find consolation and repose."[4] At the same time, Rapp continued, the economic system of the Society formed "one great machine, the principle wheel of which, when in motion, puts all the rest in operation, for common interest of the whole."[5] For the Harmonists, nature and the machine worked hand in hand in a community that was built in

---

[3] Karl J. R. Arndt, George Rapp's Harmony Society, 1785-1847 (Philadelphia: University of Pennsylvania Press, 1965), 66.
[4] [George Rapp], Thoughts on the Destiny of Man (Harmony, Indiana: The Harmony Society, 1824). Reprinted, (New York: Augustus M. Kelley, 1971), 11.
[5] Ibid, 70.

preparation for the millennium. Whatever made the community even more perfect, including economic prosperity, was both acceptable and necessary.

The balance of elements within the Harmony Society gradually emerged as it grew from its narrowly religious origins in the German Duchy of Württemberg. There, George Rapp (1757-1847), a vineyard worker and weaver living in the rural village of Iptingen, which was about twenty miles northwest of Stuttgart, rejected the rules and authority of the established Evangelical Lutheran Church and preached the Radical Pietist belief that the inner faith of the individual transcended the authority of the organized church. Rapp and his followers were among the numerous groups of Radical Pietists who believed in a return to a primitive Christianity to prepare themselves for the millennium. By 1776 Rapp had withdrawn from the church and was holding private religious services, despite the admonitions of the authorities. His pacifist views and his objections to public schools created a widening chasm between his followers and city officials. During the next few years Rapp was imprisoned briefly, his followers were fined for infractions of state laws, and the abrasive relationship between these separatists and the secular and religious authorities continued.[6]

By the turn of the century it became apparent to Rapp that Germany was no longer a suitable location for his religious beliefs; and so, after looking into the possibility of emigrating to France with his followers, Rapp finally decided that the combination of religious toleration and good land in America made it a perfect place to establish a religious community. In a letter from America to a disciple in Germany in 1804, Rapp expressed his conviction that there were opportunities available in the United States. "I shall never return to Germany," he wrote. "If my citizenship still continues, I will give it up. I am already a citizen here."[7]

While Rapp and a few of his followers examined land in Ohio and Pennsylvania, emigration of the Harmonists from Germany began. In July of 1804

---
[6] Arndt, George Rapp's Harmony Society, 1785-1847, 18-22.
[7] John S. Duss, The Harmonists, A Personal History (Harrisburg, 1943). Reprinted (Ambridge, Pennsylvania: The Harmonie Associates, 1970), 9.

the first group arrived in Baltimore, and by September two more groups had landed in Philadelphia. Not all of those who came to America settled in the community chosen by Rapp. Some purchased land in Ohio, and others formed a community under the leadership of Dr. P.F.C. Haller near present day Williamsport, Pennsylvania.[8] By December Rapp had purchased 4500 acres of land on the Connoquenessing Creek in Butler County, Pennsylvania. This property, thirty miles northeast of Pittsburgh, was to be the first of three Harmonist settlements.

An important event in the history of the community took place in February of 1805. At their village, named Harmony to represent the belief that it would be a model community combining the desired religious, social, and economic elements, the Articles of Association establishing the Harmony Society were signed by about 500 persons who contributed a total of $23,000 to the community. Some of the wealthier members contributed hundreds of dollars from the sale of their property in Germany, while others brought only their belongings.[9] There were five major points in the Articles, all of which were surprisingly free of dogmatic religious statements. Since the Harmonists were fleeing the established religion in Germany, it appears that they had little desire to make their own religion rigid and formalized.

The first of the Articles declared that the "subscribers renounce & remit all Estate & property . . . to Geo. Rapp and his Association . . . as a free gift or Donation for the Benefit & use of the Community there." Second, members agreed to abide by the laws and regulations of the community. Third, if any members withdrew from the community they would "demand no Reward, either for ourselves, or children, or those belonging to us." In return for their

---

[8] For a discussion of Haller's community see Joseph H. McMinn, Blooming Grove, A History of the Congregation of the German Dunkers (Williamsport, Pennsylvania, 1901), and Russel Gilbert, "Blooming Grove, The Dunker Settlement of Central Pennsylvania," Pennsylvania History, XX, 1 (January, 1953), 23-41.
[9] John A. Bole, The Harmony Society: A Chapter in German American Cultural History (Philadelphia: America Germanica Press, 1904), 9.

membership in the community the members received the privilege of attending religious meetings and of getting an education. Fourth, Rapp and his "Associates" promised to supply "the necessaries of Life, as Lodging, Meat, Clothing &c; and not only during their healthful days, but also when one or more of them became sick or otherwise unfit for labor." The fifth and final Article stated that if anyone left the community he would be entitled to a refund of "the value of his or their property brought in without interest."[10]

The paternalistic nature of the Harmony Society that characterized it throughout its existence is evident in the Articles. It was assumed that George Rapp was the leader of the community and that any policy not included in the Articles was determined by him.[11]

In return for this, Rapp had the obligation of providing the members with the physical and spiritual necessities of life. Although all of the Harmonists were working toward the common goal of creating a community within which they could prepare for the millennium, the shape that the community took was largely determined by George Rapp and his adopted son, Frederick Reichert Rapp (1775-1834). This relationship, with George the spiritual leader of the Society and Frederick the financial genius, served the community well for many years, but also became a source of some friction during the height of the Society's prosperity in Economy, Pennsylvania.

Since George Rapp did not advocate a community of goods when the group was in Germany, it appears that the conditions in America rather than a philosophical conviction led to its establishment. What was reported as a difficult first winter in Pennsylvania may have convinced Rapp that the only hope for survival and prosperity was the establishment of a communal system of production and consumption. However, the Harmonists went beyond the

---

[10] Duss, 419-420.
[11] When George Rapp signed the agreement for the purchase of land in Pennsylvania it was "Georg Rapp mit Gesellschaft" (George Rapp with the Society). See Arndt, George Rapp's Harmony Society, 72-73.

economic communalism that physical conditions dictated by providing education, health care, and housing for the community.

In addition to the economic and social benefits promised by a communal system, the Harmonists also had a Biblical precedent to follow. Like a number of other religious communitarian societies in the eighteen and nineteen hundreds, including the Shakers and the Society of Separatists of Zoar, Ohio, the Harmonists put to practical application the Biblical injunction found in Acts which states that "the multitude of them that believed were of one heart and one soul; neither said any of them that ought of the thing He possessed was his own; but they had all things in common." According to Harmonist philosophy on this matter

> Men view the treasures of heaven as a common stock; why not consider then the treasures of the earth in the same light? It is reasonable to suppose that he who cannot learn to share with his brother in this life, will not expect to find happiness in the heavenly society of men, unless he first learn and practice the social virtues here among his fellow creatures.[12]

The Harmonists, like the other sectarian communal societies, had a strong religious basis for their communism and thus were able to make the community a moral as well as an economic necessity. Unlike the Pilgrims, another group forced to adjust to conditions in a new environment, who adopted communism only to carry them over a difficult time and then abandoned it, the Harmonists maintained their communal system throughout their history. The apparently pragmatic nature of the Harmonists and of other Pietistic groups stemmed in part from their emphasis on setting up communities similar to those of the primitive Christian church described in the Bible. These Pietists were free to innovate and experiment as long as the Bible provided authority. The result was a combination of Biblical authoritarianism with experimental and pragmatic activism.[13] The Harmonists, no

---

[12] George Rapp, Thoughts on the Destiny of Man, 16.
[13] Sidney E. Mead, "Denominationalism: The Shape of Protestantism in America," in Paul Goodman, ed. Essays in American Colonial History (New York: Holt, Rinehart and Winston, 1967), 561.

less than the Puritans who followed a course of economic individualism, had their own "City Upon a Hill," but one based on communism and paternalism. If one reads God's grace in terms of economic success, it appears that both groups were blessed.

Beginning with Plato's The Republic the nuclear family has been seen by a number of utopian visionaries and practical communitarians as an institution which diminished the individual's dedication to the community as a whole. According to Plato, the nuclear family diverted man's energies and interests from the community, where they rightly belonged, to the husband, wife, or children. Plato's solution to this problem was a community of wives for the Guardians (the community leaders) so that they could satisfy their sexual desires without becoming involved with a family. In the sixteenth century Thomas More's response to the exclusiveness of the nuclear family was to retain the monogamous family while at the same time to have members belong to a larger "family" of from ten to sixteen members who would gather together for meals with other families. Another alternative was suggested by Charles Fourier, the nineteenth century French reformer, who saw marriage as a repressive and destructive element in society and contended that all members of his Phalanx would be allowed to indulge in sexual intercourse outside of the institution of marriage. According to Fourier, if men and women could relieve their sexual tensions, they would devote their energies to the needs of the community.

These philosophers and reformers did not consider sex in itself to be evil, but saw the intimate and exclusive relationships formed by monogamous marriages as decreasing dedication to the "state." Philip Slater has hypothesized that the more totalitarian the society, "in terms of making demands upon the individual to involve every area of his life in collective activity, the stronger will be the prohibition against dyadic intimacy."[14] In that it creates the possibility of a self-

---

[14] Philip Slater, "On Social Regression," American Sociological Review, XXVIII, 3 (June, 1963), 339-369. Slater observes that it is possible to have a prohibition of dyadic intimacy while at the same time encouraging sexual promiscuity, thus revealing "that the basis of the proscription is not

23

sufficient and exclusive sub-unit that is not emotionally dedicated to the larger society, the monogamous marriage poses a threat to that society.

In America many of the successful nineteenth-century communitarian societies were either celibate or in some way eliminated the nuclear family as a means of maintaining group dedication, while most of the unsuccessful communities did not advocate celibacy. Celibacy was a "commitment mechanism"[15] by which members sacrificed something valuable. "In the eyes of the group and in the mind of the individual, sacrifice for a cause makes it sacred and inviolable. It also represents a gesture of trust in the group, indicating how important membership is."[16]

In addition to the benefits to the community as a social structure, celibacy was also desirable for the Harmonists as a means of spiritual preparation for the millennium. The Harmonists believed that before the fall, Adam was a dual being who had both the male and the female sexual elements within himself. In such a person sexual intercourse was unnecessary. However, after the fall of Adam, which resulted from his desire for companionship upon seeing the animals of the world pass before him, a female counterpart was created. In his fallen state man's sexual elements became separate, making all intercourse contrary to God's original design and therefore sinful. The Harmonists believed that the Biblical command to "be fruitful and multiply" referred to man before his fall. In his

---

fear of sexuality but fear of libidinal contraction." Both Fourier's system and that advocated by John Humphrey Noyes at Oneida are examples of this combination.

[15] See Rosabeth Moss Kanter, Commitment and Community, Communes and Utopias in Sociological Perspective (Cambridge: Harvard University Press, 1972), 245. In Kanter's study "success was measured by length of time in existence; a system had to exist as a utopian community for at least twenty-five years, the sociological definition of a generation, in order to be considered successful." In a broader interpretation of the "success" of a communal society, Donald Pitzer has emphasized the developmental aspects of a commune; in this paradigm, the success of a community may be based on the goals of the group and its ability to use various organizational structures to adapt to changing conditions. This could include a change from a strictly communal structure of a group to capitalist structure that still maintained some of its religious, social, or historical influences.

[16] Ibid, 76-77.

innocent state Adam theoretically could reproduce by a commingling of his male and female elements.[17]

John Duss, a member of the Society during its last years, stated that celibacy may have been adopted as a temporary measure, but once adopted, Rapp searched out all passages of Scripture in support of the custom. The superior purity of the brother-sister relationship of the members was constantly eulogized, and as time went on marital relationships were more and more derided.[18]

Celibacy, it should be noted, was never a formal tenet of the Society, but rather was strongly recommended to the members by George Rapp as being a condition of holiness. In describing the practice of celibacy to Edward Page in 1822, Frederick Rapp said "We do not encourage the state of matrimony, because physical propagation cannot take place in the following of Jesus, since those who belong to Christ crucify not only their flesh but also their lusts and desires."[19]

Throughout the history of the Society formerly married couples remained together and George Rapp even married some couples at New Harmony who could not repress their "lusts and desires." Those couples who continued to have children were the Ralls, who had four between 1814 and 1829; the Schwarts, who had six between 1813 and 1826; the Vogts, who had six between 1805 and 1819; and the Killingers, who had eight children between 1808 and 1830.[20] Even George Rapp's son, John, was married, and his daughter, Gertrude, lived with George for many years after John's death in 1812. These, however, were the exceptions. By the 1830s the Harmonists became more and more firm about celibacy until by 1840 it was virtually a tenet. The records of the Society show there were sixty-nine births between 1814 and 1824 and only twenty-five between 1825 and

---

[17] Aaron Williams, The Harmony Society at Economy, Pennsylvania (Pittsburgh, 1866). Reprinted. (New York: Augustus Kelly, 1971), 98-102. Williams' book was read and approved by the Trustees at Economy before it was published and so might be considered to be the "authorized" version even though Williams was not a member of the Society.
[18] Duss, 28.
[19] Karl J.R. Arndt, A Documentary History of the Indiana Decade of the Harmony Society, II: 363.
[20] Duss, 28.

1830.[21] Those who did not live the celibate life were often made to feel inferior in the community and left voluntarily,[22] or they were given homes near the outskirts of the village.[23] In the event known as the great schism in 1832 Count Leon convinced a number of members to abandon the celibate life and leave the Society. Over the Society's century-long history, celibacy was both a unifying and a divisive factor. While for some celibacy was an effective binding "commitment mechanism," for others, including many in the group that left the community, it was a difficult, if not impossible, discipline to maintain.

The first few years at Harmony, Pennsylvania, were difficult ones, but the Harmonists were hard working and dedicated people, and by 1814 they had built a village that was comfortable and relatively prosperous. With the operation of fulling, hemp, oil, cotton, and grist mills and the cultivation of the land, they had, in the way envisioned by Thomas Jefferson, "placed the manufacturer beside the agriculturist." An indication of the rapid economic growth of the Society and of its economic diversity can be seen in the following figures from the Annual Reports of 1811 and 1814, even though only those enterprises showing the most substantial growth are given.[24]

	1811			1814		
	Outlay	Receipt	Profit	Outlay	Receipt	Profit
Hatmaker	$650.45	890.33	239.88	1055.24	2130.95	1075.71
The Inn	414.40	1591.68	1177.28	1543.54	5860.09	4316.55
Weaving	15.47	212.62	197.15			
Cloth manufacture				15,113.48	28,183.86	13,070.38
Shoemaker	636.45	1292.70	596.35	1092.98	3338.65	2245.67
Harnessmaker	292.78	474.67	181.89	571.30	1672.52	1101.22
Physician	321.86	375.50	53.64	729.96	1537.16	807.20
Whiskey						7700.00
Woolens						24,987.00
Totals			$2246.19			$55,203.732

---

[21] Arndt, George Rapp's Harmony Society, 418.
[22] Ibid, 358.
[23] See Chapter 2.
[24] These and other figures appear in Arndt, George Rapp's Harmony Society, 125-126.

These figures reflect that the Society had developed an economy that consisted of getting money from outsiders who came to Harmony to obtain the services of the physician or to stay in the inn, as well as exporting products such as whiskey, woolens, woven goods and shoes to the region. Thus, between 1811 and 1814 the total profits in these areas increased by 2500 percent. By 1814 the total receipts of the Society, excluding those from the agents in the outside world, amounted to over $100,000 and the profits to over $70,000. By 1814 the Society had expanded its economic influence by establishing agents at different points in the East through whom goods could be purchased and sold. As Karl Arndt has observed, "in the ever-increasing plans for manufacture and agriculture the leadership of the Society indicated its growing familiarity with those things that were in demand in the markets of the world outside."[25] The Harmonists may have been, to a large extent, religiously, socially, and linguistically isolated from their outside neighbors, but they were practical enough to realize that their prosperity depended upon an interaction with the economic markets of the outside world. They were, said Arndt, "in the world but not of it." The Harmonists, like the Shakers, were a communal society that was able to maintain its religious ideal while at the same time financially competing with the outside world in a capitalistic setting and still prospering.

The success of the Harmonists was due partially to their hard work, their dedication, and their economic astuteness, but it was due also to conditions in the United States over which they had little control. The Harmonists, in arriving in Pennsylvania in 1804, were in the right place at the right time. If they had arrived fifty years earlier, when the country was experiencing a gradual but not spectacular economic growth, they might have become like the communitarians at Ephrata who were supported mainly by a self-sustaining agricultural economy. Thirty years later the Harmonists would not have had the technological

---

[25] Arndt, George Rapp's Harmony Society, 127.

sophistication to compete with the manufacturies in urban centers nor would they have found cheap land near a growing city such as Pittsburgh. They did, as we will see, eventually resettle in their third village of Economy on the banks of the Ohio River, but by that time they had learned how to compete in the market. As it was, the Harmonist's economic growth coincided with the decline of finished goods from England as a result of the Non-Intercourse Acts of 1807-1808. As Douglass North has observed,

> The closing of the import trade was effective in promoting the rise of domestic manufactures, and capital which had been devoted to shipping and foreign commerce was partially absorbed in a rapid growth industry. Before 1808, only fifteen cotton mills had been built in the United States. By the end of 1809 eighty-seven additional mills had been constructed, and capacity had been increased from eight thousand spindles in 1808 to thirty one thousand at the end of 1809 and an estimated eighty thousand in 1811. Other branches of manufacturing also made substantial gains through 1814.[26]

It is significant that the Harmonists decided to move their community to the West at a time when the English goods were beginning to be imported to America after the War of 1812. Even during the war industrialization had continued to expand in England and by 1815 the English were able to offer their goods at lower prices than their competitors. During the years 1815-1818 "a combination of technological leadership, the ability of English manufacturers to dump upon the American market . . . and the auction system of distribution proved disastrous to a good deal of American manufacturing."[27]

The Harmonist response to the lower prices in the East was to move to the West where the competition from England and the East was not so great. In the Pittsburgh area transportation costs from the East were higher and prices lower than in the western market. According to a letter from a Harmonist in 1813, the Louisville price for boots, an important product of the Society, was two dollars

---

[26] Douglass North, The Economic Growth of the United States, 1790-1860, (New York: W. W. Norton & Company, 1966), 56.
[27] Douglass North, 61-62.

higher than it was in Pittsburgh. And Cossacks (a type of shoe), he continued, sell for "ten to eleven dollars, fairtops backstrap for twelve to thirteen dollars. Here [in Pittsburgh] we sell cossacks for nine dollars, backstraps for eleven dollars."[28] At this time the Harmonists realized that to prosper they needed to locate nearer to a larger water route. Harmony was located near the Connoquenessing Creek, which proved inadequate for effective shipping. Thus, in 1814, the Society moved from the Pittsburgh area to the West, where prices were higher and where the market was expected to expand. Another economic reason for the move was that the Harmonists were interested in the cultivation of the grape vine and believed that the soil and warmer climate in their new location were conducive to better grapes than those grown at Harmony.

For the Harmonist leaders, community prosperity and unity were far more important than the sense of place. Indeed, the Society defined "community" not in terms of physical location but rather in terms of a gathering of like-minded individuals, a fellowship, or, in German, *gesellschaft*, dedicating itself to creating a holy society in preparation for the millennium. For the Harmonists, their community of saints would be even more prosperous, and therefore a more shining example to the world, on the banks of the Wabash in Indiana.

By 1815 the Harmonists had sold their Pennsylvania property and settled in New Harmony, Indiana.[29] Although they were attacked with a debilitating fever the first year, the work proceeded and they began to create a second community in America. The rapidity with which they built this new town is impressive. By the end of 1818 over two hundred buildings had been erected. In a letter to a friend, Frederick Rapp expressed the sense of purpose that the Harmonists had in Indiana. "As our principles are both in a religious and political way to serve men," he wrote, "we have more opportunity here than we had in Pennsylvania to make

---

[28] John C. Andressohn, "Twenty Additional Rappite Manuscripts," Indiana Magazine of History, XLIV: 1 (March, 1948), 102. The prices are probably for dozens of pairs.
[29] Although the Harmonists called their second town Harmony, I have used the present name of the town to avoid confusion.

of a wild country, fertile land and gardens of pleasure."[30] As at Harmony, Pennsylvania, George Rapp assumed the duties as the spiritual leader of the community and Frederick Rapp was in charge of financial matters. Certainly at all three Harmonist villages this uniquely balanced leadership system was of great importance in establishing and strengthening the community. In addition to his financial genius, Frederick was also largely responsible for the architecture of the Harmonist buildings, and as an admirer of fine art was responsible for establishing an art collection at Economy.[31] The younger Rapp was also a cultured man who appreciated music and attended concerts in the outside world when he was away from the community on business.

Like other successful communitarian societies in America, the Harmonists created a hierarchy of leadership. This "authority hierarchy . . . presumably limited the members' access to the ultimate wielder of power in the community and thus enhanced the sense of awe surrounding the demands and dictums of the system. In addition, the hierarchy insulated the top leaders from violations of their symbolic properties of infallibility and truth."[32] By tending to the financial matters of the Society, which involved numerous trips to the outside world, Frederick Rapp helped preserve George Rapp's sanctity as a spiritual leader. When Frederick died in 1834, George assumed the duties of the financial manager of the community but appointed two sub-agents to take care of the outside business details.[33] Thus, Rapp maintained his power and sanctity by controlling the community finances yet not soiling his hands by limiting unnecessary contacts with those in the outside world. Of course since George Rapp did not speak English and Frederick did, it would be logical that this adopted son would be the one to negotiate with the outside world. In any event, the Harmonists managed to

---

[30] Quoted in Duss, 26-27
[31] See Chapter 3 for a fuller discussion of the art collection.
[32] Kanter, 117.
[33] Williams, 47.

interact with the outside, and yet the leader could remain within the village virtually all the time.[34]

By 1818 the Harmonists had cleared many of their over 20,,000 acres in Indiana for farming, had replaced the original log structures with sturdy brick and frame buildings, and had increased their agricultural and manufacturing output. Visitors to New Harmony were impressed with the dedication of the inhabitants and with the successful combination of agriculture and industry. Thomas Hulme, an English farmer who made a tour of the western states, praised the skill of the Harmonists and the sense of community exhibited within the Society. Visiting the town in the summer of 1819, Hulme said that

> The town is methodically laid out in a situation well chosen in all respects; the houses are good and clean, and have, each one, a nice garden well stocked with all vegetables tastily ornamented with flowers . . . . Having refreshed ourselves at the Tavern, where we found every thing we wanted for ourselves and our horses, and all very clean and nice, besides many good things we did not expect, such as beer, porter, and even wine, all made within the Society, and very good indeed, we then went out to see the people at their harvest, which was just begun. There were 150 men and women all reaping in the same field of wheat. A beautiful sight! The crop was very fine, and the field, extending to about two miles in length, and from half a mile to a mile in width, was all open to one view, the sun shining on it from the West, and the reapers advancing regularly over it.[35]

Accounts by Hulme and other English travelers may have been influential in publicizing the Harmony Society abroad and making its existence and prosperity known to such men as Robert Owen, the Welsh-born manufacturer and social reformer who bought the community in 1825. Like Hulme, many English reformers believed that a system of social harmony based on a combination of agriculture and industry could be brought about without the religious excesses and supposed "slavery" of some communities. For example, Charles Dickens

---

[34] The importance of the constant presence of the leader of the community can be seen in the failure of Robert Owen's community at New Harmony. Unlike Rapp, Owen was at his experiment only briefly.

[35] Thomas Hulme, Journal of a Tour in the Western Countries of America: September 30, 1818-August 7, 1819, in Reuben Thwaites, Early Western Travels (Cleveland, 1904-1907), X: 53.

commented on the dullness and rigidity of life in the Shaker community he visited.[36] Although there were some critical comments, almost all of the visitors felt that the Harmonists were comfortable and economically successful.

But the Harmonists decided to move again. Why, with the group's apparent success in Indiana, did the leaders of the community make this decision? There are several reasons. First, by 1820 it was becoming obvious to the Rapps that their community on the Wabash was not as economically sound as it should be. The Society was increasing both its prosperity and its production, but the expectations of a vast economic market in the West failed to materialize. In addition, an American economic crisis in 1819 almost destroyed the woolen industry of the Harmonists. The lack of a protective tariff, which the Rapps constantly urged in communication with members of Congress (another example of the Society interacting with the outside world when their economic interests were an issue), created a keen competition with foreign goods and, despite the quality of the Harmony woolen goods, sales lagged. A letter from Frederick to Samuel Patterson, a friend and business associate, revealed Rapp's concern with the economic policy of the government. "It is very desirable," he wrote,

> that the efforts of those patriotic members now in Congress would meet with success in their endeavors to lay heavy duties on all such foreign commodities which could be manufactured in our own country if the undertakers were better supported by government. Where else may the now languishing farmer look for a market to sell his surplus produce but to numerous and extensive manufacturing establishments in our country. While the latter are forsaken, the former, after toils and perils in quest of a market for the fruits of his industry, arrives at his journey's end where the

---

[36] For a discussion of the attitudes of English visitors and the influence of the Harmony Society on English settlements in the Midwest, see Arndt, George Rapp's Harmony Society, 268-286. Arndt says that "the accounts of the English travelers publicized the example of the Harmony Society as a communist society and thus kept before Englishmen a concrete example of the complete feasibility of the communistic system." 285. As late as 1848, Robert Russell, in America Compared with England, suggested that the German communistic societies could be models for more English settlements. "They are," he said, "harbingers of a new and more glorious state than that which any people have ever enjoyed. And the day will come when the names of Rapp and Bimeler [the leader of the Zoar Society in Ohio] will be associated with those of Washington and Jefferson." xviii.

great influx from every direction has gutted the shores and warehouses with superabundance.[37]

Finally, the relationship of the Harmonists with their neighbors was not as pleasant as it had been in Pennsylvania where there were more Germans. Harmonist correspondence indicates that there were some hostile feelings towards them as a result of their bloc voting practices and their ability to underprice competitors in the area.

On April 11, 1824, Frederick Rapp advised Richard Flower, a friend of the community, to advertise the Indiana property in England. Within a year terms were reached with Robert Owen, and the Harmonists were on their way to a third home in America. The history of Robert Owen's "failure"[38] at New Harmony is revealing. Had the Owenites attempted to set up a completely new village, their failure could be attributed to inexperience or to the unsuitability of the land and location. But since the Harmonists had been successful, the failure of the Owenites was not primarily the result of these factors. The paradoxical fact is that the religious Harmonists were much more practical than the secular Owenites. Judging from the comments made by the Owenite inhabitants of New Harmony, what the village lacked were people to run the machines and till the fields.[39] While Robert Owen was a successful manufacturer in Scotland, he failed to apply sound business and organizational practices to his American experiment and as a result saw it end in failure. There was also a lack of leadership at the Owenite village. If Robert Owen had been more interested in staying at New Harmony to oversee some of its practical needs, and less interested in publicizing his social

---

[37] Harmony Society Archives, Harmony Letter Books, 1822-1825. Letter dated February 12, 1824.
[38] Pitzer would not use this term and argues that while "the Owenites at New Harmony only lived communally from 1825 to 1827... the Owenite movement went on for another 40 years through publications, lectures, labor unions, and social reform efforts." (Personal communication, July, 2008)
[39] One of the best sources of information concerning the Owenite experiment is Robert Dale Owen, Twenty-Seven Years of Autobiography: Threading My Way (New York, 1874). See also the excellent chapter in Arthur Bestor's Backwoods Utopias and Donald Pitzer's "The New Moral World of Robert Owen and New Harmony," in Pitzer, America's Communal Utopias, 89-133.

theories, his experiment might have succeeded. As it was, the sense of community that the Harmonists gave to New Harmony left when they did.[40]

The Harmonists purchased a relatively small amount of land (3,000 acres as compared to over 20,000 acres in Indiana) on the Ohio River about twenty miles southwest of their previous site in Pennsylvania. The name that the Harmonists gave their new town on the Ohio reflected their philosophical views. "Economy," derived from the German *Oekonomie,* signified to the Harmonists what they termed "the Economy" and referred to the combination of their religious practices, their method of communal living, their social life, and their beliefs. In Walden Thoreau used the term in a similar fashion. For him "economy" referred to more than a manipulation of financial matters; instead it meant a completely integrated way of life in which the inner and outer self are coordinated. For the Harmonists the town of Economy was the ideal community and a proper place of residence until Christ appeared for his thousand year reign, which George Rapp predicted would take place in 1829. The name "Economy" also connoted a well balanced and profitable form of agricultural and manufacturing production. At their new location the 3,000 acres of land were certainly not enough to increase their agricultural production significantly, but they were ideally situated on a major route between the east and west and could take advantage of the commerce stimulated by the neighboring city of Pittsburgh.

As in their other locations, at Economy the Harmonists built a thriving village in a short period of time. By 1830 almost all of the important structures at Economy, including the cotton and woolen mills, the granary, the feast hall building, the church, and George Rapp's house, were built. The location on the Ohio was a favorable one for the Harmonists, for their economy rapidly expanded during their first decade there. Between 1820 and 1840 the Harmonists sold an

---

[40] For a comparison of factors affecting success in nineteenth century communitarian societies see Kanter, 61-138.

average of over $100,000 worth of goods a year, including such items as cloth, hats, shoes, rope, flour, and whiskey.[41]

During its greatest years the Harmony Society was a close knit community serving the physical and religious needs of its members. A major reason for the success of the Society was that it managed to balance effectively a number of elements. The Harmonists were, at the same time, religious idealists who had separated from the established church to set up a religious community, and practical communitarians who were aware of the secular and economic needs of the community; they combined agriculture and industry in such a way that they were self-sufficient, prosperous, and somewhat immune to the economic fluctuations of the outside world; finally, the Harmonists were a socially isolated community, admitting to membership only those few who would adhere to their particular philosophy, yet they recognized the necessity to interact with the outside world in order to maintain a degree of social, religious, and financial independence.

In spite of the overall success of the Society, however, from time to time there were discordant elements within the community. Usually the dissatisfaction of an individual or a small group centered around the practice of celibacy or of the authoritarian nature of George Rapp.[42] Occasionally individuals who left the community sued George Rapp to recover what they felt was owed them after years of work. A major split in the Society took place between 1831 and 1833 with the arrival of a self-proclaimed messiah, Count Leon, "Archduke Maximilian of the Stem of Judah and the Root of David." Rapp had expected Leon (whose real name is thought to have been Bernhart Mueller) to be a prophet who would

---

[41] Daniel Riebel and Patricia Black, A Manual for Guides, Docents, Hostesses and Volunteers of Old Economy, (Ambridge, Pennsylvania, 1970), [n.p.]
[42] The major periods of discord within the community were 1805-1807; 1818-1827; 1831-1833; 1847-1851; and 1888-1893. The most objective discussion of legal proceedings brought against the Society by former members is Arndt's George Rapp's Harmony Society. For a less objective analysis of the legal situation during the demise of the community see Arndt's George Rapp's Successors and Material Heirs, 1847-1916 (Rutherford, New Jersey: Fairleigh Dickinson University Press, 1971). In this book Arndt is very critical of Rapp's rigidity and "hypocrisy."

lead his people into the millennium, and therefore he and his entourage were allowed to reside at Economy for a short period of time. Leon, whose philosophy seemed to appeal to those who in one way or another were dissatisfied with some aspect of the community, persuaded almost one third of the 750 members to sign a petition denouncing George Rapp. Many of the signers of the petition may have done so as a result of Leon's position that celibacy should be abolished. Of the 250 members whose names appeared in the Pittsburgh Gazette on February 10, 1832, denouncing both George and Frederick Rapp, a large number (112) were between the ages of 21 and 40.[43] Broken down into groups, the list shows the following distribution:

Age	Number of signers
21-30	56
31-40	56
41-50	21
51-60	13

It is also significant that a large proportion of those whose names appeared in the newspaper had resided in the Society for five years or less. To be precise, ninety-one of them had arrived in the community in 1827 or later. Of the seventy-nine members who had been in the community since 1807 or who were born in the community, fifty-seven were forty years old or younger. These figures suggest, although by no means prove, that the individuals who left the community were those who were young enough to have children and were dissatisfied with policy of celibacy within the community, and those whose allegiance to the Society was not very strong because they were relative newcomers.

After some months of hostility, public charges and counter charges, legal maneuvers, and a public investigation of the claims of the Leon faction, an agreement was reached in March of 1832, whereby the 250 members who sided with Leon left the Society in return for a sum total of $105,000. That it was not

---

[43] The fifty-five members on the list under the age of 20 were children who did not sign the petition.

the lure of relatively cheap lands or the mainstream of American life that convinced the seceders to leave Economy is revealed by the fact that this group, under the leadership of Leon, pooled their money in a common treasury and settled at Phillipsburg (now Monaca) a village on the Ohio River north of Economy. By August of 1833, however, the community treasury there was empty and the group, called the New Philadelphia Society, was dissolved.[44] A number of the seceders also helped to form the communal society of Bethel in Missouri, and some joined the Mormons.[45]

The Leon affair created a serious schism in the Harmony Society, but it may have had the beneficial effect of cleansing the community of those who were dissatisfied. More important to the gradual decline of the Society were the deaths of George and Frederick Rapp. According to John Duss, with the death of Frederick in 1834, the decline of the community began, with "the desultory abandonment of a positive economy and the ushering in of an era of external investments to take the place of internal production."[46] This change in the economic focus of the Society, however, was not fully realized until after the death of George Rapp in 1847 and the decreasing efficiency of the Harmonist mills by the 1850s.[47] In 1851 the wealth of the Society was at least a million dollars, not including the numerous land holdings in other areas. By this period

> the chief assets of the Society no longer consisted in the land, industries, workshops, homes, and equipment of Economy itself, but in external investments – bonds, stocks, mortgages, notes. And thus the economy of the commune was no longer a positive and dynamic one; foreign investments outgrew domestic production; it had become principally a money economy.[48]

---

[44] Arndt, George Rapp's Harmony Society, 496-512.
[45] Arndt, George Rapp's Harmony Society, 517-520. For a discussion of the fate of Leonard and his followers see Karl Arndt, "The Genesis of Germantown, Louisiana," Louisiana Historical Quarterly, XXIV (April, 1941), 378-433.
[46] Duss, 91.
[47] Bole argued that the change in the economy of the Society came in 1868 with the death of R.L. Baker, the Trustee.
[48] Duss, 115.

Some idea of the outside investments of the Society can be seen in the 1855 interests, which included the Little Sawmill Run Railroad, the Cleveland and Pittsburgh Railroad, the Perryville and Zelienople Plank Road, the Bank of Kentucky, Brighton Bridge, and the Ohio and Pennsylvania Railroad. The community also had oil drilling operations on their outside lands after 1859.[49] By the 1870s the Harmonists had laid out the town of Beaver Falls, sold lots there, and encouraged manufacturing enterprises by investing in such businesses as the Beaver Falls Car Works, the Beaver Falls Steel Works, the Beaver Falls Cutlery Company, and many more.[50]

In addition, with its members aging and numbers declining by the Civil War period, the Society began to hire outside help, a move which must have slowly eroded the sense of personal contribution to the workings of the community. By the 1860s, changes in the internal makeup of the Society and changes in the economic situation in the outside world gradually transformed Economy into a communal society which used capitalist means to preserve itself.[51]

By the last quarter of the nineteenth century, with most of the members in old age and the original religious fervor softened by the absence of George Rapp and the challenge of a wilderness which needed to be transformed into a garden a distant memory, the Harmonists were on the way to extinction. Charles Nordhoff, who visited Economy in 1874, observed that

> neatness and Sunday quiet are the prevailing characteristics of Economy. Once it was a busy place, for it had cotton, silk, and woolen factories, a brewery, and other industries; but the most important of these have now ceased; and as you walk along the quiet, shady streets you meet only occasionally some stout, little old man in a short, light-blue jacket and a tall and very broad-brimmed hat, looking amazingly like Hendrick Hudson's men in the play of Rip Van Winkle.[52]

---

[49] See Karl Arndt, "The Harmonists as Pioneers of the American Oil Industry," German-American Review, XII, 1 (October, 1945)7-9; 25.
[50] Arndt, George Rapp's Successors and Material Heirs, 242-246.
[51] For the economic history of the Harmonists after the Civil War see Arndt, George Rapp's Successors and Material Heirs.
[52] Ibid, 64-65.

The effects of celibacy and the failure of the Society to seek new members were evident by the last decade of the century. In 1892 there were only thirty-seven members; there were eighteen in 1894; ten in 1897; eight in 1902; and four in 1903.[53] In 1905, one hundred years after these idealistic and pragmatic Germans carved their first village from the Pennsylvania woodlands, the Society was legally dissolved.

The history of the Harmony Society reveals that as residents of a communal group the Harmonists had a number of virtues. They were economically successful throughout their history, they managed to balance their agriculture and manufacturing, they adapted their economic system to changing demands of the outside world, and they created villages which satisfied the physical, spiritual, and economic needs of most of the members. On the other hand, even though the Harmonists were somewhat adaptable in economic matters, by the 1850s they were unable to compete successfully with more efficient manufactures in the outside world. To do so might have destroyed the very basis of their community; if the Harmonists had decided to compete with other manufacturing interests by retooling machinery and hiring larger numbers of outside laborers, they most certainly would have been forced to reevaluate their concept of the good and holy society. Thus, the Harmonists were adaptable, but only within the limits of their philosophy. It is both a statement of their dedication and a commentary on their plight that they were trapped between two worlds: one, a village economy with an emphasis on religious values and interpersonal relationships; the other, an industrialized society with its attendant conditions of urbanization and impersonality. With both of their leaders dead by 1847, the Harmonists lost the most important vestige of their old world and were faced with the complexities of a new one. Their ultimate extinction seems to be a tribute to what Rapp represented, and an inability or unwillingness to abandon his vision for a new one.

---

[53] Bole, 9.

Chapter 2

The Town Planning[1] of the Harmony Society

Without exception, the visitors who came to the Harmonist towns and who left written records were favorably impressed with their locations, regularity of plan and attractiveness. When John Melish visited Harmony, Pennsylvania, in 1811, he said that after coming from Pittsburgh through country that was "rather rough and uncultivated" he reached the top of a hill and saw, "at a little distance, the town of Harmony, elegantly situated amid flourishing and well cultivated fields." Melish then noted that the town was "regularly laid out" with a village square, streets crossing one another at right angles, and a quarter acre lot provided for each family.[2] An English visitor to New Harmony, Indiana, in 1823, said that the town was "regularly laid out into straight and spacious streets, crossing each other at right angles . . . [with] neat and commodious brick and framed houses which are extremely well built, the uniform redness of the brick . . . giving to the place a brightness of appearance which the towns of England are quite destitute of."[3] Finally, Economy, Pennsylvania, the third home of the Harmonists and their showplace was described by Charles Nordhoff in the 1870s:

> Economy has, in truth, one of the loveliest situations on the Ohio River. It stands in the midst of a rich plain, with swelling hills behind, protecting it from cold winds in winter; a magnificent reach of the river in view below: and tall hills on the opposite shore to give a picturesque outlook . . . . Streets proceed at right angles with the river's course; and each street is

---

[1] The idea of a profession and practice of "town planning" was not yet a part of early nineteenth century America, but I am using the contemporary phrase to suggest the Harmonists' concept and execution of the creation of a physical community that would meet their religious, social, and economic needs.

[2] John Melish, Travels in the United States of America in the Years 1806, 1807, 1809, 1810, and 1811 (Philadelphia, 1812.) Reprinted in An Essay on Commonwealths (New York, 1822), 56

[3] William Hebert, A Visit to the Colony of Harmony in Indiana. London, 1825. Reprinted in Harlow Lindley, Indiana As Seen By Early Travellers (Indianapolis: Indiana Historical Commission, 1916), 329.

lined with neat frame or brick houses, surrounding a square in such a manner that within, each household has a sufficient garden.[4]

When the Harmonists came to America they did not settle in an established town, nor did they purchase property that had roads and buildings. Instead, they created a completely new village by clearing the lands, establishing roads, and building structures. They created their towns according to the religious, social, and economic necessities of establishing a communal village in preparation for the millennium. Since they rejected the established Lutheran church in Germany, they were not burdened by the need to create a village that resembled the ones that they had come from, nor were they compelled to create towns similar to those that they saw in America. The United States was a *tabula rasa* that gave them the freedom to reject much and adopt some of their European heritage. A break from established Lutheranism necessitated a break from the physical world they knew. And this new world could be used to provide the inspiration and economic stability that they needed to establish their new religion.

While there is nothing revolutionary about the planning of the Harmonist villages, especially compared to the elaborate communities proposed by such utopian visionaries as Charles Fourier and Robert Owen, each was a practical rather than a theoretical solution to the changing needs and attitudes of the Society. Fourier's aesthetic ideal was based on that of the eighteenth century aristocracy, and "he would have looked with disdain upon the enforced simplicity, the drab middle-class members, customs and dress that made their way into most nineteenth utopian visions."[5] Although Robert Owen purchased the second Harmonist village, New Harmony, he had ambitious plans for his utopian community, as seen in a drawing of Owen's ideal village as made by the architect Stedman Whitwell (Figure 2). It shows an enclosed city which looks like a combination of a medieval *bastide* and an eighteenth century London square,

---

[4] Nordhoff, 64-65.
[5] For a discussion of Fourier's Phalanx, see Jonathan Beecher and Richard Bienvenu, The Utopian Vision of Charles Fourier (Boston: Beacon Press, 1971), 235-245.

quite unlike the practical towns that the Harmonists built. While Owen planned to replace New Harmony with a community based on his ideal village and even had a number of bricks made in preparation for the construction, it was never started. [6] As a reflection of the more practical town plans not just envisioned but completed by the Harmonists, a visitor to Economy said that one "should not . . . imagine some fairy temple, but merely a very common, clean, and tastefully built garden city with factories, and at the edges of town the incidental buildings needed for farming."[7] There is some irony in the fact that the visionary Owen purchased a ready-made village, while the more pragmatic Harmonists created three completely new and different communities.

The Locations of the Villages

The locations of the three villages built by the Harmonists reveal a gradual change that took place in the economic system of the community. The site for the first town was chosen by George Rapp, who, with his son and two followers examined land in Pennsylvania, Virginia, and Ohio before the first large group of Harmonists arrived in America. Although Rapp wanted to purchase a tract of land in Ohio, his petition to Thomas Jefferson for an extended repayment schedule was rejected and the down payment was more than the group could afford. And so the site finally chosen, in Butler County, Pennsylvania, was not their first choice but was an affordable area consisting of rolling hills and resembling the landscape of Iptingen in Germany where George Rapp was born.[8] Since the leader of the community was a vine cutter by trade, the land was bought with an eye towards the production of wine as a major economic factor in the

---

[6] For a discussion of Owen's background and his plans for New Harmony see Donald Pitzer's "The New Moral World of Robert Owen and New Harmony," in America's Communal Utopias, 88-133.

[7] Quoted from Wilhelm Weitling who visited Harmony in 1851, in Karl Arndt, George Rapp's Heirs and Material Successors (Rutherford, New Jersey: Fairleigh Dickinson Press, 1971), 35.

[8] Interview with Daniel Reibel, Curator of Old Economy Village, June 12, 1972.

Society. While it was true that the hillsides provided good drainage for the vines, Rapp's choice of Butler County may have been a rash one for he underestimated the duration of the Pennsylvania winters. As a result, the quality and production of wine at Harmony were never up to the expectations of the Society.[9] It is possible that Rapp understood the difficulties of making good wine in such a climate and that his insistence on growing vines was less a logical decision than one driven by economic necessities and by his attempt to recreate some part of his German experience.

In addition to Rapp's belief in the suitability of the Butler County site for the cultivation of the vine, the area was chosen for its general fertility, for the Connoquenessing Creek, which provided power for the mills, for its location near to German speaking neighbors, and probably for its isolation from major urban centers. At Harmony the Society planned to build a village with an economic base of an agricultural production of grains and wines which would become a commercial center for the area. They quickly adapted to their surroundings and turned to the production of other items, such as cloth, woolens, hats, and shoes. Evidence of the profitability of these manufactured items is seen in the receipts for cloth manufacture; it rose from $197 in 1811 to $13,070 in 1814, and by 1814 the Society realized a profit of almost $25,000 in the sale of woolen goods. The Harmonists, like other successful communal groups in the nineteenth century, including the Shakers, the Society of Separatists at Zoar, Ohio, and the Inspirationists at Amana, Iowa, interacted financially with the outside world in order to achieve prosperity. To a remarkable extent the Harmonists managed to control their contacts with the outside in spite of the fact that they even built an inn at each village to accommodate (and get the hard cash of) visitors who came to the community on business matters or merely out of curiosity's sake.[10]

---

[9] Aaron Williams, The Harmony Society at Economy, Pennsylvania (Pittsburgh, 1866). Reprint (New York: Augustus M. Kelley, 1971), 60.
[10] However, as shown in Chapter 4, the artifacts of the Society indicate that there was an increasing American influence on certain forms.

By 1811 the Society had built grist, oil, hemp, and fulling mills and was providing the surrounding area with a variety of goods, including whiskey, shoes, and hats. By 1813 agents were established in Philadelphia, Lancaster, and Pittsburgh, through whom their manufactured goods could be sold. However, although the Society was prospering, the Connoquenessing Creek, which was suitable for powering the mills, was not a navigable river and could not be used to transport the increasing amount of goods that were being produced. For that purpose the Harmonists used the Ohio River, which was about fifteen miles distant. Moreover, by 1814 the leaders of the community were convinced that the growing economic market in the West could be served more efficiently and more profitably if a western location were used as a center of manufacturing and distribution.[11]

When the Harmonists moved to Indiana in 1814 they purchased over 20,000 acres of land and located their village on the Wabash, a river substantially larger than the Connoquenessing and one that was both navigable and usually accessible by steamboats from the Ohio River, the main route of transportation from the East to the West. The Wabash also provided a route to the Mississippi and thus to the important port of New Orleans. The increasing use of steam engines to power Harmonist mills freed them from the seasonal changes in the Wabash, which was occasionally unsuitable for mill operation at New Harmony, and allowed them to locate their manufacturing structures where they could be used most efficiently, that is, in relationship to the landings, the homes of the workers, and the roads.

The Indiana site was chosen also because of the milder and shorter winters there compared to those in Pennsylvania. The area was not as hilly as that in Pennsylvania, but the climate was better suited for growing grapes and to the subsequent production of saleable wine. Even though the Harmonists were not in the vicinity of as many friendly German neighbors as they were in Pennsylvania, they were less than fifty miles from the Shaker community of West Union, which

---

[11] See Duss, 34; and Arndt, George Rapp's Harmony Society, 1785-1847, 127.

flourished between 1810 and 1827. Since the Shakers and Harmonists were in agreement on a number of religious tenets, they were on friendly terms. Gertrude Rapp, George's granddaughter, even stayed with the Shakers at West Union for a short time to learn English.[12]

Another explanation for the move from Harmony, which was relatively prosperous and could have been a comfortable place for the group to remain, was that George Rapp may have felt that the religious intensity and community commitment to building a new village in the wilderness was waning and that his members needed a new challenge to make them even more dedicated to Harmonist beliefs. While there is no written or physical documentation for this interpretation, there is some material evidence which I cite in my chapter on Harmonist buildings that may help explain their third move from New Harmony to Economy.

The frontier appears to have been an unsatisfactory environment for communitarian societies. The Shakers at West Union lasted for only seventeen years, and the Harmonists left New Harmony after only ten years there. Rather than being conducive to the spread of communitarianism, the frontier seems to have had the opposite effect.[13] For the Harmonists, the fluctuating economic market in the West and the additional hostility of non-communitarian neighbors were factors in their decision to leave Indiana. John Humphrey Noyes analyzed the failures and successes of a number of American communes and reached the conclusion that

> the fondness for land, which has been the habit of Socialists, had much to do with their failures. Farming . . . is the kid of labor in which there is . . . the largest chance for disputes and discords in such complex bodies as Associations. Moreover the lust for land leads off into the wilderness, "out west," into byplaces, far away from railroads and markets; whereas Socialism if it is really ahead of civilization, ought to keep near the centers of business, and at the front of the general march of improvement.[14]

---

[12] Arndt, George Rapp's Harmony Society, 1785-1847, 251.
[13] For a discussion of the effect of the frontier on communal groups see Bestor, 230-252.
[14] John Humphrey Noyes, History of American Socialisms (Philadelphia: Lippincott, 1870. Reprinted (New York:Dover Publications, 1966), 19.

Although there is no evidence to indicate that the frontier had a negative effect on the social unity of the Harmony Society, there were positive economic benefits to be gained by relocating in a more settled and industrialized area of the country. For this reason the Harmonists made their third and final home at Economy, Pennsylvania, only twenty miles southwest of their first village and twenty-five miles north of Pittsburgh. There were significant differences between the location of Economy and those of the previous villages. First, unlike Harmony, Economy was located on the banks of the Ohio, a major trade route, rather than on the relatively small Connoquenessing. By the 1820s the Harmonists were not content to be a commercial center for the surrounding area only, but instead had intentions of becoming a major commercial center for the Ohio River Valley, certainly not on the scale of Pittsburgh, but taking advantage of the trade that Pittsburgh engendered.[15] Second, the Harmonists purchased only 3,000 acres of land at Economy as compared to the 9,000 acres that they eventually owned at Harmony and the 20,000 at New Harmony. While they were to continue with their farming and viniculture at Economy, their economic base would consist of woolen and cotton manufacturing and the production of shoes, hats, and whiskey. Finally, by returning to a climate identical to that which they had earlier felt was unsuitable for viniculture, they indicated that the production of wine may have been more a symbolic reminder of their German heritage than a major economic venture.[16]

So the three villages of the Society were situated for considerations of agriculture, of trade, and of the changing concept of the communal good, which by the 1820s included substantial economic interaction with the outside world and the introduction of manufacturing on a large scale. The combination of an efficient communal system of production and an expanding economic market in America gradually increased the group's economic interaction with the outside world and significantly influenced its choice of location. In addition, the

---

[15] Duss, 63.
[16] This is not to say that the Harmonists were unsuccessful in their wine production since sales of wine and beer were quite good.

adaptability and the economically progressive nature of the Society were revealed in its willingness twice to abandon a settled village in America for a new one. Unlike the Shakers, whose increasing numbers allowed them to create new and often similar villages in different locations while maintaining the old ones,[17] the relatively stable population of the Harmony Society dictated the abandonment of the old with the creation of the new. Also, it is significant that the Harmonists tried something new in each village to meet changes and needs within the community.

The Street Patterns of Harmonist Villages

In each village built by the Harmonists the streets were laid out in a rectilinear[18] pattern with the major streets on a north-south and east-west axis. In choosing the rectilinear plan, the Harmonists broke away from the irregular street pattern dominant, although not exclusive, in Württemberg. George Rapp's birthplace of Iptingen, for example, consisted of just such an irregular pattern which was characteristic of most medieval villages. For the Harmonists the rectilinear plan provided several advantages. As the name of the Society and of their first town indicates, the Harmonists conceived of their community as a unified and orderly entity in which all elements, spiritual, economic, social, and physical, were in harmonious proportion to one another. The geometric precision of the rectilinear plan was therefore desirable. Whereas the irregular plan is appropriate for and characterizes villages in which growth is gradual and haphazard and in which each structure is considered separately rather than as an

---

[17] The exception to this is Pleasant Hill, Kentucky, where Shaker architectural innovations included a Trustees house with elegant twin spiral staircases.
[18] The term "rectilinear" rather than grid is used since the latter implies that all the blocks in a village are of equal size and are square. These distinctions are taken from Richard Pillsbury, "The Urban Street Patterns of Pennsylvania Before 1815: A Study in Cultural Geography." (Unpublished doctoral dissertation, Pennsylvania State University, 1968), 82. A condensed version of this work is "The Urban Street Pattern as Cultural Indicator: Pennsylvania, 1682-1815," Annals of the American Association of Geographers, LX (September, 1970),428-466.

integral part of the whole, the rectilinear plan is especially suitable where the village is seen as an entity, though capable of expansion. Second, the rectilinear plan is the logical one if an equitable distribution of property is necessary, as it was in the communal philosophy of the Harmonists.[19] By using this pattern the Harmonists could apportion rectangular plots which fitted neatly into the predetermined pattern.[20]

The irregular street pattern which characterized most medieval European villages such as Iptingen (Figure 3) often resulted from a conflict of private and public interests for property fronting the streets, with the stronger interest appropriating as much space as possible and thereby encroaching into the area of the other.[21] Since there was no such conflict at Harmony and at the other villages between private and public interests, the irregular plan would have been an unlikely development. According to the distinction made by Norman Pounds, "planted" cities in medieval Europe "were conscious and deliberate creations of territorial lords, always for their own profit," while organic towns grew spontaneously.[22] If we apply this terminology, then the Rapps "planted" their villages, not as territorial lords but as religious and economic leaders of their community. Finally, the overall structure of the Harmony Society may have had an effect on the shape of the town. As Dan Stanislawski has noted, "some form of centralized control, political, religious, or military is certainly indicated for all known grid-plans towns. When centralized power disintegrates, even if the grid pattern has been established, it disappears."[23] Under the forceful leadership of the Rapps, the Harmonists created villages which were far from random and haphazard in their planning, but instead were concrete embodiments of a vision of a harmonious society.

---

[19] However, as I show below, the Harmonists were a communal society, but not all were equal.
[20] Dan Stanislawski, "The Origin and Spread of the Grid Pattern Town," Geographical Review, XXXVI (July, 1946), 106.
[21] Howard Saalman, Medieval Cities (New York: George Braziller, 1968), 28-34.
[22] The Medieval City, 12.
[23] Stanislawski, 108.

While there are a number of theoretical reasons for a communal group such as the Harmony Society to choose the rectilinear pattern, more than likely those who proposed this pattern were influenced by similar plans in Germany and in Pennsylvania. By the time the Harmonists came to America there were a number of towns and cities in Germany laid out in an orderly and unified fashion that reflected the classical influence, which reached its peak in the eighteenth century. One of the most famous of the books describing the ideal city plan was De Architectura by Vitruvius, the first century B.C. architect and engineer. By the eighteenth century in Germany a number of Renaissance princes had absorbed the ideas of Vitruvius and his disciples and had laid out towns with a rectilinear pattern.[24] Moreover, "the systematized towns that evolved from the Renaissance seem to have been centered mainly in Württemberg,"[25] the area from which the Harmonists emigrated.

Examples of southern German towns that took on a classical pattern in the seventeenth and eighteenth centuries were Freudenstadt, Darmstadt, Mannheim, Karlsruhe, Erlangen, and Ludwigsburg. Since all of these towns but Erlangen were no more than a two days' journey from Iptingen, it seems likely that George or Frederick Rapp would have seen the rectilinear street pattern.[26] Stuttgart, Darmstadt, and Frankfurt

> were important cities, marking an area that gave encouragement to Vitruvian planning, all developing an elastic form of chessboard pattern beyond their medieval centers. Like Munich, each became classical in type, in striking contrast with the haphazard towns.[27]

---

[24] For a discussion of the "new towns" in Germany in the seventeenth and eighteenth centuries see E. A. Gutkind, Urban Development in Central Europe (London: The Free Press of Glencoe, 1964), 124-126.
[25] Frederick Hiorns, Town-Building in History (London: G.G. Harrap, 1956), 262.
[26] The distances from Iptingen are as follows: Freudenstadt, 40 miles; Darmstadt, 65; Mannheim, 40; Karlsruhe, 20; Erlangen, 120; Ludwigsburg, 15; and Stuttgart, 20. It should be noted that the Harmonists came from other villages than Iptingen.
[27] Hiorns, 259.

Ludwigsburg, a town to the north of Stuttgart and only fifteen miles east of Iptingen, may have been the model for those who planned the Harmonist towns.[28] Founded at the beginning of the eighteenth century by the Duke Eberhard Ludwig, "the town takes its rectilinear pattern and roughly square shape from the elongated rectangle and north-to-south axis of the *schloss* [castle] and its garden, and is essentially Vitruvian in quality."[29]

It seems reasonable to assume that one of the Rapps had been to Ludwigsburg, for not only is the street pattern there rectilinear, but the architecture and the formal gardens of Ludwig IV show marked similarities to features at Economy. If the Classical influence on town planning was centered in the Württemberg area, it is more than likely that a stone mason such as Frederick Rapp would have been aware of it.[30]

Even if the Harmonists were not influenced by the rectilinear plan in Germany, they must have been aware of its existence in Pennsylvania. The influence of Philadelphia's rectilinear pattern on other American cities in the nineteenth century was substantial. "For many of the towns that sprang up later during the westward march of urbanization, Philadelphia served as the model. The regular pattern of streets and one or more public squares were features that became widely imitated."[31]

The classical innovation of the rectilinear plan "reached its full importance in the United States only in Pennsylvania, where the plan first attained regional significance in this country."[32] In addition to the classical revival in Europe and America, the Penn proprietorship, which laid out Philadelphia in 1682, was directly or indirectly responsible for the introduction of the rectilinear street

---

[28] Frederick Rapp, the adopted son of George, was a stone mason and possibly an architect in Germany. He is considered to be the one who laid out the Harmonist towns.
[29] Hiorns, 261.
[30] The similarities between Ludwigsburg and Economy were made in a lecture by Ralph Griswold, the landscape architect of the Old Economy restoration.
[31] John Reps, Town Planning in Frontier America (Princeton: Princeton University Press, 1969), 222.
[32] Pillsbury, 437.

pattern throughout Pennsylvania.[33] When the Harmonists came to America in 1804 there were almost one hundred towns in Pennsylvania using the rectilinear pattern. If they were not influenced by the regular street pattern that they saw when they arrived in Philadelphia, they may well have been by those towns that they saw in Pennsylvania on their way to Harmony.

Another explanation for the shape of the Harmonist villages is that the Rapps were influenced by Johann Valentin Andreae's ideal Christian town described and illustrated in his Christianopolis of 1619, which would have been familiar to both Rapps in Germany, Frederick as a stone mason *cum* town planner, and George as a religious leader. This Community of Christians envisioned by Andreae had some similarities to the towns that the Harmonists built; while Christianopolis had a large circular temple and council hall in the center of the town and numerous residences and civic gardens, the Harmonists had a pavilion-temple at Economy, a Feast Hall Building in the center of the town, and gardens for the family dwellings.[34] However, the plan of the ideal town in Christianopolis is more similar to the idealistic concept drawn by Stedman Whitwell for Robert Owen than it is to the more practical and traditional plans of the Harmonists. And while the Rapps may have been aware of Andreae's book when they were in Germany, there is no evidence that it was in the Harmonist library, so whatever influence it may have had, it was perhaps more general than specific.

Thus, there were a number of factors which may have influenced the Harmonists in their use of the rectilinear plan such as they used first at Harmony and then at the other villages (Figure 4). As a communal society, the Harmonists needed a village plan that could be divided into roughly equal segments, and one whose regularity and order appealed to their vision of the harmonious society. They also wanted a plan that allowed for the most efficient use of space. As Germans, the Harmonists were more than likely influenced by the classical street

---

[33] Ibid, 437.
[34] Donald Pitzer, "The Harmonist Heritage of Three Towns," Historic Preservation, 29, no. 4 (Oct-Dec. 1977), 6.

plans in Württemberg, although one could argue that the creation of a planned community was even a part of the history of medieval cities and that George Rapp saw himself in the role of community aristocrat. But it seems likely that when the Harmonists came to America they observed the rectilinear plan of Philadelphia or other Pennsylvania towns.

The Village Square and Garden

The Harmonist villages, centered around a square at Harmony and New Harmony, and around a community garden at Economy, reflected changing economic and social patterns in the society. The classical square, which is usually formed by cutting off the corners of the blocks surrounding the principal intersection of the town, was used by the Harmonists at both Harmony and New Harmony. This form appeared during the Renaissance in Europe wherever the rectilinear pattern was used. It was introduced into Pennsylvania along with the rectilinear plan and like that pattern was related to the classical revolution. Pillsbury's study of Pennsylvania towns indicates that sixty-two of all rectilinear-plan towns examined were laid out with a classical square, and only nine with an irregular square.[35] The earlier use of the square by the Harmonists indicated that the Society was originally based on the idea of limited trade within the village and its environs. Like the market square in Germany, the squares at the Harmonist villages were gathering places for members of the community and for those from the outside world who bought the products of the Society or lodged at its inn. Unlike the village greens in New England towns which today are seen as islands of tranquility and which in the seventeenth and eighteenth centuries provided grazing grounds for community farmers and were not penetrated by the major roads, the squares at Harmony and New Harmony were directly in the path of the major roads. The town square thus was central to the towns both visually and

---

[35] Pillsbury, 120.

economically. It allowed for an architectural enclosure of space within the village and funneled traffic to that space.[36]

When the Harmonists moved to Economy, Pennsylvania, which was located on the Ohio River, the abandonment of the village square marked a change in the economic orientation of the community. By the 1820s the Harmonist economy had passed out of the village handicraft stage and into manufacturing on a large scale which depended on the markets in the Ohio Valley. At Harmony the streets leading from and into the square were the major sources of economic communication with the outside world. From these roads goods could be sent to nearby communities or to distribution points nearer to Pittsburgh. At Economy, on the other hand, the Ohio River provided the Harmonists with their main transportation route and made the streets leading into a square less important for their economic growth than they were at Harmony. During the building of Economy when George Rapp was at the new town while Frederick was still at New Harmony managing the transfer of people and goods to the new village, George wrote to Frederick indicating that he was relocating the main highway so that disruptive elements such as cattle and "poor folk" would not go through Economy: "I have made a change with the highway," he reported,

> it is impossible that it should go through town, you cannot say what kind of cattle of all kinds pass there, in addition to all sorts of lower and poor folk. On the outermost town street the other side ought to be occupied by houses and lots so that the public street will pass the town outside although it will require more and good land, and two or three streets should remain open into town, so that he who wished could come in, then the greater part which does not concern us would go by without hindrance."[37]

---

[36] Christopher Tunnard and Henry Hope Reed in American Skyline (New York: Mentor, 1956), state that "the strong medieval strain of the early settlements, to be seen in the half-timbering, the use of thatch and the overhanging second story, rarely produced the enclosed arcaded market square found in Europe. Part and parcel of the walled town, the architectural enclosure could not be expected in open towns where the individual rather than the community consented." 40.
[37] Arndt, Harmony on the Wabash in Transition, 119.

At Economy, much of the economic activity and movement was from the means of production in the village to the river; therefore, the main street in Economy (Store Street), was perpendicular to the river and provided access to the boat landing. Along this street which ran down to the river were located a number of small shops, the post office, the store, and the doctor's office. This was the commercial center of the village.

The Ohio River, then, functioned as another major "street" at Economy which allowed the Harmonists to receive raw materials from the outside and send out finished goods; it also brought travelers, perhaps emigrants to the West, to the community where they could purchase at the store items that would be used when they settled. By the time that the Harmonists moved to Economy they recognized that the village square, which had served them well in Germany and in their two previous towns, was no longer necessary. The economic focal point of the community had moved from the square to the river. In moving into the economic mainstream of America, the Harmonists abandoned an element which did not serve their communal needs at a particular time and place. It may be symbolic of the change from street to river access that when the Harmonists moved to Economy they commissioned a steamboat, the "William Penn," to be built by Graham and Philipps, shipbuilders in the Pittsburgh area.

At Economy the village square was replaced as the visual center of the town by a garden facing the Ohio River and taking up an entire village block. Although the Harmonists had botanical and pleasure gardens in their other towns, the reports of travelers suggest that none had the visual significance of the garden at Economy. Unlike many renaissance gardens characterized by a rigid formality and a geometric precision, the one at Economy was like the more "natural" gardens of the enlightenment. According to the landscape architect of the restoration of Old Economy, "it seems plain that . . . Frederick Rapp had joined the English revolt against symmetrical geometric patterns trimmed with clipped evergreens."[38] Reports of travelers indicated that the flora changed from time to time, but it usually consisted of flowers, fruit trees, vegetables, and hedges. Friedrich List, who visited the town in 1825, noted that the garden even contained cotton and tobacco plants.[39] The garden at Economy included a grotto, a greenhouse, a Classical pavilion surrounded by a moat, and a small, fan-shaped arbor. The innovative and flexible nature of the Harmonists can be seen in the moveable greenhouse that was built at New Harmony so that it could be attached to the house in late winter and early spring, but pulled away in summer. According to Victor Colin Duclos, who became a member of the Robert Owen community at New Harmony after the departure of the Harmonists,

> fronting on Church Street was a greenhouse about 20 x 40 feet, supported on rollers with lower foundation timbers twice the width of the house. On these were rails on which the grooved rollers traveled, allowing the building to be moved back and forth. In each side of the house was a liberal supply of glass windows, and the room was heated with the old style of tinplate stoves. Within this house were grown many kinds of tropical fruits, flowers, ferns, etc.[40]

John Melish mentions that at Harmony there was a botanical garden for Dr. Müller on the outskirts of town, and at New Harmony there was a garden behind George Rapp's house. The location of the garden adjacent to the George Rapp house at New Harmony and Economy reveals that the Harmonists recognized and honored the role of their patriarchal leader. Even though the garden was accessible to the rank-and-file members when they had time to enjoy it, and as such was a communal garden similar to that provided at Ludwigsburg by the civic minded Duke Eberhard Ludwig,[41] it was also a private garden like the elaborate formal gardens of German nobility or like the simpler ones that graced the homes of important figures in German villages such as the garden behind the house of the minister in Iptingen. From the piazza on the back of his house at Economy

---

[38] Griswold,. See footnote 30.
[39] Arndt, George Rapp's Harmony Society, 322.
[40] New Harmony as Seen by Participants and Travelers. (Philadelphia: Porcupine Press, 1975), n.p.
[41] Hiorns, 261.

George Rapp, who might be considered as a combination of German nobleman and minister, could admire his garden and could see the members of his community enjoying themselves during periods of leisure. Also, perhaps in the manner of a European prince, Rapp had a deer park at Economy, although this might also be considered to be a kind of community zoo as much as a private garden.

In addition to being a pleasure garden for Rapp and the other Harmonists, the garden at Economy may have served a symbolic purpose in representing the community as a garden of beauty in the wilderness. The garden, like the town itself, was somewhat isolated from the everyday activities of the world. In the words of George Rapp,

> There is no stopping nor retrograding in the Kingdom of Heaven, but a pressing forward to the goal where a temple of God is erected in a green and tranquil, and delightful valley, that those who are susceptible of light may find consolation and repose, and worship in the holy Tabernacle, in unison, in order and in harmony.[42]

Throughout Rapp's Thoughts on the Destiny of Man are images comparing the Society with a garden. For example, Rapp says that the cooperation of the group "is the production of our time, and will certainly blossom and bear fruit;" the existence of luxury and pride in the outside world "could not destroy the germ & fruitful tree, the branches of which are destined to overspread the earth & spontaneously unite and flourish in perpetual bloom"; and in such a Society, "where the great design is mutual prosperity, and the indissoluble friendship, the exertions of all, in the useful employment of arts or sciences, for the common happiness, is a pleasing exercise for the members in a pure and delightful climate, and on the green & flourishing plains of peace."

The garden at Economy, located at the center of town, served as a constant reminder to the Harmonists of their religious purpose. In addition, it served as a

---

[42] Thoughts on the Destiny of Man, 11.

pleasure garden which honored George Rapp and a place of repose and relaxation for the members of the community.

The Locations of the Buildings

The existence and location of the structures at Economy, Pennsylvania, reveal that the Harmonists provided, to an extent unusual in western Pennsylvania in the second quarter of the nineteenth century, for the religious, social, educational, cultural, physical, and economic necessities of the inhabitants. At all three communities there was a core area at the center of the town which provided basic services for the Harmonist and for the outsider. At Harmony, the core area surrounding the village square included the community kitchen, the store, church, hotel, the homes of George and Frederick Rapp, a warehouse, and the doctor's office. At New Harmony, two of the community dormitories, in addition to the above structures, were also located in the village core. At Economy, the core area included the George and Frederick Rapp houses, the garden, church, feast hall building, granary, store, post office, and the doctor's office. Surrounding this core area at all three villages was a ring of family dwellings and shops, and beyond this the fields and buildings related to agriculture.

The changes in the locations of structures from village to village and the adoption or abandonment of particular buildings were determined by a number of factors, all of which indicate that the Harmonists (or at least George and Frederick Rapp) had a general idea of what the physical nature of their ideal village should be, but were flexible enough to change elements when it seemed necessary.

At New Harmony, as a solution to the housing of the large number of celibate young people in the community during the Indiana period,[43] four dormitories, accommodating approximately seventy Harmonists each, were constructed. Two of these were located in the village core directly on the square and two were a block from the square. At Economy, however, no such dormitories for the

---

[43] Most of these would have been the children born before celibacy was urged in 1807.

unmarried were constructed. It may well be that by the end of the Indiana period there was some discontent expressed by these members and the Harmonist leaders felt that a potentially disruptive element in the community should not be housed separately. In a letter from George to Frederick Rapp in 1824, during the transitional period from New Harmony to Economy, George cautions Frederick

> to be watchful of the young people, especially of the two sexes, also in the house, for instance when you by change are quite a bit away from the house turn it over to the old woman and to Johanna, so that nothing goes on whereby I would be insulted. Lock up these letters or burn them so that someone may not read them and discover everything.[44]

What was George referring to when he uses the term "discover everything"? Was there something that took place that would embarrass the community? Interestingly, when Frederick, en route from New Harmony to Economy, wrote to Romelius Baker giving instructions on what should be done at New Harmony before the Owenites arrived, he said that the "kettles in the community kitchen [of dormitory 2?] should all be removed, and the stoves torn down, so that nothing more of it can be seen."[45]

The locations of the hotels provide another insight into the changing Harmonist attitudes. Whereas those at Harmony and New Harmony were centrally located in the village square where they would be easily accessible to travelers and visitors, the hotel at Economy was a block from the stores and shops along the major road, Store Street. This change suggests that the Harmonists no longer saw the hotel as an economic necessity even though its social function was still recognized. By removing the hotel from the village core the Harmonists were able to accommodate visitors while at the same time keeping them at a distance from the center of town. As a structure used by outsiders, the hotel at Economy was placed where it would be convenient to travelers, but not distracting to the members. The decreasing importance of the hotel might also be indicated by the

---

[44] Arndt, Harmony on the Wabash in Transition, 151.
[45] Ibid, 401.

fact that it was built of wood, while those at the previous villages were of brick construction.

The Harmonist use of steam engines to power the factories freed them from the necessity of locating these structures along the banks of the river. At Harmony the mills were placed along the Connoquenessing Creek, making water the major source of power in their first village. At New Harmony, on the other hand, the cotton gin and cotton factory were located to the east of town and one grist mill was to the south of town;[46] each was situated in relationship to the fields, rather than to the Wabash River, which was to the north. At Economy, the cotton and woolen mills were located along the banks of the Ohio River, but on a bluff approximately eighty feet above it. The Harmonists were thus free from the threat of flooding and yet able to have manufacturing operations.

Most of the commercial structures which omitted noxious odors were placed in the outer ring of each village where they would be less noticeable to the inhabitants than if they were located near the center of the community. For example, the distillery, tannery, dyer's shop, slaughter house, soap maker's shop, and pig sties were located on the perimeters of the village.[47] At all three villages the wind direction was from the southwest and would therefore have kept the odors away from the village core. The only exception to this was at Economy, where the dyers' vats were situated in such a manner that the prevailing winds would have blown the odors into the rest of the village.[48]

One major structure the community built only at Economy, the Feast Hall Building, was located at the center of town. The largest building in the core area, it was used by the Harmonists for social, religious, educational, and cultural

---

[46] There was also a water powered grist mill on a cut-off of the Wabash River.
[47] See John Larner, "Nails and Sundrie Medicines, Town Planning and Public Health in the Harmony Society, 1805-1840," Western Pennsylvania Historical Magazine, XLV, 2 (June, 1962), 125. Larner observed that the only exception to this plan is the slaughter house at New Harmony, which is located near the center of town. However, the map drawn by William Pickering in 1824 shows a warehouse where Larner has located the slaughter house. The slaughter house is not shown on Pickering's map.
[48] Wind data for the three Harmonist towns were obtained from the United States Weather Service.

purposes. In addition to the Society's Feast Hall, where the group gathered during various community celebrations, the building housed a museum that was open to the Harmonists and the general public, a school, and a library. At the previous villages the Harmonists used the church for social and religious gatherings, but by the 1820s the leaders must have recognized the need for a separate building which would serve a number of non-religious, or semi-religious, needs of the community. In its size and central location, the Feast Hall was a practical response to the changing needs of the members, who, by the Economy period, seem to have had more leisure time than they had in the previous settlements; it was also a focal point that indicated to Harmonists and outsiders the opportunities available to those who lived in a religiously oriented society.

Another large and centrally located building at all three villages was the granary.[49] Given that the economic systems at Harmony and New Harmony had a large agricultural base there is nothing significant about the central locations of the granaries. However, since the economy at the village of Economy was based largely on manufacturing, the location of the granary at that village may have been partially a reminder to the Harmonists of their German heritage. In most European rural villages the granary was located at the center of the town where it was used by all. For the Harmonists at their third village their granary was a constant reminder of their German roots, their ties to the land, and their well being. While it would have been more practical to locate all of the granaries near the fields, it was more reassuring to the Harmonists to know that they had a storehouse of food if bad times or the millennium should arrive.

The location of a number of houses at the Harmonist villages reveals that even though the Society was communal and members supposedly equal, there was a certain degree of social stratification. The most obvious example was the centrally located, large, and relatively elegant house built for George Rapp. When the Reverend William Passavant visited Economy in 1840 he noted that not only was

---

[49] There were other granaries at the towns than the centrally located ones at New Harmony and Economy.

Rapp's house the most elegant in town, but that those houses located near to Rapp's were inhabited by "the most influential members, and those who originally invested the largest capital," and that "those . . . whose interest was little or nothing, inhabit the squares most distant from the center."[50]

A similar arrangement seems to have existed at Harmony and at New Harmony. A map of Harmony drawn in 1832 from memory by a member shows that the Bentels, the Wagners, Dr. J. Christoph Müller, and Joseph Neff, all of whom brought money or important services into the community (Müller was the physician), had homes close to the village square. Similarly, at New Harmony many of the homes in the blocks surrounding the square were inhabited either by members who had been in the Society since its founding and who had positions of some importance, or by those who had made large financial contributions to the group. Among the former were George Schmidt, David Lentz, Joseph Dengler, George Foerstner, Johannes Langenbacher, and Johannes Bamesberger. Those who contributed their money were Jacob Neff and Jacob Schreiber. Neff and Peter Schreiber, Jacob's father, were "regarded by George Rapp as the men who gave the society the capital necessary to begin its industry."[51] It may also be significant that of the four couples who had large families, two, the Ralls and the Vogts, had houses on the perimeters of New Harmony. Of the other two, the Schwarts lived two blocks from the village square; there is no record of the location of the Killinger's house. Were the locations outside of the center of town been a subtle form of community disapproval for a couple's failure to practice celibacy?[52] In addition, there is no record of the location of the house of the Jerimias Stag family, the only African-American family in the community,

---

[50] W. A. Passavant, "A Visit to Economy in the Spring of 1840," Western Pennsylvania Historical Magazine, IV: 3 (July, 1921), 145.
[51] Arndt, George Rapp's Harmony Society, 103.
[52] Information on the locations of families at New Harmony is from maps at Old Economy and from a map drawn by Don Blair in "Harmonist Construction," Indiana Historical Society Publications, XXIII, 2 (1964). Blair's map is based on that drawn by William Pickering in 1824.

although some evidence suggests that at Economy the Stag house was on the outskirts of the town.

Most of the houses on the outskirts of town were probably inhabited by the farmers, however, who needed to be near the stables and fields. The self-contained nature of the community and its German origins are shown by the locations of the farmers' houses within the village proper rather than away from it, as was common in most of the agricultural communities in America. A typical American farm family would live apart from the daily activities of the town except for those times when they needed to use the town for selling or purchasing goods. The Harmonists, on the other hand, lived in the town and left it only for their agricultural work. Although a few members of the Society were allowed to travel and reside in the outside world for short periods of time, most remained within the village. This was but one way in which the community leaders insured that the lures of cheap and fertile land did not tempt members away from the town. Those who took care of the animals and those who tended the fields and harvested the crops lived in the village and returned there at the end of day. Isolated farms, like nuclear families, both potentially disruptive to the good of the community, were eliminated by the Society.

A balance of personal and economic elements within the Society by the time the group settled in their third village is seen in the fact that at Economy no one block was completely residential or commercial, but instead a combination. At both Harmony and New Harmony some village blocks consisted entirely of dwellings. At New Harmony, for example, six blocks consisted of family houses only. At Economy, however, although some blocks were predominantly residential, all had at least one, and usually three or four buildings which were important in the economic system of the village.

The roads at all three villages provided communication with the outside world, although at Economy the Ohio River to a certain extent tended to decrease the economic importance of the major roads there. As the Harmonists moved from Harmony to New Harmony and finally to Economy, they widened the major streets and also changed the relationship of the buildings to the streets. At Harmony the buildings fronted the streets with only a narrow sidewalk between the buildings and the street in the German style. A recent visitor to Rapp's home town in Germany has said that

> While Iptingen is not laid out on a grid as is Harmony (and New Harmony and Economy), there are architectural similarities. Buildings are built right up against the street with the same kind of steep-pitched roof the Harmonist used in Harmony to shed heavy snow. A rare few still have wood casement windows not unlike those the Harmonists used in their first large permanent building in Harmony, the 1807 store...[53]

At this early date in their history the Harmonists may still have been conditioned by their European heritage which dictated the most efficient use of space within a village as a result of a scarcity of land. At New Harmony and Economy, on the other hand, the buildings were set back from the street by an area of grass and sidewalk. At Economy there were five-foot broad sidewalks and ten-foot areas of grass between the street and the sidewalk. The streets at Economy were also graded, and although there are no visitors' comments to indicate that the streets were paved, excavation of the main street of Economy during the process of restoration revealed a cobbled and graded street.

An example of the Harmonist combination of practicality and aesthetics was their planting of trees in the village and in the fields. Frederick Rapp believed that Lombardy poplars prevented malarial fever and had hundreds of them transported from Harmony to New Harmony when the Harmonists moved.[54] At Economy mulberry (as well as cherry) trees were planted along both sides of the streets to provide silk for Gertrude Rapp's silk industry. During a visit to Economy in the spring of 1840, William Passavant commented on the efficiency of the Harmonists in their planting of trees in the fields. He observed that

---

[53] John Ruch, "A Visit to Iptingen," Communal Societies, 26: 1 (2006), 85.
[54] William Wilson, Indiana, A History (Bloomington: Indiana University Press, 1966), 41.

if the land was too steep for the plough it was covered with rows of white mulberry trees to supply the silkworms with leaves. If there was a danger of a run washing away, its banks were found lined with willows. If ground was found too marshy for the purpose of agriculture, it was planted with a species of osiers for the manufacture of baskets.[55]

At Harmony and New Harmony water was provided from wells and pumps located throughout the village. At Economy the Harmonists developed a system in which water was supplied from springs and a reservoir to a number of barns, shops, and other structures which needed a continuous supply of water, as well as to some of the dwellings. Most of the drinking water was obtained from the pumps placed at convenient locations throughout the town. Although Frederick Rapp may have seen a similar system of piped water in Philadelphia that had been operating there since 1800[56] or the New York water system which was used in the last quarter of the eighteenth century, it was George Rapp who was instrumental in setting it up. In a letter of July 5, 1824, he stated

> This week two wood-water pipe drillers are coming. We will lead Hoesler's spring which is along the highway, into the city. It has a fall of 25 feet to the middle street. A few days ago I discovered a spring which runs strongly and never dries up and which has at least an 80 foot fall down to the city.[57]

At first pipes consisted of hollowed out logs placed end to end and fitted together with metal pieces, but at a later date ceramic pipes were used to replace those sections of the line which were rotting away.[58] The Harmonist water system was in no way unique, but considering that Pittsburgh had no such system until 1828,[59] the Harmonists' achievement of providing fresh water for drinking, sanitary purposes, and fire protection was no small one.

---

[55] Passavant, 147.
[56] Larner, 137.
[57] Quoted in Arndt's George Rapp's Harmony Society, 310.
[58] For a discussion of the process of boring logs see Daniel B. Reibel, "Non-Metallic Water Pipe and Pump Log Tools," The Chronicle of the Early American Industries Association, XXIV, 2 (June, 1971), 17-21. During the restoration of Old Economy both wooden and ceramic pipes were found.
[59] John Duffy, "Smoke, Smog & Health in Early Pittsburgh," Western Pennsylvania Historical Magazine, VLV, 2 (June, 1962), 104.

Like the water system, there were other elements in the village that were by no means unique or revolutionary in themselves, but which were parts of an exceptionally well-planned community for fewer than one thousand residents.[60] Another example of the practical nature of the Harmonists is that they used their steam engines not only in their factories to power the machinery, but also in their laundry and their wine-making operations. They also used steam to heat some of the factories in the winter, thereby eliminating the danger of fire from stoves while also providing fire protection in the village by water tanks in the factories and by community fire engines. Another example of the intent of the Harmonist leaders to create a model town was that not only was there a doctor in residence, but that at New Harmony and Economy there was an infirmary for the aged and ill.

****

The three villages of the Harmony Society were situated for considerations of agriculture and trade, and for the changing concept of the communal good, which by the 1820s included a substantial amount of interaction with the outside world on economic terms. The adaptability and the practical nature of the Society were revealed in its willingness to abandon a settled village for a new one, to alter or discard some of the elements of the previous village, and to create new elements in the new village.

The street patterns at all three towns show that the Harmonists abandoned the typical street pattern of the rural German village, perhaps being influenced by the rectilinear plan that existed in both Germany and Pennsylvania as a result of the classical movement. The Harmonist villages centered around a square at Harmony and New Harmony, and around a community garden at Economy. The earlier use of the square was appropriate for a society based on the idea of limited trade

---

[60] In 1831, before the major schism, there were about 750 Harmonists at Economy.

within the village and its environs; with the gradual expansion of the economy and the community's growing interaction with outside markets, the square was seen as unnecessary and the garden was created as the focal point of the village. By the time the Harmonists settled at Economy their economic system had passed out of the village matrix and into the world at large. The abandonment of the square also indicated that the Harmonists were practical communitarians who could reject an element of their German heritage when it did not serve their American needs. Unlike the Shakers, whose communities were frequently laid out in a line along a main road with no central square, the Harmonist villages were characterized by their rectilinear quality and by the dominance of a square or central garden. And while a Harmonist square may have functioned like a New England "common," as communitarians the Harmonists did not need a place that was "common" and available to all since in theory everything was in common. In New England private property surrounded a commons; at a Harmonist village all was shared.

Certain structures at the Harmonist villages reveal that the Society experimented with particular forms in order to provide for the religious, social, educational, economic, and cultural needs of the inhabitants during different periods. At New Harmony the Harmonists built four dormitories to house the young celibates, and they built a large church that was used for both social and purely religious purposes. At Economy, the dormitory system was abandoned, and a separate Feast Hall Building served as a community center.

The locations of some of the dwellings indicate that there was a degree of social stratification within the community: those who were in positions of authority were often located near the center of the village, while some of those who continued to have children had houses at the outskirts.

There is no doubt that the Harmonists were aware of the values of a planned community. None of the three villages occupied by the Society was settled in a haphazard fashion; since the size of the Society remained relatively stable, the leaders were able to visualize the ultimate shape of the community and to improve each subsequent village. As such, the three Harmonist villages are noteworthy and significant contributions to town planning in America.

Chapter 3

Harmonist Buildings

It is not surprising that there was no one architectural style common to the American communitarian societies that flourished in the eighteenth and nineteenth centuries. Since communitarian groups originated in different periods, had various national origins, and exhibited a wide variety of philosophies, it is only logical that building styles and functions differed from community to community. The most famous of the communal groups in America, the Shakers, for example, had an essentially rural Anglo-Saxon membership and a philosophy of aesthetics which stressed simplicity, regularity, and order. As a result, the typical architecture of the Shakers, whose first communities were in New England, evolved from the simple dwellings, barns, and public buildings common in the New England countryside.[1] On the other hand, the eighteenth century community at Ephrata, Pennsylvania, had a distinctively late medieval architecture that was characterized, in the *Saal* and *Saron* by a steep roof, small windows, and shed dormers (Figure 5). Even though this style of architecture was more common in the sixteenth than the eighteenth century in Europe and was unique in America in these buildings, the Ephratans imitated a mode that, to them reflected the austerity of the medieval monastery and cloister.[2] Finally, there were plans for ideal villages by such utopian reformers as Robert Owen and Charles Fourier who advocated the creation of communities consisting of buildings which combined a number of past and contemporary architectural styles, including the

---

[1] D. M. C. Hopping and Gerald R. Watland, "The Architecture of the Shakers," Antiques, 72 (October, 1957), 335. Even generalizations about the simplicity of Shaker architecture should be qualified by reference to the elegant Trustees' House at Pleasant Hill, Kentucky, with its twin spiral staircases.

[2] The physical community at Ephrata was in fact called The Cloister.

Georgian, the Greek Revival, and the Gothic Revival,[3] and adapted them to a radical social arrangement (Figure 1). Thus, the styles of the proposed villages of Owen and Fourier were based less on national origin than on the peculiar vision of the leaders who saw that with a change in social arrangements there had to be a corresponding change in the physical form of the community.[4]

The architecture of the Harmonists is unlike that of any of the above groups. The Harmonist villages contained characteristics from the group's German medieval heritage, from the Georgian style that was prevalent in eighteenth century America, and perhaps to a greater degree, especially in the public buildings, from the German Renaissance style.[5]

It may seem uncharacteristic for a communal society that was to a great degree isolating itself from the outside world and consisted of a large number of uneducated peasants and craftsmen to use a style of architecture representative of high rather than of peasant culture. But Frederick Rapp, the financial manager and community architect of the Harmonists, had been a stone mason in Germany and may have had some training as an architect. It is likely that Rapp, whose artistic

---

[3] Donald Drew Egbert, Socialism and American Art (Princeton: Princeton University Press, 1967), 15.
[4] For comments on the architecture of the proposed Owenite villages and Fourierist phalanxes see J. F. C. Harrison, Quest for the New Moral World: Robert Owen and the Owenites in Britain and America (New York, 1968), 254. and Jonathan Beecher and Richard Bienvenu, eds., The Utopian Vision of Charles Fourier (Boston: Beacon Press, 1971).
[5] In my discussion of Harmonist buildings I will use the terms "renaissance," "classical," and "neoclassic." "Renaissance" is a general term to describe the style of architecture that emerged in the sixteenth century in Germany and which was influenced by the revival of classical Greek and Roman forms. "Classicism" refers to a philosophy of architecture that contains those elements of formality, balance, and order that were used by the Greeks and Romans. In its purist form, Classicism in architecture was a strict imitation of the principles laid down by Vitruvius. According to Russell Sturgis in A Dictionary of Architecture and Building (New York: Macmillan Company, 1905), the term "neoclassic" is often synonymous with "renaissance." Both terms suggest the application of Classical, rather than medieval or Gothic, elements in architecture. There is no one building at Economy that is purely neoclassic in its use of classical elements. But there are a number of elements in the architecture and town planning that show that the Harmonists were increasingly influenced by Classical rather than medieval forms. For further examination of the relationship between German Renaissance architecture and Harmonist buildings see the discussions below of the Feast Hall Building, the Dormitory, the Pavilion, and the Grotto.

talents are seen in some drawings that he did in America, was aware of renaissance styles in the major cities of Württemburg.[6]

A study of the architectural forms used by the Harmonists in their three villages provides a number of insights into the aspects of institutional persistence and institutional change in the Society. The ways in which the Harmonists maintained, abandoned, or modified their German cultural traditions are illuminated in the forms and functions of buildings at the three communities established by the Society in America. In addition, particular changes in architectural styles for buildings with similar functions indicate changes that took place in the cultural, social, or religious thought of the community. Furthermore, since the Harmonists were a homogeneous German group, their architecture often reveals characteristics which are more closely related to their national origins than the architecture of Germans in non-communitarian settings who were influenced by styles of other nationalities and who lived in villages and towns which consisted of an amalgam of various national architectural styles.

Harmonist Dwellings

Like many of the successful communitarian societies in nineteenth century America, the Harmonists modified the traditional nuclear family for social and religious reasons.[7] Some communitarians, such as the Perfectionists at Oneida in upstate New York, created a system of "complex marriage" which allowed members to have sexual intercourse with a number of other members. The dyadic relationship condoned by the outside society was abandoned by the Perfectionists and in its place a "family" of some two hundred members lived in separate apartments in the Community Home.[8] Communitarians such as the Shakers

---

[6] There is little information concerning the German years of Frederick Rapp.
[7] For statistics relating to "commitment mechanisms" in American communes see Kanter, 80.
[8] Noyes, 641. For a discussion of living patterns at Oneida by a member see Pierrepont Noyes, My Father's House: An Oneida Boyhood (New York: Farrar & Reinhart, 1937).

advocated and practiced celibacy and lived in dormitories which housed approximately seventy men and women with living quarters on opposite sides of the dormitory. The Harmonists were similar to the Shakers in their advocacy of celibacy. But since celibacy was adopted as a tenet rather than a rule after the Harmony Society was formed by a large number of married people, the ultimate form that the Harmonist "family" took emerged gradually over a period of years.

Since the practice of celibacy was not instituted until three years after the Harmonists began building their first village, Harmony, Pennsylvania, most of the houses there were one or two-story log, frame, or brick structures similar in form to those that the members had lived in when they were in Germany. The only exceptions at Harmony were the few larger buildings occupied by the wealthier or more prestigious members. Even though the Harmonists had a communal form of production and distribution, in the early years those who had brought the most money into the community had the largest houses. For example, those houses at Harmony which were somewhat larger than the typical house were the ones occupied by the George Rapp family, by Frederick Rapp, by the community physician, Dr. Christoph Müller, and by the Langenbachers, the Bentels, and the Wagners.[9] After the Harmonists left Harmony, however, the only large dwellings built were those for George and Frederick Rapp, who were the religious and financial leaders of the community and as such were seen to deserve a house which would complement their positions. The membership would not mind George Rapp living in a bigger home, but members living in various sized houses might cause some jealousy and discontent. By the time the Harmonists moved to Economy in 1825 the family unit, or "household," had evolved into a group of some three to eleven members of both sexes living together in a dwelling that was similar to those of other "households." The typical "family" may have consisted of a husband, a wife, perhaps a child who was born before celibacy was advocated, and other adults who may or may not have been related. At the head of

---

[9] I discuss the relationship between social status and the locations of the dwellings in Chapter 2.

the "household" was a man, after whom the dwelling was named, such as The Baker House.

In their everyday living arrangements the Harmonists were much less formal than the Shakers, who had rigid rules defining virtually all aspects of activity in order to eliminate any possibility of unacceptable relationships between the sexes. For example, a Shaker "sister" and "brother" could not pass on the stairway, nor could they talk together without a third member being present.[10] The Harmonists had no such rules. Their flexibility is revealed in the fact that while they were urged to practice celibacy, they were not forced to, although there may have been a fair amount of social pressure. For the Harmonist a measure of freedom was available within the limits of his or her own household group. They were members of a society which had a communal system of production and distribution and which put community identity ahead of individual identity, and yet they were also members of an intimate group of people who lived in what was essentially a private dwelling. The institution of the household group tended to eliminate the exclusiveness engendered by the nuclear family and yet provide a sense of belonging to a group smaller than the community as a whole.

The most common type of Harmonist dwelling was the two-story frame or brick building with exterior dimensions of 24' x 32', although other types and sizes, such as the smaller log building which was often temporary, were also erected. An indication of the efficiency and of the foresight that the Harmonists had in building their villages was their practice of erecting the temporary log cabins back from the street so that they would not interfere with the later construction of the permanent brick and frame dwellings which were located along the street.[11] When Elias Pym Fordham visited New Harmony in 1818, four years after it was established, he noted that "The houses, logbuilt, are placed at

---

[10] Shaker regulations are reprinted in Edward Deming Andrews, The People Called Shakers (New York: Dover, 1963), 266-268.
[11] Karl Bernhard, Travels through North America during the Years 1825-1826 (Philadelphia: Carey, Lea and Carey, 1828), II, 162.

regular distances, and are each surrounded by a neat kitchen and flower garden, paled in."[12]

Describing New Harmony a decade later, Victor Colin Duclos observed that there were frame and brick buildings as well as some of the remaining log structures:

> In the town and surrounding suburbs there were a great many rudely constructed log cabins which were the homes of these industrious people in the first years of the settlement, many without floors and undoubtedly built for temporary use while the more substantial buildings were being erected. In the town limits were constructed about twenty substantial two story brick buildings.....There were about the same number of frame buildings two stories in height. The dwelling houses both frame and brick were built after the same design with the door opening into the yard....[13]

Since the Harmonists pre-planned their villages rather than erect them haphazardly they knew exactly where each building was to go. A letter from Abishai Way, an outside business partner of the Harmonists, to Frederick Rapp in 1824, indicated that the Harmonists were buying prefabricated parts of what were essentially colonial style buildings from outside suppliers. This, said Way, was an example of an American influence on the "otherwise Swabian style of living."[14] Thus, when they moved from New Harmony to Economy *en masse,* the entire community was provided fairly quickly with shelter that could be abandoned when a more substantial dwelling was completed. Since most of the brick and frame dwellings at each Harmonist village were the same size, a modular system of construction was used. Timbers were cut to a modular length at the saw mill and stored until they could be used in a particular building. A town plan of Economy showing the dwellings which existed in 1840 was drawn for the Historic American Buildings Survey (Pennsylvania #1176). This plan designated four types: A, the most common, was a brick two story dwelling; B was similar in size but of frame construction; D was a log dwelling; E was a brick two-story

---

[12] Arndt, A Documentary History of the Indiana Years, I, 390.
[13] Lindley, New Harmony as Seen by Participants and Travelers. (Porcupine Press, 1975), n.p.
[14] Arndt, Harmony on the Wabash in Transition, 39.

structure slightly smaller than A. There were also a few single-story frame houses. The relatively large number of log buildings at Harmony was indicative of the fact that during their first years in America the Harmonists built dwellings that were simple and inexpensive (Figure 6). By the time the Harmonists came to Economy the log house was used mainly as a temporary shelter while the permanent house was being built. The exterior measurements of common Type A and B houses show that most were constructed on the eight foot module. Seven of these houses chosen at random from the Historic American Buildings Survey had the following exterior measurements:

> 32' 4 1/2" x 24'3"
> 32' 4 1/2" x 24' 4"
> 32' 3" x 24' 6"
> 32' 4" x 24' 3"
> 32' 6" x 24' 2"
> 32' 3" x 24' 2"
> 32' 2" x 24' 7"

According to Don Blair, who studied the construction of the Harmonist dwellings at New Harmony,

> timbers were prepared at the mill and marked with the proper erection numbers in much the same manner as used by the modern prefabrication building. When a house was to be erected, the proper number of each item was taken to the site and the framework assembled on the ground, the final adjustment thus being made under conditions which did not require that the weight of the timber be supported. When the actual erection was under way, the pieces fitted together without difficulty because of this intermediate step.[15]

The basic exterior form of the brick and frame dwelling was similar to that found in some dwellings in George Rapp's home town of Iptingen, although those in George Rapp's German village were frequently half-timber structures. This essentially Germanic form is two stories high with a gable roof and a center

---

[15] "Harmonist Construction," Indiana Historical Society Publications, XXIII, 2 (1964), 57.

chimney.[16] A characteristic architectural element of the family dwellings at Economy was the placing of the single door on the gable end and facing the garden rather than the street. This too was typical of many of the small dwellings in Southern Germany which had gardens or small courtyards which were accessible from the house rather than from the street.[17] It is significant that at Economy most of the private dwellings had doors that opened onto the private gardens at the side of the houses whereas the public structures, including the George Rapp house, had doors opening onto the street. The private gardens for each household served both practical and personal functions. Even though most of the food was distributed to the households from the stores and communal fields, the individual gardens provided the members with their daily vegetables and fruits and allowed some sense of individuality. In addition, the love of flowers and of gardening that has been seen as a characteristic of the German people[18] was given expression within the Society by the household gardens.

One of the basic differences between the Harmonist dwellings and those that the Harmonists were familiar with in Germany was in the use of materials. While the Harmonists were most familiar with the half-timber house in Germany (George Rapp was born in such a house),[19] the only structure at Economy having this form of construction is the Granary. There are probably a number of reasons for the Harmonist choice of a brick facing on their dwellings: there was an

---

[16] For a discussion of the Continental house that characterized the Mid-Atlantic region see Henry Glassie, Pattern in the Material Folk Culture of the Eastern United States (Philadelphia: University of Pennsylvania Press, 1971) 54-55, and Richard Pillsbury and Andrew Kardos, A Field Guide to the Folk Architecture of the Northeastern United States (Dartmouth, New Hampshire: Geography Publications at Dartmouth, n.d.) 45-56.
[17] Raymond Bonin, ed., Le Württemberg (Tübingen, 1950), 28.
[18] Oscar Kuhns in The German and Swiss Settlement of Colonial Pennsylvania (New York: Henry Holt and Company, 1901), 23, says that "A love of flowers has always been the characteristic of the natives of the Palatinate, and this love is quite as noticeable in Pennsylvania as in the home-country. Benjamin Rush has noted the importance of the cultivation of garden vegetables by the Germans: 'Pennsylvania is indebted to the Germans for the principal part of his knowledge in horticulture.'"
[19] There is a photograph of Rapp's house in Arndt, George Rapp's Harmony Society, 16. Characteristic of this medieval dwelling type, Rapp's house in Iptingen has a much steeper roof than the typical Harmonist dwelling.

abundance of wood in America to fire bricks; brick was a much more durable material than wood and provided better insulation and protection from fire; Harmonist leaders who saw the extensive use of brick in Philadelphia and realized its advantages; and since the classical influence is evident in a number of buildings at Economy, Frederick Rapp may have seen the half-timber form as incompatible with the order and regularity that the classical form symbolized. What is important is that the Harmonists were influenced by their German heritage in using the essentially continental form, but they did not imitate it blindly. When the Harmonists built their early dwellings at their first village they often imitated Germanic styles with steeply pitched roofs; however, when they settled their final village they brought lumber for prefabricated type, American style houses.

The Baker House[20] at Economy is a good example of the typical Harmonist dwelling. From the outside the house is simple and unpretentious (Figure 31). The major characteristics identifying this as a Harmonist house include the door on the side, the flat brick lintels above the windows, the stone foundation, the absence of two windows on the door side due to the inside stairway along the wall, the denticulated cornice, and the occasional lean-to addition which gives the Baker House an appearance similar to a New England saltbox except for the brick construction. The lean-tos, or annexes, were more common at Economy than at the previous villages[21] and were probably added to the dwellings after a decision was made to abandon the dormitory system that was used at New Harmony. If this was the case, the annexes would have provided room for those who had lived in these dormitories. Why, then, did the Harmonists not devise a house form that would have accommodated those members from the dormitories who moved to Economy? There are two probable explanations. The first is that the Harmonists were familiar with the form that they built at their two previous villages and did

---

[20] Named after Romelius Langenbacher (changed to Baker) who lived in the house from 1826 to 1868.
[21] A drawing of the locations and shapes of the structures at Harmony made by a member shows that almost all of the dwellings at Harmony were without lean-tos.

not want to abandon the modular system that had served them so well. The addition of the annex, therefore, did not involve any major structural changes in the basic building and the prefab lumber could easily be used. The second explanation is that the Harmonists had planned to build dormitories at Economy but realized after they arrived there that the dormitory system should not be continued.[22] If this was so, those who were in the New Harmony dormitories could be relocated in existing households.

The floor plan of the typical dwelling consists of an entrance hall, a kitchen, a combination living room and bedroom on the first floor, and two bedrooms on the second floor. The annex contains one or two bedrooms on the first floor. Some imaginative historians have suggested that the pacifist Harmonists did this so that the women would confront and apparently dissuade any hostile visitors from violent actions. But a more reasonable explanation is that since the women got up first to fix breakfast, they slept close to the kitchen. One of the characteristic continental traits of the Harmonist dwelling is the stairway, which is located in the corner next to the door of the house rather than in the middle of the first floor. The farm houses most common in the Mid-Atlantic region

> combine Georgian with earlier folk features – Old Rhineland peasant interiors stuffed into stylish eighteenth century shells. They are two rooms deep, have internal gable-end chimneys, a placement of windows and doors which approximates symmetry, and a low pitched roof like the Georgian houses, but they lack most of the stylish trim, the broad open stair has been replaced by a narrow boxed-in medieval stair which curls up in one corner, the hall-way is absent, and the house has a three or four-room continental plan.[23]

The houses built at Economy lack the internal gable-end chimney and instead have the central chimney that was typical of the Württemberg dwelling but otherwise similar to what Henry Glassie calls the continental house. A non-Harmonist Pennsylvania-German house with a floor plan that is similar to that of

---

[22] A few large dormitory-type buildings were erected at Economy, but they probably housed outside workers.
[23] Glassie, 54.

the Harmonist dwelling is the famous Müller House at Milbach, Pennsylvania, built in 1752. This plan "repeats faithfully a Rhine valley type, with a three room arrangement . . . with a central chimney. The mainroom was a *kuche*, a combined kitchen-dining room of ample size, with a winding stair at the corner near the door. The rest of the house was divided into a *stube* (living room) and *kammer* (bedroom)."[24] While the Müller house is somewhat larger than a typical Harmonist one and there is no partition between the hall and the kitchen as there is at Economy, the arrangement of the rooms is virtually identical (Figure 7). The architecture of the Harmonist dwellings reveals a number of things about the aesthetic and social concerns of the community. First, the floor plan, the door opening onto the garden, and the boxed-in staircase are elements of a rural and basically medieval German heritage that the Harmonists transferred from Württemberg. Second, the absence of such medieval Germanic elements as the half-timber construction, herringbone patterns and strap hinges on the doors, casement windows, and steep roofs, and the presence of a low pitched roof, brick construction, and a roughly symmetrical placement of sash windows reveal that the architect-builder (more than likely Frederick Rapp) was adapting certain elements of Georgian architecture to the Harmonist house. Finally, subtle and drastic changes in the housing for the members of the Society show that there were changing conditions within the community. Most of the dwellings at Harmony were log, frame, or brick structures for the single family, although there were a few larger structures for the wealthy and influential members. When the Harmonists moved to New Harmony, however, only the George Rapp house was significantly larger than the others, an indication of the growth of his prestige and the general equality of the rest of the members. One might speculate that the

---

[24] Hugh Morrison, Early American Architecture (New York: Oxford University Press, 1952), 543. For a discussion of German architectural characteristics, see also Thomas Jefferson Wertenbaker, The Founding of American Civilization: The Middle Colonies (New York: Charles Scribner's Sons, 1938); Wiliam Murtagh, Moravian Architecture and Town Planning (Chapel Hill: The University of North Carolina Press, 1967); and Thomas Waterman, The Dwellings of Colonial America (Chapel Hill: The University of North Carolina Press, 1950).

changes in the size of the dwellings reflected the changing relationship between the members and George Rapp. Whereas at Harmony Rapp's authority may have been threatened (actually or theoretically) by the wealthy members of the community, and at New Harmony by the large number of youngish members living in dormitories, at Economy these threats were seemingly eliminated. Interestingly, the threat came from outside in the person of "Count Leon" whose influence led to the defection of a number of young members.

Also during the New Harmony period the Harmonists built dormitories for the unmarried members of the community that were similar in function to the Shaker dormitories. But at Economy the dormitory system was abandoned and most members lived in the two-story frame building with annexes attached. The nuclear family that arrived in America in 1804 was gradually transformed to the "household" at Economy, having undergone a period of experimentation at New Harmony during which the nuclear family (though celibate), the household, and the large dormitory families existed side by side.

Harmonist Dormitories

With the construction of the four communal dormitories[25] at New Harmony the Society departed from its European and its Pennsylvania experiences to create new and radical living arrangements for some of the members of the community. Since the Harmonists knew of and communicated with different Shaker communities, and especially with the village of West Union, Indiana, they may have been influenced by the Shaker system of housing large numbers of men and women in dormitories.[26] In 1816 George's eight-year-old granddaughter, Gertrude, spent some time living with the Shakers at West Union so that she could learn English, and when she was older she returned there to learn the details

---

[25] The Harmonists did not use this term, but referred to House No. 1, no 2, etc.
[26] They were also undoubtedly aware of the dormitory system in German monasteries and in the dormitory system at the communitarian villages of Ephrata.

of silk production. Although in Shaker dormitories the men lived on one side and the women on the other, there are no records, either written or material, that reveal what the arrangements were for separating the genders in a Harmonist dormitory. On the first floor a dormitory had a fireplace for cooking, and a dining room. Because the fireplaces in the kitchens were relatively small, community ovens in other buildings were often used for baking.[27] According to Victor Colin Duclos, who lived in New Harmony as a member of Robert Owen's community after the Harmonists had sold the village, three of the four dormitories were similar in size and style: these dormitories numbered as 1, 2, 3, and 4 by the Harmonists and called "Community Buildings" by them, were three-story brick structures 40' x 70' with hallways on both floors running the whole length of the building and which contained sixteen large apartments. Although the dormitories had gable roofs with interior end chimneys that gave them a decidedly Georgian appearance,[28] dormitory number 2 is distinct in that it has a mansard (or German gambrel) roof.[29] This building appears to have been the first public structure designed by Frederick Rapp in the German Renaissance style (Figure 8). The use of the mansard roof by builders

> originated in the desire to reduce the height of the medieval roof, especially over buildings with a double file of rooms. Although known by the name of the French architect Mansart when used on all four slopes with a level cornice, it was by no means confined to France.[30]

By the early eighteenth century variations of the mansard roof were common in Germany, especially in the public buildings of more than two stories where the architect wanted to emulate the Classical style. In the museum at Old Economy

---

[27] Donald MacDonald, "The Diaries of Donald MacDonald, 1824-1826," Indiana Historical Society Publications, XIV: 2 (1942), 219.
[28] While dormitories 1, 3, and 4 have been destroyed or altered beyond recognition, there is a photograph of number 3, and dormitory 2 had been restored.
[29] According to Wertenbaker, "Distinctive of Germany itself . . . was the modified form of the mansard roof, the gambrel with the lower slope often bell-shaped, the upper overlapping to form upper eaves," 314.
[30] Fiske Kimball, Domestic Architecture of the American Colonies and of the Early Republic (New York: Charles Scribner's Sons, 1922), 45.

today there is a photograph of a house of a well-to-do farmer in Aurich, Germany, that has a mansard roof and is stylistically very similar to the New Harmony Dormitory 2 except that the German building is half-timbered. Aesthetically the high-pitched roof form and the half-timber construction were suited to Gothic architecture with its emphasis on vertical lines, but with the more horizontal style of the seventeenth and eighteenth century classicism, the steep gable stood out as an anachronism. The mansard roof, on the other hand, made the roof a lower mass which could be brought into harmony with the building below.[31] The striking difference between the Harmonist's classically influenced dormitory and the completely medieval Sisters' House at Ephrata is indicative of the more sophisticated aesthetic philosophy of the Harmonist architect. While the Ephrata builder looked back in time for his building models (Figure 5), Frederick Rapp selectively chose from the past and present those elements that would be aesthetically pleasing and practical.

A letter from George to Frederick Rapp in 1823 reveals that Frederick was not the only designer for Harmonist buildings. While Frederick was away from New Harmony on business, "Father" George Rapp decided to alter the plans for dormitory 2, which was under construction. He wrote,

> I was called into house no. 2 and there I discovered that the upper floor with its beautiful rooms could not be lived in, because fifty persons had good and plenty [of] room in the two lower stories, and if one would put more people into it there would be too much activity of cooking, baking, and washing, &c. For that reason I changed the plan of no. 3 and am having no French roof put on it. So we are building no 2 about like no. 1.[32]

That Rapp refers to the roof as "French" indicates that he and Frederick were aware of the French classical influence that was prevalent in Württemberg in the

---

[31] Anthony Blunt, Francois Mansart and the Origins of French Classical Architecture (London: The Warburg Institute, 1941), 39. For an example of an early eighteenth century mansard roof in Germany see the photograph in Adolf Bernt, Deutsch Burgerhauser (Tübingen: Ernst Wasmuth, 1968), 196. The mansard roof of this 1710 building is almost identical to that of dormitory 2 at New Harmony.

[32] Arndt, George Rapp's Harmony Society, 242.

eighteenth-century.[33] Although the gambrel form used at New Harmony was distinctive of Germany, its origins were in the mansard roofs of seventeenth and eighteenth century France. This letter to Frederick concerning the roof styles may also suggest that the beginnings of discontent were emerging among the people in the dormitories and that George was having second thoughts about their value. In a letter to Frederick, George Rapp said that

> there is always something to adjust and to pacify as you report concerning [dormitory] no 1 is not surprising, it will still take a while before the corners have been smoothened, but who would suspect that the beautiful butterfly in the worm if one would not know that beforehand, that is what will happen with our generation, we must only wait longer, the prize, however, is of course offered only to the fighter....[34]

And another letter from George at Harmony to Frederick who is completing arrangements for the move from New Harmony warns Frederick to "be watchful of the young people, especially of the two sexes also in the house, for instance when you by chance are quite a bit away from the house, turn it over to the old woman and to Johanna, so that nothing goes on whereby I would be insulted."[35]

George also makes the unusual request that Frederick "Lock up these letters or burn them so that someone may not read them and discover anything,"[36] In a January 1825 letter to those remaining at New Harmony to finish up the transfer of the community to the Owenites, Frederick instructs that "the kettles in the community kitchen should all be removed, and the stoves torn down, so that nothing more of it can be seen."[37] What this means is difficult to determine. In any event, when the Harmonists moved to Economy, the dormitory system was abandoned and most of the Harmonists lived in the community households.

---

[33] See the chapter entitled "L'Influence Francaise Au XVIIIe Siecle" in Bonnin, Le Württemberg, 206-209.
[34] Arndt, Harmony on the Wabash in Transition, 262.
[35] Ibid, 151.
[36] Ibid, 151
[37] Ibid, 400

Without supporting evidence one can only surmise that dormitories were erected only at New Harmony because George or Frederick Rapp saw them as practical solutions for housing the young people who were reaching adulthood and for those who came to the Society unmarried during the New Harmony period.[38] A child born during the pre-celibacy period of 1804 (and even earlier) to 1807, would be a teenager during the end of the New Harmony period between 1822 and 1824. Just as the baby boomers born in the United States between 1946 and 1964 have been described as a "pig in the python" who influenced society in different ways during particular phases of their lives, the Economy teens and young adults during the New Harmony years must have created some difficulties for the Society. Since celibacy was not adopted as a tenet until 1807, most of the dwellings at Harmony, Pennsylvania, reflected the traditional family structure. Why, then, were no dormitories erected at the final home of the Harmonists in Economy? The answer seems to be that either the Harmonists members who lived in the dormitories disliked the living conditions and wanted to live in more intimate households, or that George Rapp saw the beginnings of discontent among the young dormitory dwellers and decided that the household system was best suited to the needs of the individual and to those of the community as a whole. Rather than having a large cohort of young Harmonists living together (and influencing one another) in dormitories, they were spread about the village of Economy where they would be influenced by older members of the community. An indication of the dissatisfaction with the policy of celibacy of many of the younger members of community at New Harmony is that when the schism took place in 1832 at Economy, a large number of those who left the community eventually married.

---

[38] For statistics concerning the ages of those who left Economy during the schism of 1832 see Chapter 2.

The Rapp House

The largest and most elegant dwelling constructed by the Harmonists at Economy is the George Rapp house, which was also called the "Great House," the "Big House," and the "Rapp Mansion" (Figure 35). The Rapp House actually consists of two houses which are joined together and which, presumably, were connected to one another in such a way that access to each was possible without going outside. During George Rapp's life the house was also occupied by his wife, Christina; his daughter, Rosina; his daughter-in-law, Johanna; his sister, Barbara; his granddaughter, Gertrude; Jacob Henrici, who moved into the house in 1834 when Frederick died and who, with R. L. Baker, took over Frederick Rapp's management of the external affairs of the Society; George Fleckhammer, a gardener and friend of George; Florian Keppler; Conrad Boehm, a glover and confidant of George; and Eusebius Böhm, who came to the Great House after his father, Conrad, died in 1842.[39]

The style of the Rapp House at Economy (which includes the adjoining George Rapp house that was built in 1826 and the Frederick Rapp house, built in 1828) is indicative of the strong Classical strain in Harmonist architecture, and reflects the Harmonist belief that they could create order and regularity out of chaos in preparing for the millennium. The relationship between the classical style and thought in the Age of Reason represented a major change in man's attitude towards his environment. By the eighteenth century,

> gone is the medieval "acceptance" of nature taking its course, along with the unworked materials, exposed construction, and additive composition that expressed it. This design is informed by very different convictions: that the world has a basic immutable order; that men by powers of reason

---

[39] Evelyn P. Matter, The Great House (Old Economy: Harmonie Associates, 1970), 33; and Daniel B. Reibel, A Guide to Old Economy (Harrisburg: The Pennsylvania Historical and Museum Commission, 1972), 30.

can discover what that order is; and that, discovering it, they can control environment as they will.[40]

Thus, although some historians have concentrated on the strong mystical strain in the Harmonist philosophy, one can see that the Harmonists were in some respects heirs to the Age of Reason in their aesthetic expression.[41]

Both the George Rapp house and the Frederick Rapp house are two and a half story brick buildings with gable roofs.[42] However, as a result of the double end chimneys on the Frederick Rapp house being connected with horizontal brick parapets, that building has a much more purely Georgian appearance than does the George Rapp house, and suggests that Frederick, who spent much time in the outside world in his business and cultural affairs, was more Americanized than George. The non-Georgian elements of the George Rapp house include the truncated gable roof, which was common in Germany,[43] and the porch, or piazza, on the rear. This piazza may have been inspired by similar ones on Pennsylvania farm houses or by the balconies on Swiss influenced houses in southern Württemberg (Figure 9).

In the 1880s the Harmonists altered the truncated roof and made it a gable. One might speculate that at a period when the Harmonists were becoming more and more involved in business ventures in the outside world they changed the

---

[40] Alan Gowans, Images of American Living (Philadelphia: J. B. Lippincott Company, 1964) 116-117.
[41] For a discussion of the symbolic and mystical elements in the Harmony Society see Hilda A. Kring, "The Harmonists: A Folk Cultural Approach" (unpublished Doctoral dissertation, University of Pennsylvania, 1969. Kring tends to find symbolic significance in many of the designs at Economy; however, although there was a strain of mysticism, as I show there was also a consistent classical motif.
[42] The George Rapp House was completed in 1826 and the Frederick Rapp House sometime between 1828 and 1831.
[43] For numerous examples of truncated and hipped roofs in Württemberg see photographs in the following: Schönes Schwabenland (Stuttgart, 1968); Adolf Bernt, Deutsch Bürgerhauser (Tübingen: Ernst Wasmuth, 1968); Otto Heuschele, Württemberg: Bilder eines deutschen Landes (Frankfurt, 1969); and Otto Siener, Württemberg (Tübingen, 1950).

appearance of what was in effect their business office from the more Germanic style to one that resembled the typical American roof.[44]

The three front doors of the Rapp House are early Georgian in style, with the center one having a triangular pediment above Doric columns and a fan window. The end doors have a semi-circular transom with a flower design that Hilda Kring suggests may be the symbolic rose of the Harmonists, but which more than likely is patterned after a design in one of the numerous eighteenth-century architectural handbooks. An almost identical design can be seen in the transom of the Port Royal house at Frankford, Pennsylvania, which was built in 1764.[45]

The increasing use of Classical elements in architectural design is evident in the changing treatments of doorways at the three Harmonist villages. There is a gradual abandonment of stone-carving in the doorways of the public buildings and an adoption of the Georgian pilasters, transoms, and pediments in wood.[46] The elaborate and sometimes symbolic carved lintels that were common in Rhine Valley houses[47] were incompatible with the order and regularity of the Georgian style. At Harmony, for example, there were at least four doorways with relatively elaborate carvings, ranging from the braided pattern around the door of the store, to the rose, lily, and Virgin Sophia motif in the lintel of the warehouse[48] (Figure 10). At New Harmony, the only documented use of a carved lintel was that of the rose motif in the lintel of the 1822 cruciform church. At Economy, however, the doorways of the public buildings do not have this characteristically German

---

[44] When restoration began in the 1930s the roof was restored to its original lines with the truncated roof.
[45] The entrance hall of the Port Royal house has been re-erected in the Winterthur Museum. For a photograph see Gowans, 159.
[46] Of course, one has to realize that there are more remaining buildings at Economy than there are at New Harmony. So often archival drawings of buildings at New Harmony are used to help understand what existed there.
[47] Wertenbaker, 297.
[48] The symbolism of these figures is discussed in Chapter 4.

stone-carving and instead exhibit the more Americanized Georgian style. The only example of a carved lintel at Economy is that on the flax house.[49]

The emergence of the Georgian doorway can be seen at Harmony, where the Frederick Rapp house has a rather simple Classical pediment and engaged pillars (Figure 11). By the time the Harmonists completed their final village, this early form of architectural expression by Frederick Rapp had evolved into the balanced and proportioned Georgian doorways of the Rapp House and the Feast Hall Building.

In its functions, the large and relatively elegant Rapp House combined the religious and the secular concerns of the community. It served as the dwelling for George Rapp and his family, and in its elegance honored his position as the religious leader of the Society. A visitor to the town in 1826 noted the apparent incongruity between the communal philosophy of the Harmonists and the obvious superiority of Rapp's dwelling, which, he said, "speaks rather freely against the equality he preaches to his people." Yet this same visitor observed that the house existed "without exciting jealousy or becoming a stumbling block."[50] Even though the comparative opulence of the Rapp House might have disturbed those who expected all of the dwellings in a communal village to be identical, this probably would not have disturbed most of the Harmonists.[51] These Germans created a commune in which all were equal in God's eyes, but they were also a religious group who reorganized the nuclear family into an extended one of men and women whose spiritual "father" was George Rapp. Complete equality would have been unthinkable to most of the members. They accepted the paternalistic elements as both practically necessary and spiritually desirable. Just as the minister in a German town was provided with a suitable house, so was George

---

[49] While the flax house is no longer standing, there is a photograph of the doorway in the museum archives.
[50] Bernhard, II, 162.
[51] There were, however, a number of instances of individuals who left the community because they felt that George Rapp was too authoritarian and rigid. Historian Karl Arndt became increasingly critical of George Rapp's authoritarian nature in his studies of the group.

Rapp. The Harmonists, it should be realized, were at the same time radical communists who were reforming society by the creation of a utopian village, and conservative peasants maintaining the sense of community that they knew in Germany through the master-peasant arrangement that was so much a part of their heritage.

The size and elegance of the Rapp House were not merely to honor George Rapp, but were also public relations elements designed to impress visitors from the outside world. "This house," one writer reported,

> dominates the villages in the same manner that George Rapp dominated the lives of the Society. The road through town . . . [passed] the Great House so all the world's people could see what a great leader George Rapp was and, as he expressed it, "what a united people could do."[52]

The main doorway of the Rapp House fronts on the street rather than on the side as do those of the household dwellings, and as such gave Rapp the disadvantage of less privacy than the average member. This arrangement allowed Rapp to suitably welcome visitors such as social reformers and business associates. Rapp was shrewd enough to realize that in his business dealings the Harmony Society had to appear as successful as possible. It seems likely that since Frederick Rapp was the financial leader of the community his house was used to welcome business associates (and perhaps some friends from the outside world) while George's house was used to receive other visitors.[53] That the appearance of the Rapp House was important to the Harmonists is indicated by the fact that the front of the building is faced with brick in a Flemish bond pattern while the back of the house uses a common bond. The Flemish bond was more decorative than the common bond; however, it was more difficult to produce.[54] Since the visitors saw

---

[52] Daniel Reibel, "Preface" to Evelyn Matter's The Great House (Old Economy, 1970), iii.
[53] Almost all of the visitors who left written reports of Economy mentioned that they were welcomed into the George Rapp house and dined or had a glass of wine with George.
[54] Charles M. Stotz, The Architectural Heritage of Early Western Pennsylvania (Pittsburgh: The University of Pittsburgh Press, 1966), 27. Stotz notes that this practice was not unique to the Harmonists.

only the front of the Great House it was not necessary to use the Flemish bond where they could not see it on the rear of the house.

Seen from this perspective, the size and elegance of the Rapp House were not incongruous with the communal system of the Harmonists. In its style the Great House shows that the Harmonists accepted Classical trends and that they were more contemporary than many other communitarian societies in nineteenth century America. Donald Drew Egbert has noted that "The same up-to-dateness can be seen in the buildings of the Mormons and of the Oneida Community, especially after these groups had obtained a certain amount of wealth, and with it more awareness of worldly fashions."[55] Unlike the Mormons, however, the Harmonists did not imitate the Greek revival style which was becoming popular in the 1830s, but instead incorporated those elements of style common in their near past.[56] Thus, the Georgian elements at Economy were popular in America in the last half of the eighteenth century while in the first half of the nineteenth century, when Harmony was built, the Greek revival style was in vogue. In its function, the Rapp House served as a combination minister's home, duke's palace, and merchant's office, accommodating both the community and those who visited from the outside. It is, in some ways, a testament to the strength of the Harmony Society and a symbol of the power exercised by George Rapp.

The Feast Hall Building

Dominating the northwest quadrant of the village center at Economy and separated from the Rapp House in the southwest quadrant by the main street, is the Feast Hall Building (Figure 32). These two structures, along with the Church, which is facing the Great House, stand as reminders of the peculiar balance the Harmonists maintained between their leader's strength, the religious purpose of

---

[55] Egbert, Socialism and American Art, 9.
[56] Egbert noted that "the early Mormon temple at Kirtland, Ohio, completed in 1836, was a naïve mixture of the late Georgian and the new Greek Revival and Gothic Revival styles," 9.

the community, and the social, cultural, and intellectual needs of the members. Both are marked by features of Germanic and Classical architecture; both present an impressive face to the world, with their Georgian doorways and their elaborate Flemish brickwork on the sides fronting the streets. In terms of mass, however, the Church fails to assume the visual significance of the 54' by 120' Feast Hall building with its uniquely Germanic gambrel roof. In fact, the church, which is 50' by 80', seated only seven hundred members, while the Feast Hall itself seated up to one thousand. There are a number of possible explanations for this. First, the Harmonists may have intended to carry their philosophy of celibacy to the extreme of having a separate house of worship for the men and the women. If this were the case, the Harmonists never built the second permanent church. A more logical explanation is that since the church was not begun until 1828, the year of the completion of the Feast Hall Building, the leaders may have realized that their members would not increase and that they did not need a church that would accommodate more than the approximately seven hundred members at the time. A third explanation for the larger size of the Feast Hall is that more room was needed there for the movement of people during the serving and consumption of meals.

The similarity of the Feast Hall Building at Economy to Dormitory number 2 at New Harmony is striking and clarifies the meaning the building held for the Society. Although the Dormitory is smaller (50' by 70'), both buildings have almost identical gambrel roofs with dormers, suggesting that for the Harmonists the Hall was connected with their communal way of life. Settling in Economy, they adopted the system of individual "family" households; yet they constructed the Feast Hall, with its feast hallroom, or *saal*, on the second floor, in the style of their recently vacated dormitory. Significantly, the purpose of the Feast Hall was to reinforce group solidarity by counterbalancing the individualization allowed at Economy by allowing members living in the households to have their own gardens. Typically, the Harmonists gathered in the *saal* for group ceremonies and meals at Easter, the *Pfingfest* (six weeks after Easter), the Fourth of July, which, coincidentally was an American celebration and also the date in 1804 when the Harmonists arrived in Baltimore on the *Aurora*, the *Erntfest* (a harvest festival in the late summer, the *Liebesmahl* (a religious love fest), Christmas, and the Harmoniefest, which celebrated the founding of the Society on February 15, 1805.[57]

The practice of group celebrations may have been familiar to the Harmonists in Germany, for there, beginning in the Middle Ages, guild feasts in guild buildings were important parts of the life of the community. Originally these buildings had a guild office and archives for general administration on the lower floor and a hall for general meetings on the upper floor.[58] For the members of the guilds the feasts served to remind them of their common bond and of the advantages that they received as a result of their group solidarity. The feasts served a similar purpose for the Harmonists. Unlike the church services, the feasts were more festive and social in nature even though they too had religious functions.

The structure of the Feast Hall Building, with its Germanic gambrel and hipped ends, fairly uncommon in Pennsylvania, suggests that the Harmonists here drew from their German heritage. Even though the gambrel roof was a common feature in Germany in the seventeenth and eighteenth centuries, there are relatively few of these buildings in Pennsylvania. The explanation seems to be that the gambrel roof is well suited for large, public buildings, since it gives added space on the second or third floor.[59] However, most of the early public buildings in Pennsylvania were erected by English, rather than German, immigrants who

---

[57] Daniel B. Reibel and Patricia Black, A Manual for Guides, Docents, Hostesses, and Volunteers of Old Economy (Ambridge: The Harmonie Associates, 1970), n.p.
[58] Howard Saalman, Medieval Cities (New York: George Braziller, 1968), 37. For a discussion of guilds see George Clune, The Medieval Guild System (Dublin: Browne and Nolan, 1943), and George Renard, Guilds in the Middle Ages (London: G. Bell and Sons, 1918, reprinted by Augustus M. Kelley, 1968).
[59] The hotel at Harmony also had a gambrel roof.

had no proprietary interests in the colony.[60] Significantly, a number of gambrel roofed buildings were constructed by the Moravians, who, like the Harmonists, were a communal group that established entire villages. For both communities the gambrel was used in what can be called public buildings, such as the halls and dormitories.[61] The German gambrel roof, with its upper slope often overlapping to form an eave, was one of the German architectural reflections of the renaissance that was used by the Harmonists, German immigrants who had both the inclination and the wealth to build "public" buildings, that is, communal buildings within the Society. Moreover, there were educated members of the community who would have been aware of Renaissance buildings in the Stuttgart area.[62]

In addition to the Harmonists' use of the Renaissance styles in the construction of the Feast Hall Building, they may also have drawn upon their memory of the *Rathaus*, or town hall, which served as the cultural center of the German village, and has been noted previously, the mansarded roofed farmhouse in Aurich, Germany, is similar to Dormitory number 2 at New Harmony and the Feast Hall building. It is worth noting that there was no building like the Feast Hall Building at their two earlier settlements; perhaps the Harmonists by this time were becoming more aware of their image as successful settlers of German ancestry, or perhaps with the pressures of gaining a foothold and becoming successful behind them, the Harmonists felt the need for a structure which would

---

[60] G. Edwin Brumbaugh, "Colonial Architecture of the Pennsylvania Germans," The Pennsylvania-German Society Proceedings and Addresses, 1930, XLI (1933), 8.

[61] Examples of gambrel roofed buildings at Moravian settlements are the Boys' School and Whitefield Hall at Nazareth, and the Bell House at Bethlehem. One of the few private dwellings with a gambrel roof is the George Müller House at Milbach, Pennsylvania. For a discussion of European variations of the gambrel, see Henry Lionel Williams and Ottalie K. Williams, A Guide to Old American Houses, 1700-1900 (New York: A. S. Barnes and Co., 1962. Thomas Jefferson Wertenbaker in The Founding of American Civilization: The Middle Colonies (New York: Cooper Square Publishers, 1963) said that the gambrel style might have been dominant in Pennsylvania had the German immigrants been wealthy and aware of the renaissance buildings in their homeland.

[62] In a lecture on the Harmonist gardens, Ralph Griswold, the landscape architect of the restoration of Old Economy, said that the similar roof design between the older parts of the palace of Ludwig IV, Duke of Württemberg, at Ludwigsburg, near Stuttgart, suggests that Frederick was influenced by the palace architecture.

serve their demands for social and cultural activity. The economic shift in the Society from agriculture, to manufacturing, to growing external investments may have provided the members with more leisure time than they had experienced at the previous villages. Also, the Society seems to have institutionalized the feast as a community experience by the time they settled in Economy.

Certainly the architectural detail inside as well as outside of the Feast Hall Building demonstrates a deliberate attempt on the part of the Harmonists to build in the style that was in vogue when they left Germany. Like the Rapp House, the Grotto, and the Pavilion, the Feast Hall (or *saal*) is marked by the classical style that was dominant in both Europe and America in the middle of the eighteenth century. On either side of the *saal*, which measures 95' x 49', are nine columns which are connected by flat arches known in French as *anse de panier,* or handle of a basket, and are painted to resemble marble. Similarly, at the ends of the *saal* are four non-structural painted columns, in the classical *trompe l'oeil* fashion. Not only are columns painted on the walls, but the "shadows" of the columns are also painted to give a greater illusion of reality (Figure 33). The ceiling of the *saal*, which has an arch like to those connecting the columns, is painted blue and is similar in color to the roof of the Church which was described as "Heaven's blue"[63] by an outsider, and which may have had some symbolic significance. This same blue was used for the Harmonist window shades; coincidentally, similar blue was used by the Shakers on their interior walls.

There are several similarities in the construction and interior details of the Feast Hall Building and the Church in addition to the color of the ceiling. A drawing done by a Harmonist, possibly Frederick Rapp, shows the framework of each building and reveals that in spite of the different roof lines, each was based on the same system of interior framework. Also, the *anse de panier*, which was a relatively simple arch made from segments of circles with different radii, is used in the Church. Finally, although some historians have suggested that the doors at

---

[63] Agnes M. Gormeley, "Economy -- A Unique Community," Western Pennsylvania Historical Magazine, I:3 (July, 1918), 128.

either end of the *saal* and half way up the back wall were used by George Rapp to watch or speak to the members gathered at the feast, it is evident from the similar door which leads to a balcony in the Church that balconies were planned for the Feast Hall but never completed, perhaps for structural considerations. There is also some evidence that the areas accessible by the doors on either end, and above, the feast hall were used to store some of the extra tables and benches, especially after the population declined.

In addition to the Classical elements mentioned above, the front door of the Feast Hall is Georgian in style, with a triangular pediment, a fan window, and engaged columns. All of these Classical details were out of style by the 1820s, when Greek revival was the architectural vogue, but the Harmonists continued to use them throughout the orderly village they were creating in preparation for receiving their God. Unlike the more ascetic Shakers, who eschewed most forms of ornamentation in both their public and private buildings, the Harmonists were well aware of and used "worldly," although slightly out of date, styles in many of their structures.

The Harmonists were neither too elegant nor too wasteful in their attempt to honor God and impress the world. This is obvious in two details of the Feast Hall Building. First, the well-designed Georgian door at the front is not repeated at the rear, where a much simpler style, without a pediment, columns, or a fan window, is employed. Second, the pattern of brickwork varies on the Feast Hall, as it does also on the Rapp House. On the south and east sides of the building, which would have been seen by visitors, the pattern is the rather elaborate Flemish, in which five stretchers alternate with one row of headers.

The importance of the Feast Hall is not restricted to its second floor *saal* and to its stylistic qualities. The first floor, which was divided into a number of smaller rooms, housed a museum, an adult school and library, a printing room, and a band practice room, all unusual for a community west of the Alleghenies with fewer than one thousand inhabitants. These features make it quite clear that the Harmonists were not intellectually stagnant, as some of their more critical contemporaries claimed. Thomas Hulme, who visited the Harmonists when they were in Indiana, praised their skill but felt that they were too subservient. "I observe," he said, "that these people are very fond of flowers, by the bye; the cultivation of them, and music, are their chief amusements. I am sorry for this, as it is to me a strong symptom of simplicity and ignorance, if not a badge of their German slavery."[64]

The Feast Hall Building amenities also demonstrate that at Economy the Harmonists were concerned about not merely surviving, as they were when they arrived in America, but with providing for their social, intellectual, and aesthetic needs. And, perhaps not incidentally, they provided Frederick Rapp and Dr. Johann Christoph Müller, two of the community's most important members, with space to pursue their intellectual and cultural interests.

Two of the rooms on the first floor of the Feast Hall were used for the museum, which was open from 1827 to 1853. The museum was set up by Müller, who was not only a physician with a university degree, but a botanist and a musician. The collection was eclectic, in the tradition of the German *Wunderkammer,* or wonder room, where objects of botanical, zoological, geological, historical, and artistic interest were displayed with little apparent order.[65] At the same time Dr. Müller did not want to display the type of oddity common in similar museums. When collector Albert Koch wrote to Müller in 1830 offering a lamb with 18 feet, two tails, and four ears, the doctor replied, "I do not consider Natural aberrations and birth defects an unusual, remarkable natural phenomenon. One looks at that with pity and horror. For my part I would

---

[64] Thomas Hulme, Journal of a Tour in the Western Countries of America (London, 1828), 57. Reprinted in Reuben Thwaites, Early Western Travels (Cleveland, 1904-1907), X, 53-60.
[65] For a discussion of the Harmonist museum, see Daniel B. Reibel, "The Harmony Society Museum," Harmonie Herald, November, 1969. The nature of early American museums is discussed by Herbert Katz and Marjorie Katz in Museums, U.S.A (Garden City, New Jersey: Doubleday & Company, 1965), 1-27. See also George H. Daniels, American Science in the Age of Jackson (New York: Columbia University Press, 1968); George Smallwood, Natural History and the American Mind (New York: Columbia University Press, 1941) 57-129; and Water M. Whitehill, A Cabinet of Curiosities (Charlottesville: University Press of Virginia, 1967).

not give a dollar for it. Our museum would not have it."[66] A description of the museum at Economy was made in 1839 by an English visitor, James Silk Buckingham, who noted that the museum contained quadripeds, birds, reptiles, fishes, insects, minerals, antiques, paintings, and drawings.[67]

The paintings were purchased in New York or Philadelphia by Frederick Rapp, who, as designer-builder, concert-goer, connoisseur of art, and financier, was a kind of communitarian equivalent to Thomas Jefferson. This art work at the museum may have been his way of indulging his artistic interest within the confines of a communal society, but they were also available for the typical Harmonist as a means of broadening his or her knowledge. The Harmonists did admit outsiders to the museum for a small fee. When it served its purposes, the community was willing to allow the general public a glimpse of the workings of the Society. In this case the museum was an example to the outside world of the superior advantages available in a religious commune. The museum was one of the first open to the general public in western Pennsylvania and between 1827 and 1834 over 12,000 people paid the ten-cent admission fee to visit it.

Correspondence in the Old Economy archives reveal that the museum purchased such items as "forty-eight varieties of birds, including cuckoos, larks, and a black-eared Wheatear," animal and mineral specimens, and such scientific instruments as microscopes, a telescope, a static electricity machine, a pantograph, and an air pump, insects, butterflies and shells. In 1826 the Society purchased twenty-eight boxes containing "A Museum of Natural Curiosities, paintings, etc." from J. W. Sturm for $4,000.

The museum was one of the first open to the general public in western Pennsylvania and between 1827 and 1834 over 12,000 people paid the ten-cent admission fee to visit it.

---

[66] This quotation and several other in the discussion of the museum are found in display descriptions at the recent reconstruction of the museum at Old Economy Village.
[67] James Silk Buckingham, The Eastern and Western States of America (London, 1942), II, 225.

After the defection from the community of Dr. Müller in 1832 during the great schism, and the death of Frederick in 1834, the growth of the museum stopped. After Frederick's death George Rapp, who apparently may not have been as interested in the museum as Frederick or Dr. Müller, wrote to naturalist Thomas Say in New Harmony saying that the museum was for sale. In 1853, six years after the death of George Rapp, the collection was sold to Dr. B.W. Morris of Pittsburgh and had a short life in that city at Apollo Hall on Fourth Street. Perhaps the demise of the museum indicates that it was the devotion and interest of such leaders as Dr. Müller and Frederick Rapp that kept it going rather than the demand of the general membership of the Society.

Harmonist children received a basic education in writing and reading German and in arithmetic until they were about twelve years old, when they were apprenticed.[68] In the Harmony Society Library (and now in the reconstructed museum) is a science book for children, *Naturgeschichte für Kinder (Natural History of Children)* that has engravings and descriptions of animals, birds, reptiles, shells and flora. The adults at Economy were allowed to take evening classes in the Feast Hall in such subjects as singing, science, handicrafts, and drafting. There still remain in the archives a number of architectural and technical drawings made by students in a class probably taught by Frederick Rapp[69] (Figure 34). Other rooms on the first floor of the Feast Hall which served the cultural needs of the Harmonists were the rooms for the printing press and the band room, where members of the Society practiced for the periodic concerts. It is difficult to determine just how educated and cultured the members of the Society were, but John Duss sheds some light on the changing nature of the membership. "In the early days," he said

> the Society could boast of experts in mathematics, chemistry, physics, men who were conversant with the Latin, Greek, French, German and

---

[68] See Melvin R. Miller, "Education in the Harmony Society, 1805-1905," (doctoral dissertation, University of Pittsburgh, 1972.)
[69] One of these drawings is discussed below in the section on Harmonist churches. See additional comments in Chapter 3.

English languages. Some had been trained in the best German university traditions. Learning among the Harmonists was thus at its apex in the early days. But the clearing of three forest areas and the building of three beautiful communities, left little time for academic education. The younger generations therefore received instruction only in the common branches.[70]

The somewhat practical nature of the Harmonists, including George and Frederick, was more than likely a reason for the success of the community. One might contrast their down-to-earth approach to community building and maintenance with that of Robert Owen, whose theoretical approach to building a community led to its early demise as a functioning village. The Duke of Saxe-Weimar described some of Owen's "inventions":

> One of them consisted of cubes of different size, representing the different classes of the British population in the year 1811, and showed what a powerful burden rested on the laboring classes, and how desirable an equal division of property would be in that kingdom. The other was a plate, according to which, as Mr. Owen asserted, each child could be shown his own capabilities, and upon which, after a mature self-examination, he can discover what progress he had made. The plate has this superscription: "Scale of Human Faculties and Qualities at Birth." It has ten scales with the following titles...: Self Attachment; Affections; Judgment; Imagination; Memory; Reflection; Perception; Excitability; Courage; Strength.... A slide that can be moved up and down shows the measure of the qualities, therein specified, which each one possesses, or believes himself to possess.[71]

Of course, while the Harmonist leaders were practical men in many respects, they were also deeply spiritual and even mystical in some of their thinking and both Rapps believed in the pseudo-science of alchemy.

Taken as a whole, the Feast Hall Building reveals a number of things about the Harmonists. Its use for both communal feasts and cultural activities shows that the Harmonist leaders found it necessary to stress communal solidarity and yet at the same time allow for a certain degree of individualization and self expression. The style of the building shows the Harmonists' willingness to imitate the

---

[70] Duss, 156.
[71] Arndt, Harmony on the Wabash in Transition, 813.

Germanic and renaissance structures known to them in Germany as well as to adopt Classical features. And the fact that the Feast Hall was used for cultural and educational purposes at Economy suggests that by the late 1820s, with the community financially solvent and most of the important structures built, the Harmonists had a greater amount of leisure time than they had at their previous villages and that the leaders provided constructive outlets for this leisure.

Harmonist Churches

In all, five churches were erected by the Society at their three villages: one at Harmony in 1808; two at New Harmony, in 1815 and 1822; and two at Economy, in 1824 and 1831. The Harmonists, like the other non-conformist religious groups in seventeenth and eighteenth century Europe, did not equate the church with worship of God and tended to eschew the architecture of the established church since it represented the corruptions and worldliness to which organized religion had fallen prey.[72] For the Harmonists the entire community was a "church." As Karl Arndt has observed, the Harmonists considered themselves

> a congregation and a church having a divinely ordained and prophesied mission. In the first articles of agreement the Society had been called a church and the words church (*Kirche*) and Congregation (*Gemeine*) had been used interchangeably to designate the organization.[73]

Because of this concept the building itself was less of a sacred temple than it was a practical solution to providing a meeting place for religious worship and for social gatherings.

One indication of the Harmonist concept of the church as a functional structure was their practice of using the church as a storage facility for different commodities. The upper story of the 1808 Church at Harmony, for example, was

---

[72] See John Betjeman, "Nonconformist Architecture," Architectural Review, LXXXVIII, (December, 1940), 160-174. Comments on English and American church architecture are in Garvan, Architecture and Town Planning in Colonial Connecticut (New Haven: Yale University Press, 1951), 130-148.

[73] George Rapp's Successors and Material Heirs, 143.

a granary capable of holding several thousand bushels of grain.[74] At New Harmony, observed William Hebert who visited in 1823, the upper compartment of the 1815 Church was used "as a store for grain, earthenware, cotton, etc.," and that the 1822 Church had "vaults . . . appropriated to the reception of stores of various kinds."[75]

Significantly, it was not until after the Harmonists had erected a grist mill, an inn, a store house, and a saw mill at Harmony that they built their first church, or, as the Harmonists preferred to call it, as the Philadelphia Quakers did, their "meeting house." Before the construction of this church in 1808 the Harmonists may have met in small groups in George Rapp's house; but with almost 700 by 1807, that method of gathering the community must have been less than ideal! Even though the Harmonists saw no need for a church building during their first few years at Harmony and devoted their energies to creating a strong economic base for the community, it seems likely that by 1808 the leaders realized that meetings of the community as a whole were necessary to maintain group solidarity. Karl Arndt has shown that in 1806 and 1807 George and Frederick Rapp were sued by some of the community members who were dissatisfied with Rapp's leadership and with the location of the village.[76] George may have felt that the construction of a church would prevent others from leaving the community by providing a spiritual and visual focal point toward which the members could gravitate. This Church, in addition to serving the religious needs of the community, provided space for the social activities as well. Here the children received their education before the school was built, here the community gathered for song and food during the various religious feasts, and here the orchestra members practiced and gave community concerts.[77] These functions were later

---

[74] John H. Wilson, The Historic Town of Harmony, Butler County (Pennsylvania, 1937).
[75] William Hebert, A Visit to the Colony of Harmony in Indiana (London, 1824) Reprinted in Harlow Lindley, ed., Indiana as Seen By Early Travellers (Indiana Historical Commission, 1916), 335.
[76] George Rapp's Harmony Society, 99.
[77] John Duss, one of the last members of the Society, says that at Harmony much of the social program of the community revolved around the church.

taken over by the Feast Hall Building at Economy when they became more institutionalized, that is, more a planned part of the annual activities of the members.

In form, the 1808 Church was a one-story brick building with a wooden tower crowned by a hexagonal clockroom containing two clockfaces.[78] The Harmonists contracted out for the church clocks and bells. In letter from clockmaker John Eberman of Lancaster, Pennsylvania, to Frederick Rapp in 1810, Eberman says that he has written to the manufacturer of the bell. "In general," he says, "I will make you a good clock and as far as the price is concerned I cannot well give you a statement but I will deal with you in a brotherly manner." In August of the following year Eberman asks whether the Harmonists will pay his son's expenses to install the clock"[79] (Figure 12). This type of church was later modified at New Harmony and Economy, but in its basic form it provided the model for the two other structures. Although the building has been substantially altered, a town plan by a community member shows that the Church at Harmony had doors at the front and the side, probably to allow for separate entrances for men and women, and also had oval windows above the doorways similar to the ones above the side doors of the churches at New Harmony and Economy.

When the Harmonists moved to Indiana, one of the first structures erected was the 1815 Church, located, as was the Church at Harmony, in the village square. Although the first structure at Harmony other than the dwellings was the Granary, at New Harmony the now prosperous community built their church first. Sketches and visitors' descriptions of this Church reveal that it was a two-story frame building with an outside tower crowned with a hexagonal belfry containing a large and small clockface.[80]

---

[78] The clockworks of the Harmony church are now in the museum at Harmony. Harmonist correspondence shows that the Society clock maker made clocks for the cities of Pittsburgh and Wheeling, West Virginia.
[79] Arndt, Harmony on the Conoquenessing, 974.
[80] For sketches of the Indiana churches see William Wilson, The Angel and the Serpent (Bloomington: Indiana University Press, 1964).

In 1822 the construction of the largest and architecturally most striking of the Harmonist churches was begun at New Harmony (Figure 13). The best description of this cruciform shaped Church (which was razed in 1874) came from William Hebert in 1823. "These people," he said,

> are erecting a noble church, the roof of which is supported in the interior by a great number of stately columns, which have been turned from trees of their own forests. The kinds of wood made use of for this purpose are, I am informed, black walnut, cherry, and sassafras. Nothing I think can exceed the grandeur of the joinery, and the masonry and brick-work seem to be of the first order. The form of the church is that of a cross, the limbs being short and equal; and as the doors, of which there are four, are placed at the ends of the limbs, the interior of the building as seen from the entrances, has a most ample and spacious effect. A quadrangular story or compartment containing several rooms, is raised on the body of the church, the sides of which inclining inwards towards the top, are terminated by a square gallery, in the center of which is a small circular tower of about ten feet in height, which is surmounted with a silver globe.[81]

Traveler George Flower described the church in 1819 as having

> four entrances..., closed by folding doors, the doors were about one hundred and twenty feet from each other. The upper story was supported by twenty-eight pillars being six feet in circumference, and twenty-five feet high; the others were twenty-one feet high and of proportionate circumference.[82]

Another visitor, George Duclos, said that in the center of the church there were four columns 18" in diameter which seems to be a more reasonable size than that described by Flower. Whatever the exact dimensions, it is hard to imagine the effect that this church must have had on not only the local farmers who were used to far more modest churches, but also on those sophisticated travelers who found this oasis of architectural sophistication in the middle of what was little more than a wilderness area in southern Indiana.

---

[81] Hebert. 233-235.
[82] Lockwood, The New Harmony Communities, 31.

Why did the Harmonists build this large church (each two-story transept and two-story nave was 120' long)[83] which stylistically had little in common with their previous churches? Hebert reported that his Harmonist guide told him that the old (1815) Church, which was constructed of wood, was too hot during the Indiana summers and that the new brick church was much cooler. Another explanation is that George Rapp said that he had seen the plan of the Cruciform Church in a dream and had therefore ordered that it be built.[84] Visitor Count Bernhard who saw the Church in 1825 somewhat cynically said that George Rapp built the church "to keep his society in constant employment, so that they could have no leisure to reflect upon their situation and dependence on him."[85] Both of these explanations may have some validity, but another, and perhaps more convincing one, is that George Rapp saw the need for a large structure which would serve the social and religious needs of almost a thousand members.[86] The cruciform plan of the structure might well have allowed a number of activities at one time and would have constituted the religious and cultural center of the town (Figure 14). As suggested above, when the Harmonists moved to Economy, the Feast Hall took over the function of providing for the educational and cultural needs of the community, and there was no church of the scale of one build in 1822 at New Harmony.

In terms of architectural form, the Cruciform Church at New Harmony was a model of the "harmonic proportion" that was advocated by eighteenth century architects who were attempting to recapture the classical ideal.[87] The cruciform or Greek cross with its axial arrangement of nave and transept of equal length certainly captured the Enlightenment quest for balance, order and symmetry. Once again, the Classical strain within the Society was represented in a Harmonist

---

[83] Wilson, 48.
[84] Wilson, 48.
[85] New Harmony as Seen by Participants and Travelers, n.p.
[86] In 1818, 130 new members from Germany were admitted into the Society.
[87] See Emil Kaufman, Architecture in the Age of Reason (Archon Books, 1966); and Rudolf Wittkower, Architectural Principles in the Age of Humanism (New York: Random House, 1965).

structure. This Classical strain was also evident in the main doorway,[88] sometimes referred to as the "Door of Promise," of the cruciform Church, which consisted of attached Doric columns, a triangular pediment, and a semi-circular transom with a flower design almost identical to that found in the main doorway of the George Rapp house at Economy. In addition to the Classical elements represented by the doorway, the pediment contained a carved rose which reflected the mystical strain within the community. According to Harmonist belief, the golden rose symbolizes the New Jerusalem to come in the millennial kingdom of God on earth. Unfortunately the 1822 Church was destroyed by the Harmonists themselves. After Robert Owen's experiment at New Harmony collapsed, the church became St. Stephen's Episcopal Church. "The east wing was for years used as a ballroom, and the room south for a theater, the walls being 'beautifully frescoed and painted.' Later a part of the building was used as a pork packing establishment."[89] Finally, in 1874 Harmonist Jonathan Lentz was sent from Economy to the town of New Harmony to arrange for a wall to be built surrounding the Harmonist cemetery. He purchased the Church and had all but the east wing demolished so that the bricks could be used for the cemetery wall. While the Harmonists did not mark their gravestones, there is one exception. At Harmony, Pennsylvania, the only marked gravestone is that for George Rapp's son, John, who died in 1812. Around 1870 the Harmony Society entered into a contract to have a stone wall and carved stone gateway built for the cemetery at Harmony. One of the inscriptions (translated) read "Here rest 100 members of the Harmony Society who died from 1805 to 1815."

When the Harmonists moved to their third village they built two churches. The first was a temporary structure built in 1824. When the Feast Hall Building was completed in 1828 the church services were moved there. Finally, in 1831, the second church at Economy was finished. With this Church the Harmonist

---

[88] Although the church is no longer standing, a replica of the doorway is now a part of a school in New Harmony, and the original pediment is in several pieces in the storehouse of Historic New Harmony.
[89] Lockwood, 51.

architect abandoned the cruciform plan that had been used in the 1822 Church at New Harmony and returned to a style similar to the 1815 Church. The use of the Feast Hall for communal gatherings at Economy meant that the church was utilized for religious purposes only and therefore did not need to be as large as the cruciform church. Although the church at Economy is much more attractive in its proportions than its predecessors, it is a combination of elements of all but the cruciform structure. The similarities include the Church belfry, the renaissance cupola, and the clockfaces. In a curious statement John Duss, the last Harmonist leader, said that in 1929 "at the removal of the steeple at the old Harmonist church, enterprising citizens had salvaged the old tower clock (likely brought to America by Frederick Rapp)." Duss continued to say that "A. J. Whitehill, the expert who repaired the clock, places the date of its manufacture at about the year 1650... and that this may be the oldest tower clock in the Western Hemisphere."[90] There is no evidence to support Duss' claim and the clock mechanism that he is describing is probably the one that was in the tower of the 1808 Church at Harmony and as we have seen, the clock mechanism at the first Harmonist church was not brought from Germany but purchased from Lancaster clock maker John Eberman and now on display at the museum at Harmony, Pennsylvania. There was a clockmaker at Economy, however, and perhaps at Harmony and New Harmony as well, for in a letter from Frederick Rapp to Matthew Brown, the President of Jefferson College in Cannonsburgh who requested that the Harmonists make a clock, Frederick responded that "At present . . . we are not in a situation, or able to accommodate you. The person who devoted himself mostly to that kind of work, has left our Society . . . ."[91] This letter is dated December 19, 1832, and it is likely that the Society's clockmaker left the community during the great schism in that year.

The 1808 Church at Harmony, the 1815 Church at New Harmony, and the 1834 Church at Economy were similar, although the Economy Church was

---

[90] Duss, 412.
[91] Arndt, Economy on the Ohio, 826-827.

modified in the twentieth century. The Economy Church is a more refined one than that at Harmony, which in some ways resembled a combination of church and grain elevator. Of course, since the second floor of the Harmony Church was used to store grain, that might have been appropriate. In addition to the pleasing proportions of the Economy Church as a whole, the cupola is far more sophisticated in its execution and relation to the tower than the cupola at Harmony Figure 36). This Renaissance style cupola was quite common in Germany from the sixteenth century[92] and the architect may have patterned those at Harmony after German models or after illustrations in architect's handbooks. While the church in Iptingen that George Rapp attended still stands, its tower, unlike those built by the Harmonists, is not integrated into the church building itself and was, in fact, used as a defensive keep and the local baron's residence when it was built in the twelfth century.[93] In spite of these possible sources, the skill of a mature Frederick Rapp as architect is evident in this beautiful Church at Economy. In 1839 James Silk Buckingham described its interior as

> being perfectly plain but lofty and spacious, well lighted and ventilated and beautifully clean. There were neither pews, pulpit, altar, or other furniture; in which respect it resembled the simple interior of a Quaker meetinghouse that seats were substantial forms, or benches with a broad flat rail at the back, of unpainted wood, and without cushions. The platform for the preacher was a single elevation, or about three feet, enclosed on each side with a wooden railing, open in front where the ascent was by a few steps; and on this platform, about twelve feet by eight, was a table and a chair for the preacher.[94]

Thus, an examination of the churches built at the three Harmonist villages reveals subtle changes in the community that may not be evident from written sources. The church at Harmony, with its relatively austere facade, reflected a community struggling to become economically self-sufficient. The construction

---

[92] For a cupola almost identical to the one at Economy see the photograph of the *Schloss* at Aschaffenburg *in Gustav von Bezold*, Die Baukaunst der Renaisance in Deutchland, Holland, Belgien und Dänemark (Leipzig: Alfred Kroner, 1908), 105.
[93] Ruch, "A Visit to Iptingen," 84.
[94] Buckingham, 121.

of the Cruciform Church at New Harmony shows that the Harmonist leaders were enjoying the fruits of success and were building a structure which would, in its size and sophistication, represent the triumph of the Harmonists over their environment. Unlike the 1808 and 1815 churches, this one conveyed a sense of success, almost of contentment, and it also provided space for the social, educational, and religious functions of almost one thousand members. Finally, when the Harmonists moved to Economy they abandoned the concept of a combination church and social hall and instead constructed a Feast Hall for the social, cultural and educational functions, and a church for religious services. Although not as striking as the Cruciform Church, the last Church built by the Harmonists combined the Classical ideals of symmetry and balance with the simplicity of a religious, but not a sacred, building. It may well be that with the abandonment of the dormitory and the building of the Cruciform Church at New Harmony the leaders were responding to the threat of dissention within the community by restructuring the functions and the forms of their buildings.[95]

The Grotto, Labyrinth, and Pavilion

Further evidence of the Classical elements within the Harmony Society are the Pavilion and the Grotto in the community garden at Economy. These garden houses were common Renaissance features in Europe "intended chiefly for ornament but also for pleasure or repose. [The grotto or pavilion] . . . was purposely isolated in a garden to disassociate it from mundane affairs and . . . to serve as a retreat."[96] Visitors to Harmony and New Harmony often mentioned the existence of a "rude" structure surrounded by a labyrinth or maze of shrubs and hedges. When John Melish visited Harmony in 1811 he observed the labyrinth,

---

[95] As noted previously, a major schism occurred in 1832, so obviously the leaders could not prepare for all eventualities, especially in the form of the charlatan "Count Leon."
[96] Ralph E. Griswold, "Early American Garden Houses," Antiques, XCVIII, 1 (July, 1970), 82.

which is a most elegant flower-garden, with various hedge-rows, disposed in such a manner as to puzzle people to get into the little temple. . . The garden and temple are emblematical. The Labyrinth represents the difficulty arriving at Harmony. The temple is rough in the exterior, showing that, at a distance, it has no allurements; but it is smooth and beautiful within, to show the beauty of harmony when once attained.[97]

The purpose of the Labyrinth and Grotto at New Harmony was described in a similar way by Robert Dale Owen: "It contained," he said

small groves and gardens, with numerous circuitous walks enclosed by high beech hedges and bordered with such intricacy, that, without some Daedalus to furnish a clue, one might wander for hours and fail to reach a building erected in the center. This was a temple of rude material, but covered with vines of the grape and convolvulus, and its interior neatly fitted up and prettily furnished. Thus George Rapp had sought to shadow forth to his followers the difficulties of attaining a state of peace and social harmony. The perplexing approach, the rough exterior of the shrine, and the elegance displayed within were to serve as types of toil and suffering, succeeded by happy repose.[98]

Historically, the Grotto at Economy and the other villages had its origins in the ancient hermitages of Europe and the East; since there were rather sophisticated hermitages in Beyreuth, Germany, which is not far from Württemberg, George or Frederick Rapp may have patterned the Harmonist grottos after these.[99] According to Old Economy director Mary Ann Landis, the Grotto there "may be the only original one in the world.... Germans and Austrians built similar stone or wooden garden structures known as einsiedelei ('hermitage' or 'shelter') in the 18th and 19th centuries."[100] There were other models which the Harmonists may have followed if they had seen illustrations. The Petite Trianon at Versailles, for example, included a cave-like grotto which represented a "natural" escape from the formality of cultivated society. This is not to say that the Harmonists were directly influenced by the structures at Versailles, but as a

---

[97] Melish, II,10.
[98] Robert Dale Owen, Threading My Way, Twenty Seven Years of Autobiography (New York: G.W.Carleton and Co., 1874), 212-213.
[99] Ralph E. Griswold, Lecture (mimeograph copy), 13.
[100] Kirkland, Kevin, "Restored Grotto Stands as Unique Symbol," Pittsburgh Post-Gazette, (August 27, 2005).

Württemberg stone mason Frederick Rapp must have been very much aware of the castles and gardens built by Württemberg princes and patterned after the French models.[101] The Harmonists seem to have adapted this element of the European enlightenment period into their community and used it to support their religious philosophy (Figure 15).

While the symbolism of the Grotto has been described by visitors who got their information from the Harmonists themselves, some recent interpretations may suggest that the interior of the Grotto had other meanings. According to Hilda Kring in her folk-cultural approach, the rose in the Grotto's elegant ceiling was a dominant symbol of the Harmonists.[102] She supports the contention of John Yelland and George Hays that the panels in the Grotto

> are framed in ivory forms of the letter 'A' as in Alpha and the whole dome is supported by the Roman Ring of paganism which represents the 'O' as in Omega, . . . The Roman Ring with the golden bands circumscribing the building support one hundred and forty-four projecting blocks which in the Christian religion represents the one hundred and forty-four thousand chosen souls.[103]

While it is true that there some symbolic elements in the Harmony Society and that the Grotto itself has a general symbolic significance representing the rough exterior of man surrounding his beautiful soul, a close examination of the Grotto itself reveals that there are not 144 blocks (dentils), but far fewer. In addition, since the Greek "Omega" was represented as an Ω rather than an O it is stretching the point to say that the circular motif in the ceiling has specific symbolic importance (Figure 37). Interestingly, it was not the Harmonists who did the work on the interior of the Grotto since they did not have a skilled plasterer in the community. Instead, "the ornamental plaster work of the interior was executed

---

[101] The French influence on the Württemberg princes is discussed in Raymon Bonnin, ed., Le Wurtemberg (Tübingen, 1950). "Mais, tout compt fait, l'influence française fut plus utile que nuisible a la Souobe du XVIII siecle; elle arracha ses princes et ses elites à l'austère torpeur de leur vie provinciale et les entráina dans le movement des idées nouvelles. Jamais la France et l'Allemagne de l'Ouest n'ont été se rapprochées et ne se sont si bien comprises," 209.
[102] Hilda A. Kring, The Harmonists, A Folk- Cultural Approach (Unpublished doctoral dissertation, University of Pennsylvania, 1969).
[103] George A. Hayes, The Grotto at Old Economy (Ambridge: The Harmony Press, 1959), 2.

with great skill by William Jenkins of Pittsburgh, whose bill for 'plastering and ornamenting' the Grotto including credits for 'bording, doctoring' and [whose] purchases at the [Harmonist] store totaled $190."[104] When the Grotto was restored in 2005 David Flaharty, the restoration plasterer, said that "It has full ornamental plaster like the Pantheon in Rome. I've never worked on anything like it" and that the only other place that he had seen such sophisticated acanthus leaves is "on the ceiling in an 1830s house on the campus of Wesleyan University."[105]

Rather than having specific symbolic meaning, the design on the interior of the Grotto is essentially a Classical motif. Aaron Williams, who wrote the only authorized history of the Harmonists, described the interior of the Grotto as a "beautiful miniature Grecian temple."[106] Charles Stotz, the restoration architect, said that the interior of the Grotto is one of the earliest examples of the Greek revival style in the Pittsburgh area.[107] Thus the Grotto at Economy represents a combination of the Classical and the mystical-romantic tendencies of the Greek Revival style and cannot be confined to either tradition exclusively. Interestingly, it was not the Harmonists, but an outside artisan, who created the Grotto's interior in a style, the Greek Revival, that the Harmonists did not use for their buildings.

The other structure in the garden with a strong Classical precedent is the Pavilion, build between 1831 and 1834. The Pavilion at Economy was a "variation of the classical rotunda similar to those which enhanced many renaissance and English landscape gardens."[108] The Petite Trianon at Versailles, contained, in addition to a grotto, a Belvedere, which was a hexagonal pavilion

---

[104] Charles Morse Stotz, "Threshold of the Golden Kingdom: The Village of Economy and its Restoration," Winterthur Portfolio, 8 (1973), 155. Stotz was the restoration architect for Economy in the 1930s.
[105] Kevin Kirkland, "Restored Grotto Stands as Unique Symbol." Pittsburgh Post-Gazette (August 27. 2005).
[106] Aaron Williams, The Harmony Society at Economy Pennsylvania (Pittsburgh, 1866); Reprint (New York: Augustus M. Kelley, 1971) 67-67.
[107] Stotz, 155.
[108] Ralph Griswold, "Early American Garden Houses," Antiques, XCVIII, 1 (July, 1970), 85.

similar in its basic form to that at Economy, although enclosed rather than open and much more elaborate in detail.[109]

Located behind the Rapp house at Economy in the center of the garden and surrounded by a small moat, is a Pavilion. Within the Pavilion, which in the nineteenth century was hidden as a result of the trellis of grape vines planted around the outside of the moat, is a life-sized, carved figure of *Harmonie*, who, by the Economy period at least, was a symbol of the Society (See Cover Figure). It is likely that this "goddess" was a representation of the Biblical "Sunwoman" who the Harmonists believed would lead them from the wilderness to salvation.

This goddess in the garden was created by the famous Philadelphia sculptor William Rush and was a focal point for those in the garden. Duke Bernhard described the statue in 1826: "Mr Rapp there wants to build a temple on which a statue of *Harmonie* is to be placed. The statue was finished already. It is a colossal wooden figure by a sculptor in Philadelphia, and resembles the figure-head of a ship."[110] In 1825 the Vincennes Western Sun reprinted an article from Philadelphia that said

> At the shop of our townsman Rush, is a colossal statue emblematic of Harmony, the symmetry, ease and elegance of which make it one of his best specimens. We understand it will leave here on Wednesday for the West.... It is intended to be placed at the new settlement of the Harmonie Society, at Economy....[111]

The existence of the Classical Pavilion and the fact that the Harmonists could now afford to hire an outside plasterer and a sculptor for their aesthetic needs reveals the growing prosperity of the community by the 1830s. As a focal point for the garden and as a platform for the Harmonist musicians who periodically gave concerts to the members of the Society and to outsiders, the Pavilion, with

---

[109] For a photograph of the Belvedere see Ian Dunlop, Versailles (New York: Taplinger Publishing Company, 1970), 168.
[110] Arndt, George Rapp's Harmony Society, 334.
[111] Ibid., 244.

its beautiful "goddess in the garden,"[112] served the social and aesthetic needs at the Harmonists. At neither Harmony nor New Harmony did the community have the time to indulge its aesthetic sensibilities with such a structure. In addition, the classical elements which had been used previously are nowhere more evident than in this Pavilion with its symmetry and its elaborately carved wood finials. In no other communitarian village in nineteenth-century America is there a structure which so obviously reflects the high European culture of the renaissance and enlightenment. If, as some have suggested, the essentially ascetic nature of the Shakers is revealed in their unadorned furniture and architecture, it is equally apparent that the strong Classical strain in the Harmony Society as well as its indulgence of aesthetic needs was made manifest in the Pavilion.

The Granaries

The Harmonists built large granaries at all three villages. Wallrath Weingärtner's map of Harmony in 1815 shows a Granary, except for the Cruciform Church perhaps the largest building in the town, located near the center of town and almost behind George Rapp's house. At New Harmony the "Fort Granary" has been described as

> the largest granary of its type built by German craftsmen in the United States. Completed in 1818, the granary at New Harmony was five stories high, 40 feet wide and 70 feet long, with a tile-covered German-style hip roof. The bottom two stories are brick."[113] (Figure 16)

At Economy, one of the largest (90 feet by 38 feet and five stories) buildings in the center of the village is the Granary (Figure 34). Unlike the other buildings at Economy, which are of frame or brick construction, the Granary's first floor is of the half-timber type of construction. The Granary at Economy is also unlike the previous ones at Harmony and New Harmony, which were of frame, brick, or

---

[112] The original sculpture no longer exists. The one now at Old Economy Village is a reproduction.
[113] Historic New Harmony, http://www.ulib.iupui.edu/kade/newharmony.

stone construction. The Granary at Economy also had a "tread mill" in the attic that was powered by cattle or other heavy animals. As a part of their practicality, the Harmonists also used men treading on a wheel to draw up the bags of grain into the loft of one of their granaries, and in their distillery they used dogs to power the water pumps.

When the Harmonists abandoned New Harmony for Economy, why did they use the traditional Germanic half-timber style only on the granary there? The Harmonists preferred the use of brick because it was a cheap and practical and could be easily produced in their brick yards. Also, the brick façade was seen to represent the qualities of symmetry and regularity that were so admired by those who imitated the classical mode in architecture.

However, more than likely the half-timber form of the Granary resulted from historic and symbolic considerations although there were some practical factors as well. One of the most common forms of medieval dwellings and barns in Southern Germany was the half-timber construction. The Harmonists, as former Württembergers, were aware of this form and may have been reminding themselves of their heritage by placing it near the center of the town, the common location in medieval villages. In addition to the historical precedents for the half-timber Granary, the form might have been symbolic. The *hof*, or public barn, was a common feature of certain German Pietistic societies, especially the Moravians. In some of these groups the barn served as a symbolic and actual "Old Testament Community" treasury where grain would be stored in preparation for the famine that is predicted in both Revelation and Acts. Since fire, disease, and famine would precede the millennium, the Harmonists stocked the Granary with a year's supply of grain on the top three and a half floors and other supplies on the lower floors.[114] One could also surmise that since the Harmonists were becoming less dependent on income from agriculture and more involved in the commercial and financial world outside of the community, the large half-timber Granary was a

---

[114] Daniel Reibel, A Guide to Old Economy (Harrisburg, 1972), 15.

reminder of their agricultural roots. The half-timber form on the first floor also may have been a practical element. Since the first floor of the Granary was used to store cider, the half-timber construction provided a kind of temperature control that a stone or frame exterior would not have.

The Granary was partially prefabricated on the ground and, similar to construction techniques for the dwellings, numerals were marked on the beams to indicate where they would be placed. The first floor of the Granary was also used as a storage area for agricultural machinery and other supplies, and the upper floors were used to store some 25,000 cubic feet of grain. The Harmonists lifted sacks of grain to the storage areas by means of the enclosed hoists on the west side of the building. The ventilators were used to keep the grain aired and prevent it from rotting.

So even though the Harmonists had decided to embark on an essentially industrial venture by the time they moved to Economy, they built this large and impressive Granary in the center of town. In doing this they fulfilled the practical need for storing grain for the winter months, the religious need of providing for the famine preceding the millennium, and the emotional need of reminding the Harmonists of their ties to Germany and to the land.

The Commercial Buildings

The commercial center of the village consisted of the Mechanics Building and the Store Building.[115] These structures are located next to the cultural center of the community, the Feast Hall, and face the community garden but are separated from it by a stone wall. This combination of functions at the heart of Economy is one of its most striking characteristics. Within an area of little more than a block are buildings and gardens which satisfied the economic, cultural, aesthetic, spiritual and personal needs of the members (Figure 17).

---

[115] This building was once called the Tailor's Shop, but since it contained various commercial ventures calling it the Mechanics Building seems more appropriate.

The Mechanics Building included shops for the tailor, the barber, the shoemaker and the printer on the first floor, and on the second floor the milliner's shop and storage rooms. The Harmonist print press displayed at Old Economy is the oldest flat-bed printing press in America still in its original setting. The products made in this building were distributed to the members of the community, and large numbers of surplus items were sold to the outside world in the community store. This building is of brick construction; like the typical Harmonist structure, it has a denticulated cornice, a stone foundation, and flat lintels formed by vertically placed bricks. Beneath the building is a vaulted wine cellar similar to the one beneath the Store Building at Harmony.[116] The Harmonists pressed wine at Economy by means of a steam-operated engine after about 1844, and filled the large tuns by means of troughs, abandoning the German tradition of crushing grapes with human feet. When the wine was ready for consumption or sale, it was drawn into barrels and rolled up a rack on the stairs by means of a windlass (Figures 31, 32).

Combining practicality with aesthetics, the Harmonists placed grape vines, or espaliers, on the outside of the shop building and some other brick structures, giving the community a decidedly Germanic appearance.[117] Not only did these espaliers have the function of giving increased warmth and hence sugar to the grapes as a result of their proximity to the heat-retaining bricks, but they served aesthetic function of giving variety to the broad expanses of brick walls on the Store Building and Feast Hall. The use of espaliers at Economy gives the brick buildings an appearance of formality, which is not incongruous with the classical elements of the architecture,[118] while at the same time creating a certain rural

---

[116] Bonnin says that the wine cellar beneath the dwellings of vinecutters was characteristic of Württemberg buildings along the Nekar River.

[117] The communitarian villages of Amana, Iowa, with many German members, also used espaliers.

[118] John Reps in The Making of Urban America (Princeton: Princeton University Press, 1965), comments on "the dignity, the excellent sense of proportion of scale, and the true urban character of the remaining buildings" at Economy, 454.

quality, especially in the spring and summer months when the colors are most striking (Figure 32).

Next to the Mechanics Building on the main street is the Store Building, which provided members with their material needs and which also sold products from the crafts and industries to people from the outside world. Usually the head of a Harmonist household rather than an individual member drew items from the store, perhaps to insure that one member did not acquire more goods than others. Outsiders purchased such goods made by the Society as cloth, hats, shoes, whiskey, farm products, and leather goods. In addition, the Society bought items from the outside and sold them in their store at a profit. It has been estimated that the Harmonists grossed at least $100,000 a year during their period of greatest prosperity before the Civil War.[119]

The Store Building is of brick construction and is similar in size and appearance to the Mechanics Building. One difference is that whereas the external ornamentation on the Mechanics Building is provided by the espalier, the Store Building has solid shutters rather than the more refined louvered ones found only on George Rapp's Great House. Another difference which resulted from the function of the building is that unlike the Mechanics Building, the Store Building has two entrances from the street rather than one. There is some evidence that the doctor's office and the apothecary shop were located in this building; if so, one of the doors would have been used as an entrance for patients.

Today the interior of the store has been restored to contain items similar to those that the Harmonists sold. In addition to the cloth and shoes, and china that the Harmonists manufactured themselves (during the 1880s and 1890s the Harmonists made dinnerware under the name "Economy Potteries"), there would have been such items as glass, spices, and tea which represent the items that the Society purchased from the outside for their own consumption or for resale. Since the Store Building also served as a post office, there is a small desk with a pillared

---

[119] Reibel, A Guide to Old Economy, 18.

gallery that the postmaster/storekeeper used for collecting and distributing mail. The combination of capitalism and communism working side by side in the store business is an arrangement that typified the Harmonist economic system. The Harmonists employed a communal system of production and consumption within the community and at the same time competed in the capitalist system outside of the community. The Harmonist store is indicative of the fact that during their most prosperous years before the Civil War the Harmonists were willing to meet and interact with the outside world as long as they could do it on their own terms and to their advantage.

Harmonist Factories and Mills

Although no physical remains of the factories and mills at Economy remain today, Society records show that they were an integral part of the economic system by the late 1820s and that they were visually important in the skyline of the village. By the time that the Harmonists settled at Economy they had decided that they would base their economy on industrial production of cotton and woolen goods. They still had extensive farm lands, but these were used mainly to provide food for the members of the community.

The architecture of the Harmonist woolen and cotton factories was similar to that of factories in the outside world (Figure 19). Each was a brick structure with the upper story in the form of a clerestory monitor to provide light for the workers there. The flour mill, on the other hand, was built with the Germanic gambrel roof in order to provide extra space on the fifth floor for the storage of enough grain to last a year in the event of a famine.[120]

Until the 1840s the factories at Economy were technically advanced in the use of steam engines in a number of their operations. According to Carroll Pursell, "the steam engine was largely an urban phenomenon. For example, in

---

[120] Bernhard, II, 163.

Pennsylvania in 1838, the Pittsburgh area accounted for 133 engines and Philadelphia for 174 out of a total for the state of only 383."[121]

That the Harmonists used steam power in Indiana and had at least four steam engines at Economy reveals that they were well aware of the inventions of the outside world and were not loathe in using them to increase their efficiency. A visitor to Economy wrote that

> While the factories were being built, special members of the Society visited the better-known factories of Europe and America in order to learn; when their own factories were ready, they invited, at high cost, known experts and mechanics from whom the Society members learned all that was necessary, and not practically all the work is performed by the members themselves.[122]

At Economy the Harmonists had one engine to run the cotton and flour mills, one for the woolen mill, one for the silk mill, and one for the laundry and the wine and apple presses.[123] As early as 1826 the Harmonists had their cotton and woolen factories in operation, and according to visitor Karl Bernhard, "all the machinery is set in motion by a high-pressure engine of seventy horsepower, made in Pittsburgh. The machine pumps the water from a well fifty feet deep, sunk for the purpose." At Economy the Harmonists even had a steam laundry to efficiently clean the clothing of several hundred members.

Bernhard's description of the operations in the factories at Economy gives a rather complete picture of the processes of wool and cotton manufacturing there. Bernhard wrote that after the wool was washed

> it is picked by the old women of the community, who work on the fourth story, whence it is reconveyed by a sort of tunnel into the lower story. After the wool is separated and dyed, it is . . . returned to the mill, where it is combed, coarsely spun, and finally wrought into a fine yarn by a machine similar to the spinning jenny. As soon as spun, it is placed in the loom and wrought into cloth, this is placed in a steam fulling-mill, so

---

[121] Early Stationary Steam Engines in America (Washington: The Smithsonian Institution, 1969), 87.
[122] Arndt, Karl. "Three Hungarian Travelers Visit Economy," Pennsylvania Magazine of History and Biography. LXXIX, 2 (April, 1955), 202.
[123] Williams, 64.

arranged that the steam from the engine is made to answer the purpose of soap and fuller's earth, which is a great saving. The cloth is shorn by means of a cylinder, which upon a strong piece of steel turns.[124]

At the cotton factory, he continued,

The spinning machines are of the common kind, each of which have one hundred and fifty spools at work. . . . Many of the machines are made in Pittsburgh; most of them, however, at Economy. As this establishment has been so recently founded, it is natural enough that but few machines should be prepared or in operation.[125]

Not only were the factories technologically up-to-date until the 1840s, but the working conditions in them were exceptionally good. Bernhard observed that the factories were warmed during the winter by means of pipes connected to a steam engine, that the women in the factories had healthy complexions, and that there were vessels of fresh flowers standing on all of the machines. During one visit to the factory Bernhard was honored by hearing the sixty or seventy girls "sing spiritual and other songs" to him and George Rapp.

While Bernhard's description is similar to the many comments made by visitors concerning the girls at the factories in Lowell, Massachusetts, the working conditions at Lowell deteriorated as a result of the hiring of cheap immigrant labor; at Economy, they remained unchanged. Of course, one must realize that the Harmonist factories were in operation only until the 1850s. By that time there were two situations that made their mills unprofitable. For one thing, since the Harmonists practiced celibacy and did not admit many new members after the 1830s, by the 1850s most of the "girls" described by Bernhard were at least forty years old, and probably older. Some of the younger ones had left the community during the 1832 schism. Second, although the Harmonist mills were competitive in the first half of the century, by the 1850s their aging machinery could not produce cloth quickly and cheaply enough to compete with other manufacturers. The idyllic conditions that existed for the workers in the 1820s apparently did not

---

[124] Bernhard, Karl, Travels Through North America During the Years 1825 and 1826 (Philadelphia: Lea & Carey), II, 162.
[125] Ibid, 163.

deteriorate, but since the factories were shut rather than modernized, they did not continue after the 1850s.

Both Economy and Lowell were similar in their patriarchal system of management, but the comparison is superficial. It is true that Frederick Rapp lived in a better house than did the average worker, but unlike Kirk Boot, who was the resident manager of Lowell and lived in an elaborate house on a hill overlooking the factories,[126] Rapp was a well-loved and respected member of the community, not just the financial manager. The workers at Economy were not hired laborers exploited by a management whose prime goal was to turn a profit, but were profit-sharing members of an integrated economic, social, and religious system. When the Harmonist women walked home to their households after a day's work, they knew that they were a part of a large community; when the Lowell girls went home to the community dormitories, they knew that they were replaceable parts of an impersonal industry.

The Inns

Another indication of the practical nature of the Harmonists and of their willingness to interact with the outside world if it brought them hard cash are the existence of inns at the center of all three villages. When John Melish described Harmony, Pennsylvania, in 1810 he indicated that one of the first large buildings constructed (in 1806) was "an inn, partly of stone, 32 feet by 42 and two stories high."[127] Visitors to the villages noted that the innkeepers were genial men who spoke both German and English. Obviously the Harmonists wanted to make a good impression on visitors and also wanted them to feel comfortable eating or lodging at the inn. Arriving at the New Harmony inn in 1819, Ferdinand Ernst said that when he arrived there

---

[126] John Coolidge, Mill and Mansion (New York: Russell and Russell, 1942).
[127] Arndt, Harmony on the Connoquenessing, 454.

It seemed as though I found myself in the midst of Germany. Clothing, language customs and manners—all has remained unchanged with these colonists. They served me a stein of beer, and I was not a little astonished to find here a genuine Real Bamberg beer.[128]

Another visitor to New Harmony wrote that

The Tavern is one of the most comfortable I have met in the western country, and remarkable for its cleanliness, neatness, and good order; and the manager, while civil to all his guests, effectually prevents excessive drinking. I never met anyone of the Society at the tavern, which was evidently established for those who might have business at the store.[129]

But the inns were not always money-making ventures, for there are several documents indicating that vagabonds or those who could not pay for lodging were often allowed to stay for a while at no cost. Whether this included an overnight stay or just a glass of warm cider in the dining room is difficult to determine.

****

The Harmonists, then, planned and built three villages. Neither was an exact replica of the previous one(s). The Society modified the economic base of the community; they transmitted and abandoned certain elements of their German heritage; they adopted elements from their American environment; and they changed their concept of community needs and structures.

The success of the community was due partly to an economic flexibility marked most readily in the changing town plans of the three villages. Harmony was located and laid out to meet primarily agricultural needs; New Harmony to satisfy a growing manufacturing capacity as well as farming; and Economy to support an industrial enterprise ringed by fields which fed the community. The buildings also reflected this change. Although Harmony had its share of mills, including grist, saw, fulling, and hemp mills, they were essentially those of a

---

[128] Arndt, A Documentary History of the Indiana Decade, I, 745.
[129] Ibid, 800.

thriving farming town. At New Harmony the Harmonists increased their acreage to accommodate their plans for an expanding agricultural community that would include the cultivation of grapes for wine production, but they also constructed cotton and woolen mills in order to increase their industrial capacity. At Economy, where the climate was not ideal for the cultivation of vines, the Society abandoned that aspect of their agricultural plans, but they concentrated on the production of cotton and woolen goods in their factories.

Whereas the type of structure, mill or manufactory, reflected the changing economic structure of the Society, the style of a number of buildings demonstrated the Harmonists' use of their German heritage and their response to their American environment. Harmony, built in the exigencies of their arrival, when they had just subscribed to communalism and had not yet turned to the concepts of celibacy and the extended family, was characterized by log dwellings, public buildings with elaborately carved stone doorways and lintels, and arched cellars in at least two buildings for the storage of wine. Here, in short, the Harmonists reproduced many of the forms that they had known as peasants in Germany. Only the Georgian doorway of the Frederick Rapp house hinted at the Classical strain which became evident in the Society's second and third villages. Indeed, at New Harmony and Economy much of the medieval German heritage of the Society was abandoned. A few exceptions were the truncated gables at a granary at New Harmony and those of the Great House at Economy, the floor plans of the dwellings with the Germanic staircase in the corner, the carved lintels of the church at New Harmony and the flax house at Economy, and the half-timber form of the first floor of Economy's granary. These Germanic elements may very well have been to serve as a symbolic reminder of the Society's past when economic and social changes in the community were beginning to erode the cohesiveness of the group.

Simultaneously, the Classical element was growing in prominence. At New Harmony one of the four dormitories featured a gambrel roof, a style common to public buildings of the German renaissance. Even more striking, the second church constructed at New Harmony was of a highly stylized Greek cross design. At Economy, the Feast Hall and the Great House featured Georgian doorways, gambrel roofs, and Classical interiors with fan windows in the Great House, *anse de panier* arches and *trompe l'oeil* wall designs in the second floor *saal* of the Feast Hall.

The sources of the Society's Classical forms are open to speculation. Frederick Rapp, who designed the three Harmonist villages and was a stone mason in Germany, probably had seen and possibly even worked on the Classical buildings constructed in Württemberg in the late eighteenth century. But obviously the Classical forms appealed to the Harmonists and their leaders because they were somehow compatible with their philosophy. George Rapp's writings expressed a view of the Society as a well ordered and harmonious entity; the very names the Society gave to its towns exemplified this view.

Rapp's followers, who lived at Economy in houses made of regular and orderly brick, may have found comfort in the Germanic floor plans of the houses' interiors; but Rapp himself lived in a house with elegant paintings and furnishings. And he looked out over a garden with a Pavilion and Grotto, both nonfunctional, aesthetic structures which bespoke Classicism.

It was the Rapp House and the Feast Hall Building which were the ultimate expressions of the Harmony Society. These structures were two of the largest buildings at Economy and were emblematic of two seemingly disparate strains which combined to make the group live and prosper for a hundred years: George Rapp's strong and acknowledged leadership, and the Society's communal and basically egalitarian nature. The Rapp House, an impressive and sophisticated dwelling, stood as testimony to the Society's acceptance of Rapp's position. Whereas the wealthier and more important members had at Harmony been accorded larger houses, at Economy only George and Frederick Rapp were so honored. As the members became more equal and were given houses of equal size, George Rapp consolidated his position and that of Frederick, his adopted son. Although he shared his house to some extent – the trustees met there, important visitors were entertained there, and his family and a few of his friends lived there – George obviously enjoyed the honors which in Germany were granted the minster and the nobleman.

The reason Rapp's power was generally accepted by the members is evident in the Society's other major structure, the Feast Hall Building. Unusual, perhaps unheard of in a nineteenth century town of fewer than a thousand inhabitants, the Feast Hall served as a community center. On its first floor the members pursued lessons in drafting and handicrafts, practiced for their community band, ran the printing press, used the library, and enjoyed the eclectic wonders of the museum. On the second floor, in the *saal*, with its eighteenth century painted wall designs, the members met for community feasts and their reminder of the Society's philosophy and unity. In short, the Feast Hall represented the element which balanced Rapp's power: the weight given the needs of the Society's members.

At all three villages the home of George Rapp was larger than those of the average member, but the first two did not achieve the distinction of the Great House at Economy. At the same time, Harmonist feasts at Harmony and New Harmony were held in the church buildings; only at Economy were the needs of the members interpreted as necessitating a separate structure devoted to them. The Church at Economy was a return to the simpler style of the Society's first churches at Harmony and New Harmony; it had no elaborate Greek cross design and no functions other than those of the church.

The changing concept of communal organization and needs, then, is most obvious in the Rapp House and Feast Hall Building. Only one other architectural element of the villages contributes as clearly to an understanding of the inner workings of the Society, and that is in the dwellings and dormitories. As shown above, the Society first built primitive log cabins upon their arrival at Harmony, with noticeably larger dwellings for the wealthy and powerful. At New Harmony, however, as celibacy was espoused, and perhaps enforced to a greater degree, the Harmonists built four large dormitories to house their unwed members.

This experiment was not successful, and at Economy the Society refined further their idea of the community by abandoning the dormitories and instead constructing brick and frame dwellings of equal size to house extended families. These "households" had the relative privacy of a house of six to ten members, and the pleasures of individual kitchens and gardens, yet they had none of the potentially devisive desires and demands of either a nuclear family or a large congregation of younger, unwed members.

Interestingly, the dormitories were tried at New Harmony, which was only about thirty miles from the Shaker settlement at West Union, and with which the Harmonists corresponded. For a short period, Gertrude Rapp, George's granddaughter lived at West Union with the Shakers to learn from them. Dormitories, of course, were the form of housing the Shakers employed at all of their villages, and the Rapps were probably looking for the best way to house their own celibate members. Certainly the Shakers would have been a good example, although the less rigid social philosophy of the Harmonists may have been incompatible with dormitory living. One wonders if the younger members of the Society were put in the difficult position of being together with members of the opposite gender in a dormitory setting without the rigid rules Shakers enforced to control unacceptable behavior.

The influence of the Shakers here is highly conjectural, however, as it is for most of the American elements within the Society. What American features their architecture exhibited had seem to have resulted from general, rather than specific, environmental influences. Since Frederick Rapp visited some large cities in America in his capacity as one of the financial officers of the Harmonists, he may have been influenced by what he saw. The brick facades of the majority of the buildings at Economy, and the Georgian doorways of the Feast Hall and Great House may have been the result of what Frederick saw in Philadelphia structures.

On the other hand, since these elements were common throughout the larger towns in America by the first quarter of the nineteenth century, Rapp may have seen models in a number of locations as well as in architectural handbooks.

Thus, as the Society moved from Harmony, to New Harmony, to Economy, they abandoned many of the medieval forms that they had known in Germany, adopted a number of German Classical elements, and incorporated forms and materials common in America. By the middle of the nineteenth century Economy had a uniquely European appearance, accented by the gambrel roofs of the Feast Hall and Hotel, the pleasure garden behind the Great House, and the espaliers on the brick walls of many of the buildings. However, there was also a subtle blending of American elements so that the village was no imitation of a German hamlet or town, but instead was an orderly and aesthetically pleasing village that suited the needs of a communally and Pietistic Society. But by the Economy period the landscape also included two large factories, perhaps reflecting the group's final acceptance of an economy based not on agriculture or small manufacturing, but large scale manufacturing and numerous financial investments in the outside world. This may have been the inevitable "tipping point" of the Harmonists between an idyllic community that dealt with the outside world only when it was necessary, to one that depended on the financial and capitalistic markets of the United States.

Figure 1. Inscription on the back of a stair riser in No. 2 dormitory at New Harmony: "In the 24th of May, 1824 we have departed Lord, with thy great help and goodness in Body and soul protect us."   L Scheel
From the collections of the Indiana State Museum and Historic Sites

Figure 2. New Harmony as envisioned in a drawing by Stedman Whitwell, Robert Owen's architect

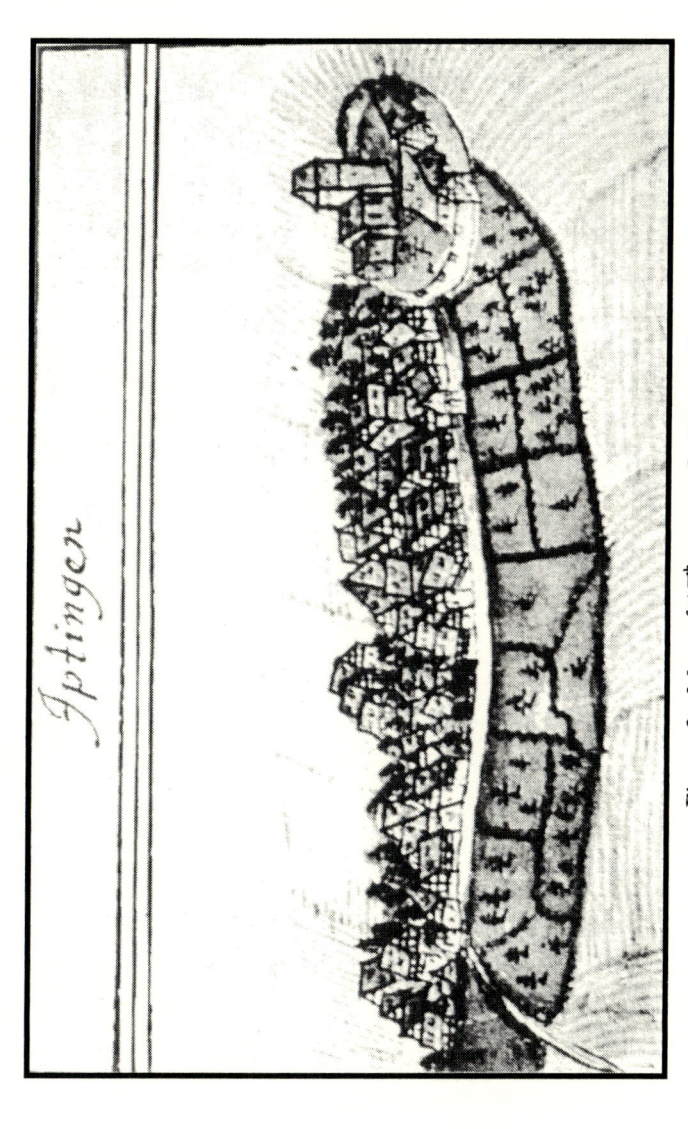

Figure 3. Map of 17th century Iptingen, Germany.
Reproduced with permission of the Hauptstaatsarchiv Stuttgart

Harmony, Pennsylvania

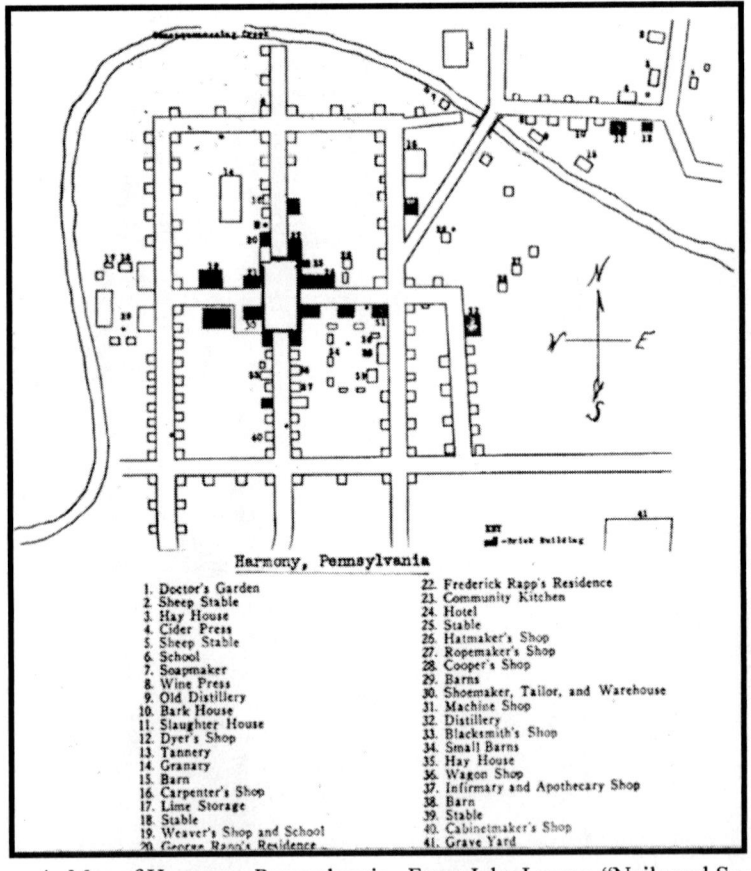

1. Doctor's Garden
2. Sheep Stable
3. Hay House
4. Cider Press
5. Sheep Stable
6. School
7. Soapmaker
8. Wine Press
9. Old Distillery
10. Bark House
11. Slaughter House
12. Dyer's Shop
13. Tannery
14. Granary
15. Barn
16. Carpenter's Shop
17. Lime Storage
18. Stable
19. Weaver's Shop and School
20. George Rapp's Residence
22. Frederick Rapp's Residence
23. Community Kitchen
24. Hotel
25. Stable
26. Hatmaker's Shop
27. Ropemaker's Shop
28. Cooper's Shop
29. Barns
30. Shoemaker, Tailor, and Warehouse
31. Machine Shop
32. Distillery
33. Blacksmith's Shop
34. Small Barns
35. Hay House
36. Wagon Shop
37. Infirmary and Apothecary Shop
38. Barn
39. Stable
40. Cabinetmaker's Shop
41. Grave Yard

Figure 4. Map of Harmony, Pennsylvania. From John Larner, "Nails and Sundrie Medicines: Town Planning and Public Health in the Harmony Society"

Figure 5. Medieval style buildings at the Ephrata Cloister

Figure 6. Log house at Harmony, Pennsylvania, ca. 1805. This structure was formerly on German Street and was moved and rebuilt in 2001 to where a similar Harmonist log house once stood

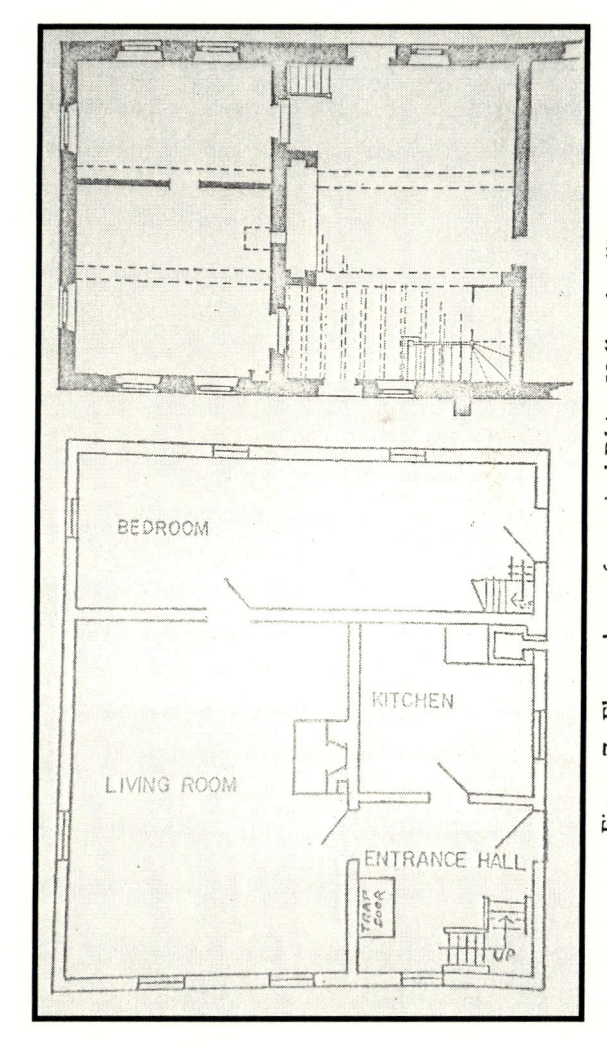

Figure 7. Floor plans of a typical Rhine Valley dwelling
Left: The Müller House at Milbach, Pennsylvania. Right: The Baker House

Figure 8. Dormitory No. 2 at New Harmony, Indiana

Figure 9. The George Rapp House from the rear

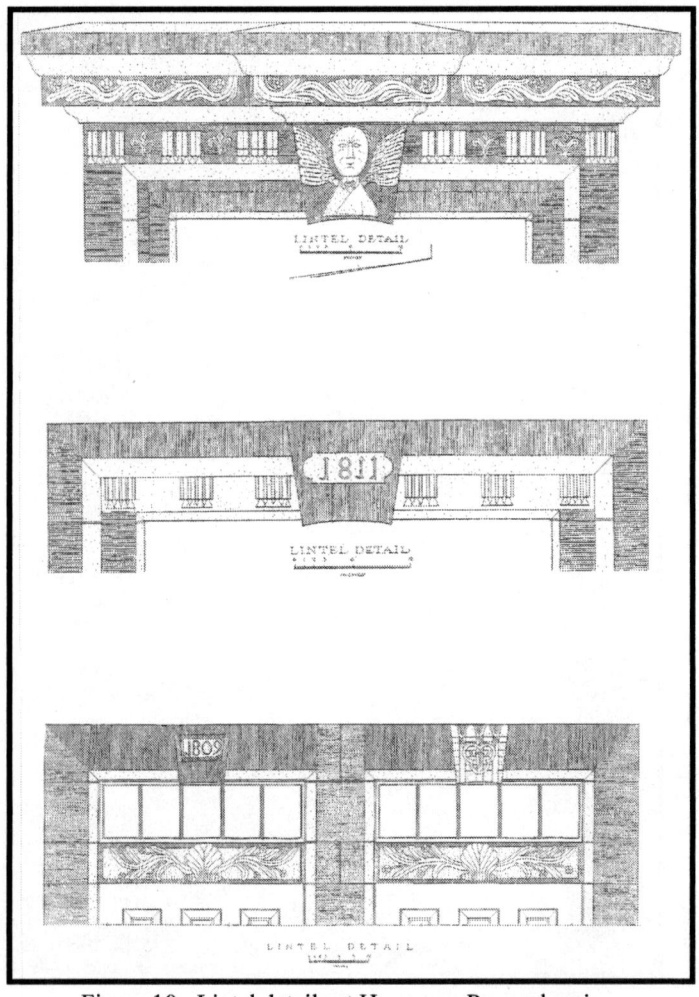

Figure 10. Lintel details at Harmony, Pennsylvania
From Charles Stotz, The Architectural Heritage of Early Western Pennsylvania

Figure 11. The classical pediment of the Frederick Rapp House in Harmony

Figure 12. Clock face from the church at Harmony
Reproduced with permission of the Harmony Museum

Figure 13. The 1822 church at New Harmony
Reproduced with permission of the Pennsylvania Historical and Museum Commission

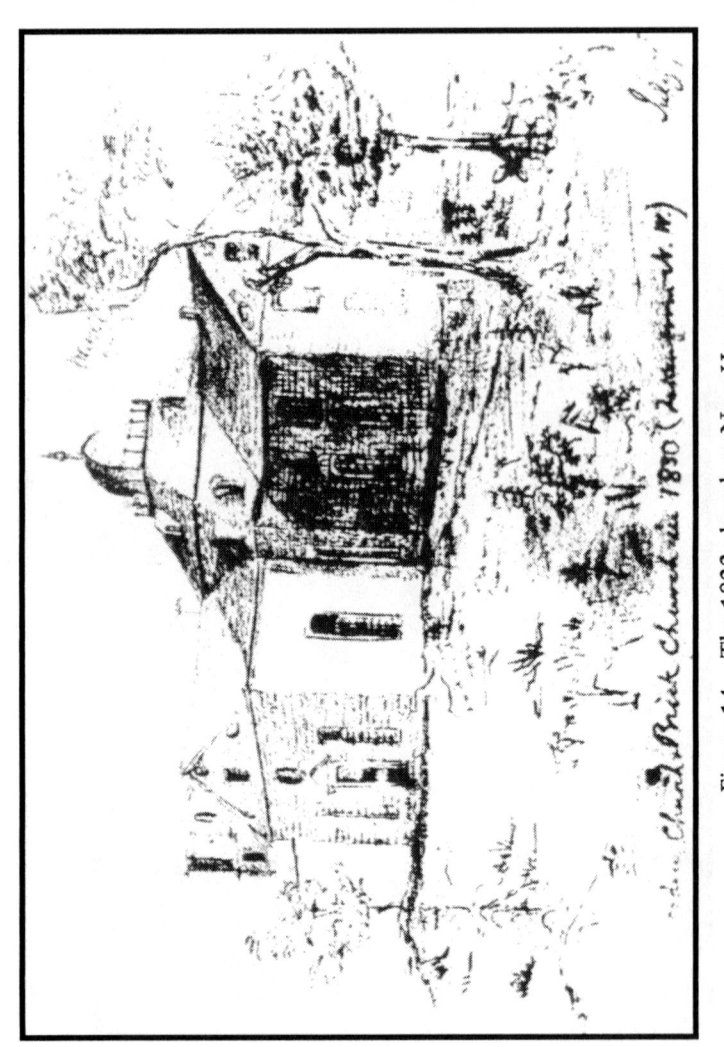

Figure 14. The 1822 church at New Harmony
Unknown artist

Figure 15. The Grotto at Economy

Figure 16. The Granary at New Harmony

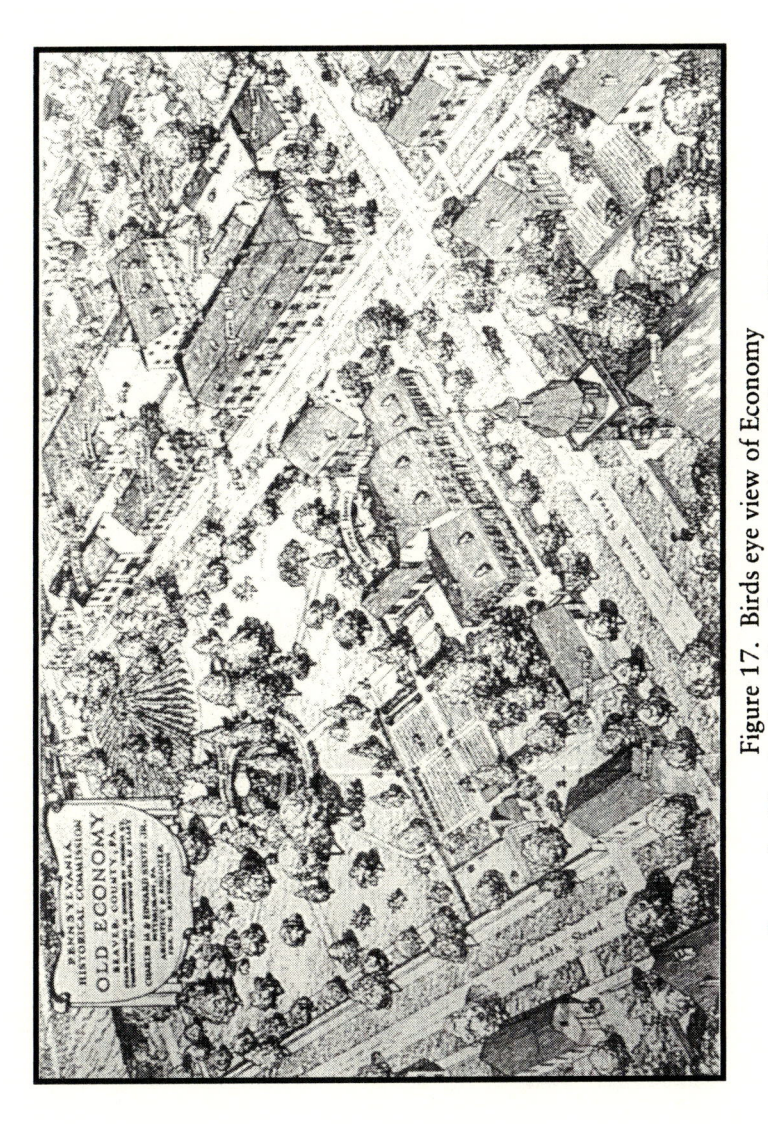

Figure 17. Birds eye view of Economy
Drawn by Charles Stotz, Jr., the restoration architect for Old Economy
Reproduced with permission of the Pennsylvania Historical and Museum Commission

Figure 18. Wine cellar at Economy

Figure 19. The 1829 cotton factory at Economy
Reproduced with permission of the Pennsylvania Historical and Museum Commission

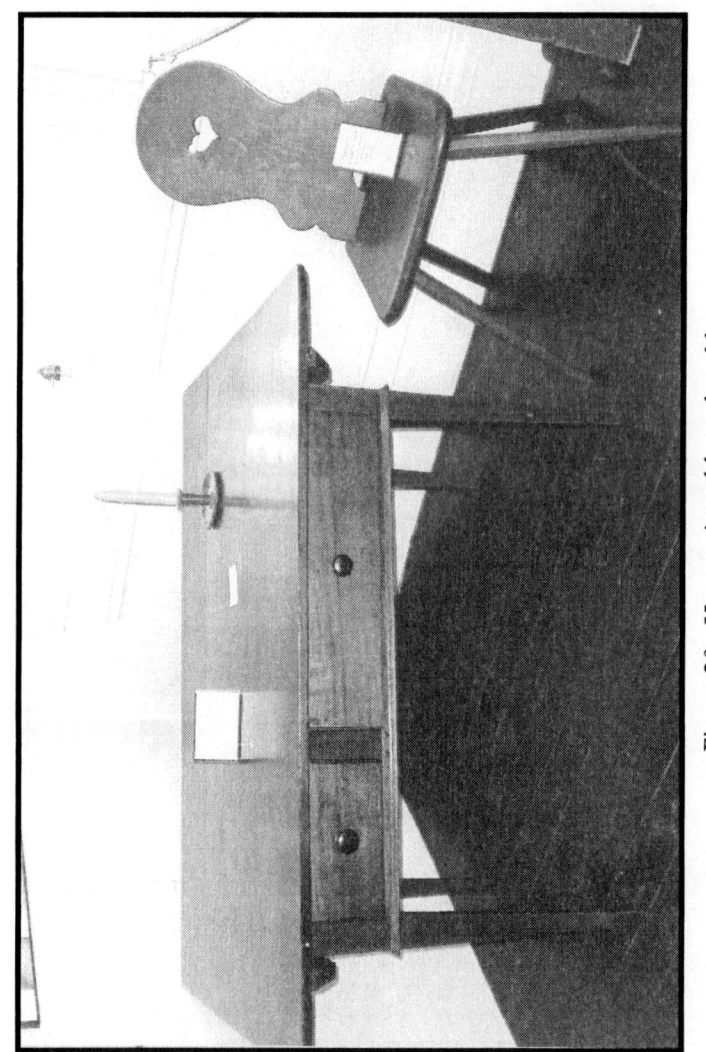

Figure 20. Harmonist table and *stuhl*
Reproduced with permission of the Harmony Museum

Figure 21. Trunk with rounded top at New Harmony
Reproduced with permission of the Working Men's Institute, New Harmony, Indiana

Figure 22. Cupboard (dish or wine) at Economy

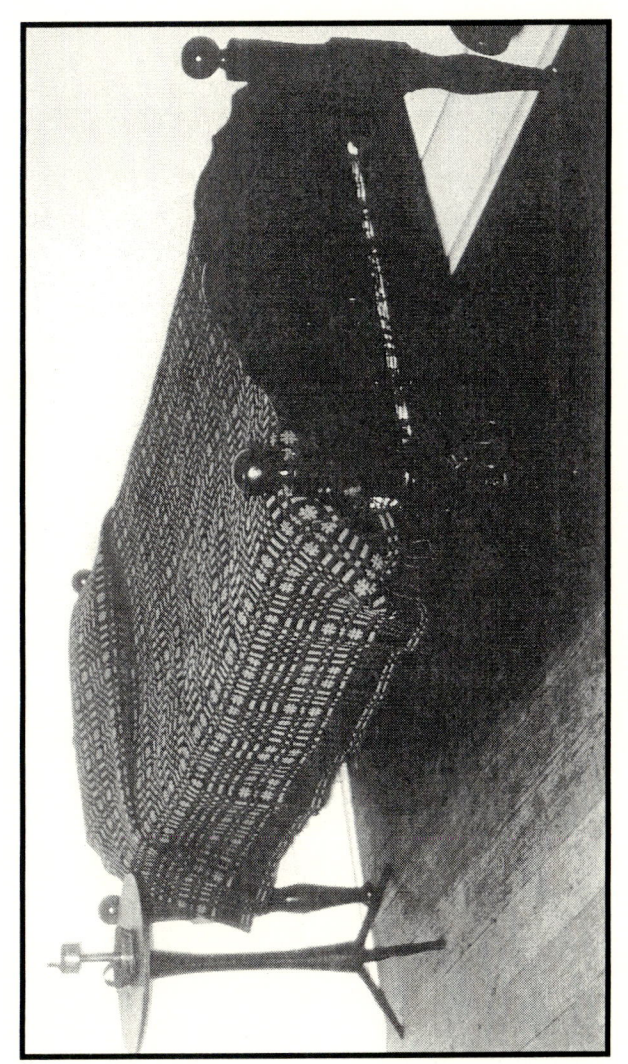

Figure 23. Single bed at Economy

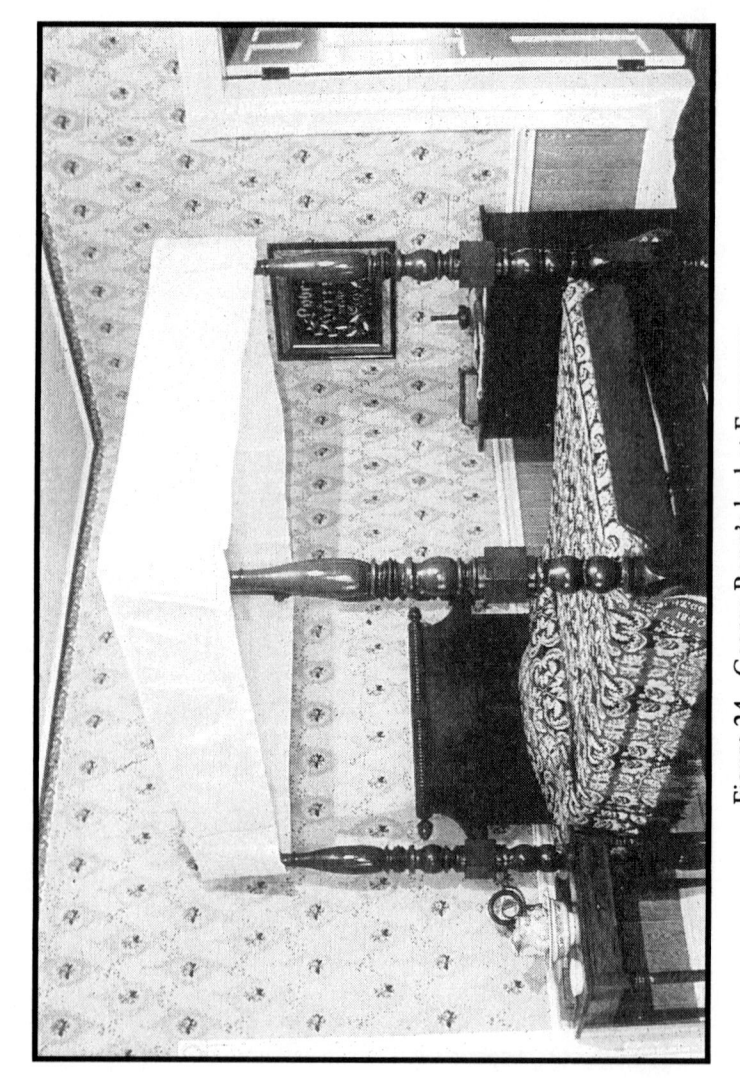

Figure 24. George Rapp's bed at Economy

Figure 25. Trustees' room in the Rapp House
Reproduced with permission of the Pennsylvania Historical and Museum Commission

Figure 26. Harmonist clothing in the 1870s
From Charles Nordhoff's The Communistic Societies of the United States

Figure 27. Rose motif from the gravestone of John Rapp at Harmony

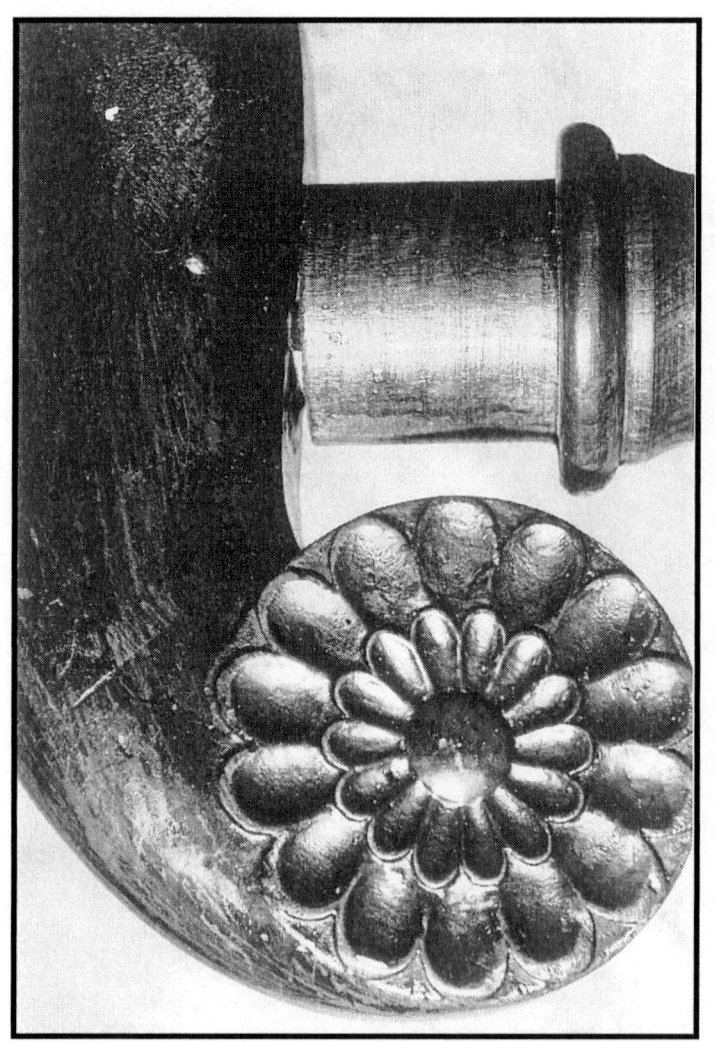

Figure 28. Newell post with the rose motif in the George Rapp House

Figure 29. Fire engine at New Harmony
Reproduced with the permission of the Working Men's Institute

Figure 30. Water pump at Economy

Figure 31. The Baker House at Economy

Figure 32. Feast Hall at Economy

Figure 33. Feast Hall interior

Figure 34. Granary at Economy

Figure 35. Rapp House at Economy

Figure 36. Church at Economy

Figure 37. Interioir of Grotto

Reproduced with permission of the Ohio Historical Society.

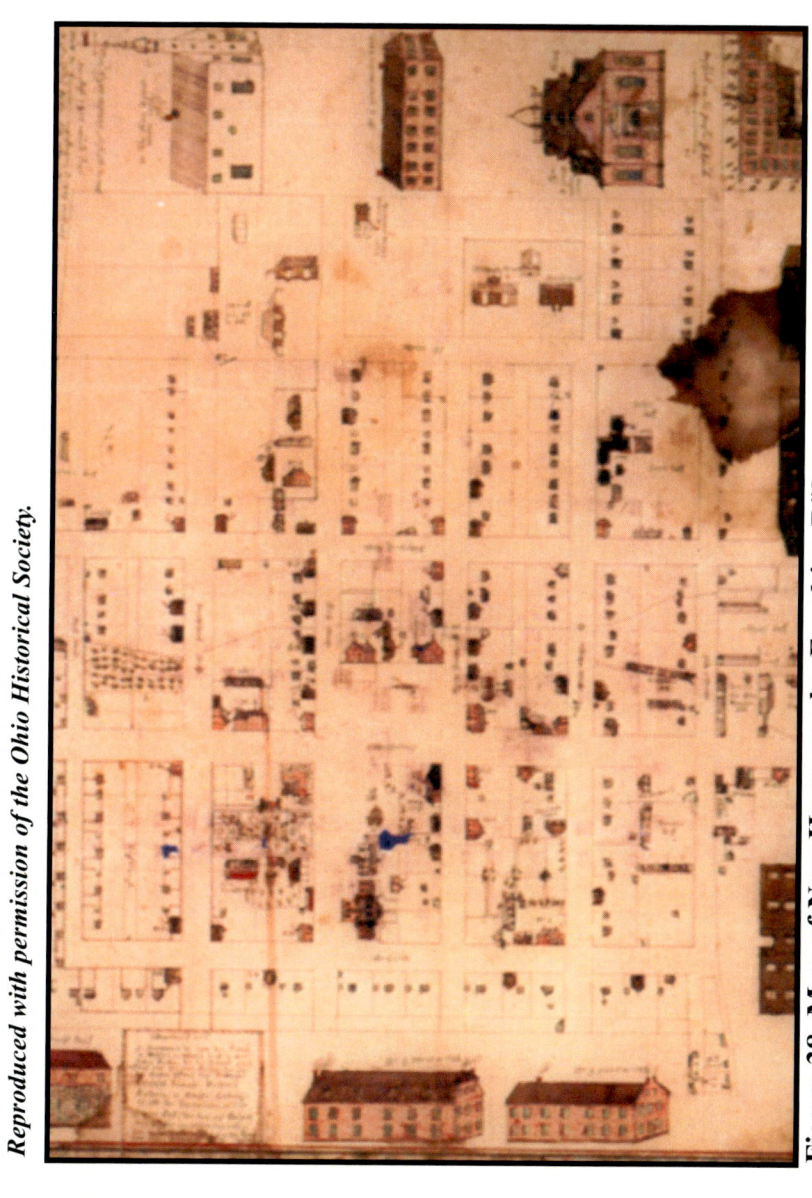

Figure 38. Map of New Harmony by Eusebius Böhm.

Reproduced with permission of the Pennsylvania Historical and Museum Commission.

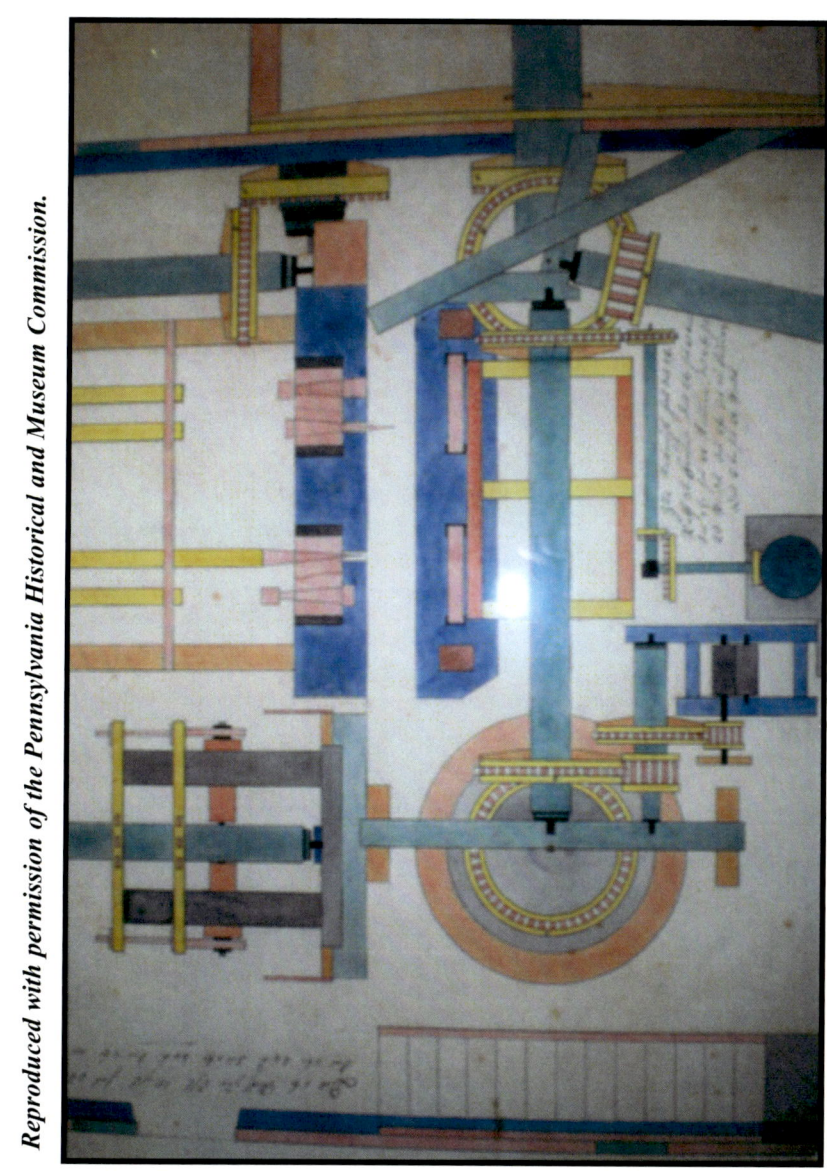

Figure 39. Drawing a factory machinery at Economy.

Figure 40. Pelican on slipware plate at Economy

Reproduced with permission of Historic New Hrmony.

Figure 41. Silk tribute piece for George Rapp.

Chapter 4

Harmonist Furniture

The communitarian society, as a result of its isolation from the outside world and its pressures towards uniformity in thought and behavior, tends to develop a material culture that is peculiar to itself and characteristic of the group philosophy. Examples of this tendency can be seen in the material culture of the Shakers, and to a lesser extent, that of the Amana Society. In its extreme simplicity and uniformity the furniture of the Shakers reflects the ascetic strain that existed within the society as well as the insistence on uniformity in all aspects of life. The less rigid social organization of the Amana Society, on the other hand, resulted in a style of furniture that allowed for a degree of variation and which was characterized by a combination of German and American elements.[1]

One of the problems in evaluating Harmonist furniture is that it is often difficult to determine the provenance of objects. When the Harmonists moved from Harmony, to New Harmony, to Economy they left no records of specific pieces that they moved with them, although they did categorize types. In an 1825 letter to George Rapp about the Harmonist furniture that was being sent from New Harmony to Economy, J. McLain listed "31 chests, 7 cupboards, 7 trunks, 4 tubs, cases and drawers, 120 bedsteads and 5 work benches."[2] Also, when the Harmony Society finally dissolved at the beginning of the twentieth century, many objects were taken by John and Susie Duss, the last members of the group, to their home in Florida, but many were returned when the couple became

---

[1] A discussion of the artifacts at Amana is Grace E. Chaffee, "An Analysis of Sectarian Community Culture," Antiques, XVI, 2 (August, 1929), 114-118, and Marjorie K. Albers, The Amana People and their Furniture (Ames: Iowa State University Press, 1990). For Shaker furniture the standard study is Edward Deming Andrews and Faith Andrews, Shaker Furniture (New York: Dover, 1950), and Religion in Wood (Bloomington: Indiana University Press, 1965).
[2] Harmony on the Wabash in Transition, 551-552.

supporters of the effort to create a museum at Economy. Duss wrote that when the General Assembly of Pennsylvania, through an intermediary who lived nearby and knew the Harmonists, asked the Dusses for some objects for the new museum, Duss replied that "Mrs. Duss had assiduously collected and preserved items of particular interest precisely for such purpose."[3] Duss further noted that he and his wife "have donated the invaluable collection of furniture, paintings, tools, silks, books and manuscripts to the . . . Pennsylvania Historical Commission."[4] Furniture brought into the Society by members may also confuse the issue of provenance. For example, Peter Kaufmann, who was a member of the Society for only a short period in 1827, sent a list of objects that he left at Economy and wanted shipped to him. These included two tables, two gilt looking glasses, eighteen chairs, two beds, and a piano forte. Given that there is no record these were returned to Kaufman, they might have become community property. And during the schism of 1832 when over 200 members left the community there are documents showing Frederick Rapp's concern about withholding items such as pots, pans, tools, and beds that the departing members wanted. As I show later, the Harmonists also purchased numerous objects, such as pianos, which they did not have the ability to create within the community, and chairs, which they could make but not in the large numbers required when moving from one village to another.

Another problem in evaluating furniture is that there are few records to identify Harmonist cabinetmakers. Two such joiners were John Daut (or Dautt) and Georg Adam Jung, both of whom probably learned their trade when they were in Iptingen. Both Daut and Jung left the Society in the 1830s. When Jung withdrew from the Society in 1832 as a result of the influence of Count Leon, he eventually received a payment of $1,875 for the twenty-five years he had spent as a community cabinetmaker. One member of the community, David König, became joiner after many years as a carpenter in the Society. In keeping with the

---

[3] Duss, 407.
[4] Ibid, 411.

communal and egalitarian nature of the society, there is no joiner signature on any of the Harmonist furniture. To contribute to the success of the entire community, the joiners also made such objects as coffins and window frames for the numerous houses that were constructed when the Harmonists moved from village to village.

Even before the departure of Daut and Jung the Society depended on outside craftsmen for some of the work. In a letter to Frederick Rapp in 1813 one of the members says that "Today is the first day that I have the carpenters and cabinet makers here to repair Leets house. They also board here...."[5] The wording of this letter reveals that these carpenters and cabinetmakers were not members of the Society but were hired from the outside, in a practice which became more common after the middle of the century. By the 1880s, according to John Duss, "the remaining shops and industries were now under the supervision of those who were not members of the Society...including Henry Breitenstein at the cabinet shop."[6] The only other documentation of a cabinetmaker who was a member of the group is a reference to a Harmonist cabinetmaker Karl Ulrich in the late 1870s. Duss described him as "a recent émigré from Württemberg,...a curly-headed, handsome young man, a superior cabinetmaker who soon became foreman of the cabinet shop." According to Peter Kaufman, the Harmonist who left the Society in 1827, "the majority of our present members consists of nothing but the best craftsmen and workers who ever existed in Rapp's Harmony...."[7]

In her study of the Harmony Society, Lisa Ann Porter said that by the middle of the nineteenth century there was not much work for the joiners:

> The shops slowly ceased to exist as economical and social factors changed the community from an agricultural and small industrial complex to an economy of capital investment. . . . The Harmonist craftsmen disappeared from the shop and the historical record.[8]

---

[5] Arndt, Harmony on the Connoquenessing, 680.
[6] Duss, 220
[7] Karl J. R. Arndt, Economy on the Ohio, 1826-1834. (Worcester, Harmony Society Press, 1984.), xiii.
[8] The Joiners of the Harmony Society, 26.

Like the furniture of the Amanans, that of the Harmonists was a combination of German and American folk styles, but in addition there existed at Economy, the final home of the Harmonists, a number of pieces in the "high" or "cultivated" tradition. The artifacts of the Harmonists reflect layers of objects indicative of the community's changes in time and place. Grace Chaffee noted this tendency in the Amana Society:

> First, there is a stratum of the very old objects brought into the community by the first members and preserved through years of struggle and persecution. Then there are evidences of a folk art, expressing the spirit and meaning of the life of the particular community. Strong traces of the influence of the old pattern and style as well as adaptations to the mode current in the world outside, are distinguishable in this folk art. . . . Finally, there is a class of objects frankly imitative of the outside world.[9]

The furniture of the Harmonists falls into similar categories. The three basic traditions influencing Harmonist furniture are German rural, American vernacular, and a combination of late Federal-early Empire and other styles that reflect the cultivated tradition.

Stylistic Tendencies of Harmonist Furnishings

The most obvious indication of the German heritage of the Harmonists is their plank chair, or *stühl*, which is a simple folk piece consisting of a back and seat made with flat planks, and with legs that are splayed but are without reinforcing stretchers (Figure 20). One of the plank chairs now at Economy has a traditional heart-shaped handhold in the back and a relatively simple outline for the back piece. The only other attempts at ornamentation are the tapered edges of the seat and the tapered, five-sided legs. The heart is a traditional motif in Pennsylvania-

---

[9] Chaffee, 115.

German arts and crafts such as *fraktur* and gravestone carvings and represents the heart of Christ.[10]

A variation of this type, but with a more elaborate back pattern and a circular handhold rather than a heart-shaped one, can be seen at Economy also, currently in the Baker House. It is possible that the Harmonists brought some of these chairs with them when they immigrated to America, but lacking evidence that joiners made this style of chair at any of the villages one can only speculate that the chairs were comfortable reminders of their life in Germany but were not made or used in any quantities at any of the communities. And since they are such simple chairs to construct, it may be that they would not be among the more valuable items that a Harmonist brought from Germany. Eventually the Harmonists abandoned the medieval, rural style in chair design by the time they settled in Economy.[11]

The numerous cane-bottom ladderback chairs at Economy show an American vernacular influence that is absent in the plank chairs. The ladderbacks usually have three slats on the back, turned stretchers, and back-post finials that often differ from chair to chair, indicating that unlike the Shaker cabinetmaker, the Harmonist had no rigid pattern that he was required to follow. Also the variations in the distance from the floor to the seat in Harmonist chairs reflect the practice of them being made for households (or even individuals) rather than for the community as a whole.

Since there has been so much written on Shaker furniture it is tempting to suggest that the Harmonist cabinetmakers were influenced by similar Shaker chairs. The Society communicated with the Shakers throughout their history, and their proximity to a Shaker village may have provided opportunities for Harmonist cabinetmakers to observe the material culture of the Shakers. Further evidence of possible Shaker influence can be seen in the slat outlines of the

---

[10] Philip Zimmerman, who has studied the furniture as a trained expert in that field believes that only one of the plank chairs now at Economy was made there.
[11] It is possible that the two *stühle* at Economy were not made there but at Harmony.

Harmonist chairs. John Cummings has shown that the slat bottoms of the typical New England chairs are flat while those of the New Jersey-Pennsylvania region are curved. Since all of the Harmonist pieces have flat bottoms, they are closer in style to the essentially New England-inspired Shaker pieces that they are to those characteristic of Pennsylvania.[12]

Even though this evidence could suggest a Shaker influence on Harmonist chairs, it is possible that both the Harmonists and Shakers were influenced by a chair type that was common in the colonies in the eighteenth century. The Harmonist cabinetmaker was undoubtedly aware of different styles of ladderbacks from New England, New Jersey, Delaware, and Pennsylvania, as well as variations in Indiana. The tapered foot found on almost all of the Harmonist ladderbacks is not typical of Shaker chairs but may be characteristic of those made in the Midwest in the nineteenth century.[13] Thus, although the Harmonists could have been influenced by the Shakers, the abundance and similarity of the ladderback in nineteenth century America makes such an attribution tentative. One has to ask, if the Harmonist joiners were influenced by the Shakers, why they did not incorporate one of the Shaker innovations, the use of flexible balls on the bottoms of the rear legs of chairs so that the sitter could lean the chair back without stressing its structural integrity? It is reasonable to assume that the Harmonists did not have an overriding philosophy that wedded material forms with beliefs as it did with almost all of the Shaker objects. Instead they combined a variety of styles that suited their needs at a particular time and place.

Another chair more indicative of American rather than of German culture is the Windsor, which is much lighter and more delicate than the *stuhl*. There are a number of unornamented Windsors at Economy today, suggesting that they were common household chairs used at the dining table. The Windsor and ladderback chairs showed the influence of the American vernacular; the plank chairs, of

---

[12] John Cummings, "Slat Back Chairs," Antiques, LXXII, 1 (July, 1957), 60-63.
[13] For examples of Midwest ladderbacks in the nineteenth century see Ralph Kovel and Terry Kovel, American Country Furniture, 1780-1875 (New York: Crown Publishers, 1965), 93-94.

which there are only two extant and whose provenance is undetermined, and the kitchen tables, carried on the tradition of the German rural. A number of pieces, however, combined the American and German styles, and are characterized by a heaviness and simplicity, both evident in the deep skirts or aprons on dressers, tables, cupboards, and blanket chests; in the simple, squared or tapered legs; and in a general absence of ornamentation.

It is likely that many of the chairs were not made by the joiners in the society but were purchased from the outside. "The Harmony Society did have the capacity to produce seating furniture. Yet with the combination of surviving invoices and the lack of credits involving chairs [in the internal accounting system of the Harmonist departments] it appears that chairmaking was not extensively pursued, especially at Economy, Pennsylvania."[14] For example, during a period of three years at Economy, 1828 to 1831,

> at least 126 chairs traveled up the Ohio from Pittsburgh. J. Hanson, a Pittsburgh merchant, charged $8.50 for a dozen of "Common chairs" and $18.00 for a dozen of "Fancy chairs," in 1828. In November 1830, John D. Davis shipped forty-eight chairs to Economy and two months later, George Cochran sent thirty-six common chairs at $9.00 a dozen. In the end, the Society selected a more efficient option for seating furniture. The purchase of chairs from Pittsburgh, where specialists could turn them out in huge quantities, permitted ... the joiners to pursue other projects within the community.[15]

This purchasing of simple furniture from the outside during the Economy period is one more example of the Society turning from internal agricultural and manufacturing to a more active dependence on the outside world in purchasing objects, and investing in land, banks, railroads, and other economic ventures.

The Harmonist kitchen tables in the Baker House and in the Great House are further indications of the German heritage of the community. These heavy, solid pieces were probably common in the kitchen or dining room of the typical Harmonist household (Figure 20). A table in the Great House kitchen has a pine

---

[14] Porter, 44.
[15] Porter, 45.

top and a walnut frame with top dimensions of 55" x 29" and overall height 33," The distance from the floor to the skirt of this table is only 20", for the Harmonists, in the European tradition, sat with their legs at the edge of, rather than beneath, the table. However there is an overhang of the table top of almost ten inches which allowed some room for the knees. Many of these tables had removable tops which could have been used to set food on the table in one room and moved to another like an oversized 1950s television tray, but there is no evidence that this was done. A characteristic German detail is the exposed battens on either end of the table. Similar tables with drawers of different sizes were a familiar type in the Palatinate; the large drawer was used for linens and the smaller one for cutlery.[16] The German origins of this table are evidenced by the numerous examples of the type in German communities in Pennsylvania.[17]

There are two extant German chests or trunks that were likely brought to America during the Harmonist migration. The first is now located in the museum at New Harmony, having been left in that town when the Harmonists moved to Economy. The significant features of this chest are the elaborate pattern of the iron band and front pieces and the painted inscription on the front:

R:S: W:[?]
V:S: 1804 *

The second chest is now at Economy and like the one at New Harmony, has wrought iron bands which encircle the entire chest, and an inscription:

Johan Georg Knoedel, von Oelbrun, 1805

---

* Records do not show any families with these initials.
[16] For drawings of variations of this type of table see Frances Lichten, Folk Art of Rural Pennsylvania (New York: Charles Scribner's Sons, 1946), 105.
[17] For a photograph of this type see Earl F. Robacker, Touch of the Dutchland (New York: A. S. Barnes and Company, 1965), 159.

According to Society records, Knoedel arrived in America on November 5, 1805, and died in 1823. It is likely that his son, also named Georg, brought the chest from New Harmony to Economy when the Harmonists moved in 1824.

Both of these chests have rounded tops, a common feature to discourage the practice of loading chests on top of one another (Figure 21). Significantly, the chests built by the Harmonists in America have flat tops and were used as blanket chests as well. Since the Harmonists controlled the details of moving from community to community they did not have to worry to damage to their chests and therefore abandoned the old style rounded tops. At Harmony there are two types of chest: painted pine and unpainted walnut or cherry, which were more expensive wood types. One walnut chest has a diamond inlay on its corners and three drawers. According to Lisa Porter, it is

> difficult to conclude that the walnut chest with three drawers, inlaid decoration and forged iron handles expressed greater prestige or position than the simple, painted chest with imported, butt hinges. . . . Tradition associates the walnut chest with George Rapp and the cherry chest with the Society's physician, Conrad Feucht. Those associations raise a question as to whether or not these objects express a hidden social hierarchy within an egalitarian community. Without proof of ownership, that question will remain unanswered.[18]

One chest currently on display at Old Economy may have come from Germany with one of the early members. This piece has a "finely crafted and engraved lock, the hasp of which has a small face chiseled into it. The lock and overall quality of the trunk indicate that it would have belonged to an early member who had some financial standing in the community." [19]

Another type indicative of the German heritage of the Society is the painted *schrank*, a large wardrobe. The *schranken* at Economy are more similar to the medieval German *schrank* than they are of the typical Pennsylvania-German *schrank*, which "declares its independence from the

---

[18] 39.
[19] From exhibition description notes.

Germanic forms by a new grace and in some instances by a new lightness."[20] Three of the schranken at Economy are not painted but are constructed of walnut and have fancy cornices and banded inlays. Since these pieces were made of black walnut rather than the more common pine, the Harmonist joiner was creating a *schrank* that was likely to be used by one of the important members of the community. Although the community members might not have resented it if George or Frederick Rapp, because of their status in the community, had more expensive furniture than the common members, but would have done so if a common member did. To show the outside world just how successful this group of German Pietists was, impressive buildings such as the Rapp House with appropriately elegant furnishings were accepted as necessary.

The Harmonist blending of two plain styles is perhaps nowhere more evident than in the few side tables extant at Old Economy. One of these, now in the George Rapp bedroom, has a single drawer with a wooden pull, exposed battens, and turned legs. A simpler piece is the side table in the Baker House. The top of this stained and varnished piece extends beyond the apron, and the apron itself has a characteristic Harmonist molding to give some definition to an otherwise plain piece. Unlike the table described above, this one does not have exposed battens, and the legs are squared and tapered rather than turned.

A slightly more refined side table is the one in Gertrude Rapp's bedroom. The inlay along the top of the table and along the bottom edge indicates that this piece was probably made for Gertrude, or for another inhabitant of the Great House, rather than for the common member.

The differences between each of these pieces are indicative of the fact that they were not mass-produced for the community as a whole, but, like those ladderback chairs constructed in the community, were made for individuals or for households. It is quite likely that the average Harmonist, however, had a table

---

[20] Stoudt, 118.

similar to the one in the Baker House rather than to the one in Gertrude Rapp's bedroom.

A third style of furniture used by the Harmonists at their final village reflects the cultivated tradition. The growing involvement of the Harmony Society with the outside world by the time they settled at Economy seems to have influenced the form of their material culture. Thus, while most of the pieces at Harmony were probably in the German or American vernacular tradition, and numerous chairs at Economy were purchased from the outside, there are a number of pieces in the Rapp House at Economy exhibiting such styles as Heppelwhite, Federal, Greek Revival, and Early Empire. It is sometimes difficult to ascertain which pieces were made by Harmonist cabinetmakers and which ones were purchased from the outside world.

One of the "sophisticated" pieces is a stained and varnished walnut and curly maple Empire secretary in the Reception Room of the Rapp House. The top of the secretary is a cupboard with two doors surmounted by a curved cornice. The base has four bowed front drawers with wooden knobs and false locks. This piece was made in the 1880s by Herman Ott, a worker hired by the community,[21] and is indicative of the fine furniture used in the Great House. Since Ott made this piece during the waning years of the community it may indicate the increasing use of worldly and sophisticated objects at Economy.

In Gertrude Rapp's room is a Heppelwhite style bureau of cherry. The four drawers of the bureau vary in height, getting larger from top to bottom. The details of this piece are very fine, consisting of inlay at the edge of the top, around the drawer fronts, and around each key hole. In addition, further detail is provided by oval brass drawer pulls. This is one of the most finely executed pieces at Economy and shows that the Harmonist cabinetmakers were capable of creating furniture comparable to that of good cabinetmakers in American cities.

---

[21] Evelyn P. Matter, The Great House (Economy: The Harmonie Associates, 1970), 29.

One of the most striking, if not the most graceful, of the Harmonist pieces in the cultivated tradition is an unusual wine or dish cupboard in the dining room of the Great House (Figure 22). This piece, which is over 5' tall and 3 ½' wide at the base, is veneered in mahogany, has six drawers in the bottom section, and two four-toed claw feet in the front and two large round feet in the back. Further decoration consists of incised circles within squares on either side of the bottom drawer. If any piece of furniture represents the difference between the Shaker and Harmonist aesthetic sense, it is this wine cupboard. One cannot imagine such a piece in a Shaker community where simplicity and "form follows function" were adhered to in both architectural and furniture expression.

Another piece in the dining room is a small, early Empire sideboard consisting of a base with side columns on separate pedestal bases, a recessed cupboard on the bottom outlined with inlay, and two top drawers separated from the bottom section by a molding with inlay.

Except for the Gertrude Rapp side table described above and a few other pieces, most of the furniture in the cultivated tradition has a simplicity indicative of the German origins of the craftsmen or of the choices made by Frederick Rapp in purchasing items from the outside. An example of the blending of a German piece with the cultivated tradition is the kitchen-type table in the drawing room of Frederick Rapp's house which is similar to the typical household kitchen table of the Harmonists but which has rather graceful Queen Anne feet. So while the Harmonist cabinetmaker imitated the cultivated styles in many pieces for the Great House, he could not escape a heritage which emphasized mass rather than delicacy in furniture. As noted by Lisa Porter,

> the members and joiners shared a common German vocabulary that manifested itself in their furniture. The retention of German styles and forms was not the result of a conscious decision to cling to European roots. Rather, this maintenance was the result of age, economics, and experience.[22]

---

[22] Porter, 27.

Occasionally there will be a piece of furniture that seems somewhat out of place, especially if one is familiar with the simple lines of Shaker furniture. One such piece at Old Economy, currently in the George Rapp house, is a sofa upholstered in green fabric.

Much Harmonist furniture, unlike that in a typical Shaker village, included traditional Germanic pieces, more elegant objects made by the cabinetmakers to reinforce the status of the group's leaders, sophisticated furniture purchased from the outside, and simple chairs (and perhaps other pieces of furniture) to meet the needs of a community in transition that needed a number of similar objects in a fairly short time period.

Furnishings in a Typical Dwelling

Today the Baker House is furnished with a selection of pieces that would likely have been found in the typical Harmonist dwelling during the 1840s.[23] As now conceptualized, the kitchen of a Harmonist household held two or three American Windsor type chairs and a small green table, the same color that is found on a chest in the Baker House and one in the Rapp House. It also contained hanging, standing, and open-shelf cupboards, a cast-iron stove, and a stone sink draining to an outside barrel which collected garbage as swill for the pigs. The walls of the kitchen and of the other rooms were painted white or light blue; the woodwork was white; the windows were covered with blue cloth blinds on rollers and white pleated half curtains.

The largest room in the household-type dwelling was a combination of living-dining room. It most probably held a Harmonist-made dining table of the Germanic type, along with several ladderbacks and Windsor chairs, a pine sideboard, a chest of drawers, a wardrobe, a settee, and a clock.

---

[23] Since visitors to Economy described the artifacts in the Great House only, my observations are based on the objects placed in the Baker House by the curatorial staff using a court required inventory of the house in 1846.

The floor of the dining-living room may have been covered with a rag rug of blue filler and yellow warp that the Harmonists themselves wove. Ironstone dishes and brown and green pottery made by the Society were used, although some purchased china may have been in the typical household in the later years of the community. Lighting for the dining room was provided by grease lights and candles.

The bedrooms contained wardrobes, or *schranken,* chests of drawers, ladderback or Windsor chairs, blanket chests, side tables, mirrors, and simple rope beds for one person, as appropriate for a community that advocated celibacy (Figure 23).

Great House Furnishings

The various styles of Harmonist furnishings and interiors, however, are not as significant in themselves as is the contrast between those styles found in the Great House and the ones in the typical household dwelling. Just as the Rapp House is larger and architecturally more sophisticated than the other dwellings, so is the furniture in that building more elegant than that in the Baker House. The increasing worldliness in the material culture of the Harmony Society was, for the most part, concentrated in the styles of the public structures and in the furnishings of the Rapp House. Although the furnishings in the typical dwelling probably underwent a change from the German rural style to the American vernacular, only in the Great House was the cultivated tradition used to any great degree.

One example of the difference in styles is the beds. Unlike the simple rope beds that were in the household dwelling, a large bed identified by a curator in the 1970s as George Rapp's and placed in the Rapp House, is not only larger but more elegant, with a ringed horizontal bar at the top of the head board characteristic of the Empire style bedsteads. Below the valance the four heavy posts are turned into vase shaped sections, and in the center of the turned posts are large, square blocks surmounting bulbous turnings (Figure 24). While one might expect that in a communal society all of the beds would be identical, that was not the case at Economy. Befitting his role as the spiritual leader of the Society, Rapp had a bed that was larger and more elaborate than those of the average Harmonist. Other examples of the elegant furnishings in the Great House (some of which have been noted previously) include a *schrank* with inlay, a dining room table with Queen Anne legs, blanket chests with inlay, and a number of Hitchcock style chairs. Comparable pieces in the Baker House are simple and unadorned *schrank*, dining room tables, painted chests, and ladderback or Windsor chairs.

The elegant and refined interior of the Great House as it appeared in the last half of the nineteenth century is nowhere better revealed than in the comments of Agnes Gormley, who visited Gertrude Rapp in the 1870s. In the sitting room, she observed,

> A row of rush-bottom chairs stands stiffly against the outer wall. The beautiful Colonial mantel bears four vases of wax fruit . . . and a fine old gilt clock, beneath which is a joy of a Franklin stove. At the side is a lovely mahogany work table, then a door over which hangs a fine copy of the "Ecce Homo" with two pianos at right angles, each covered with dark blue silk of home manufacture. Over them hang replicas of "Christ Healing the Sick," and a lovely "Nativity" said to be by Raphael Ments. . . Miss Gertrude excused herself, and in a few minutes re-entered with a tray of wine glasses through whose facets you see a ruby liquid. Then she opens a long narrow closet in the chimney corner and piles ginger cakes on an "Adams" plate and serves you . . . and we discuss the ivory carvings hanging over us and the wonderful old prints on the wall.[24]

The glasses mentioned by Gormley could be among the twelve "gilt" glasses records show were purchased from A. Cochran & Co. in Pittsburgh in 1829.

The Harmonists bought a number of fine pieces, including furniture, silver, china, and lamps, to furnish the Great House in an impressive manner. Since Philadelphia was the cultural and commercial center of Pennsylvania, the Rapps

---

[24] Evelyn Matter, The Great House, 13. Quoted from Agnes H. Gormley, Old Economy, The Harmony Society (Sewickley, Pennsylvania, 1920). Many of the pieces mentioned by Gormley are in the Great House today.

often bought their better pieces there. A letter to the R. L. Cauffman Company of Philadelphia in 1835 mentioned a number of items shipped to Economy, and noted that several were broken and some not identical with the samples. According to the writer, the Society received "bowls, printed purple muffins [sic], teapots and Sugars; one dozen of the largest dishes and several pieces of finest china were broken . . . and six dozen Japanese Cup Plates (craz'd) . . . are missing."[25]

In 1827 W.R. Griffith wrote to Frederick Rapp with a proposal for gas lighting. Griffith included an offer to Rapp to invest the amount of $20,000 to establish a gas lighting company in Pittsburgh. He also proposed that gas lighting be installed at Economy, but there is no evidence that Griffith's offers were acted on.[26] Invoices of the Society show that purchases from J. Solms and Company of Philadelphia included "German ceramic lamps, hanging lamps, stocking weaver globes, chandeliers, sperm whale oil, wicks and hanging chains."[27] Lawrence Thurmond, the former Curator at Old Economy, contended that this lighting equipment "is not of such quantity that it could have been used by the whole community, and the prices quoted by these ledger books indicate that the lighting was used mainly for the Great House and Church."[28]

In addition to the paintings, prints, and pianos described by Agnes Gormley and to the fine china, lamps, and other items mentioned in Harmonist correspondence, there were a number of other pieces in the cultivated tradition in the Great House that would not have been found in the household dwelling (Figure 25). A few of these pieces existing today include a silver tea service; a set of rush bottom Hitchcock style chairs that have a gold stenciled classic design; a blanket chest with a diamond-pattern inlay on the edges to hide the joints; a mahogany *schrank* with inlay on the doors; a candle stand with an octagonal top,

---

[25] Old Economy Archives, Correspondence Book 19, 86.
[26] Arndt, Economy on the Ohio, 171
[27] Old Economy Archives. Letter by Lawrence Thurmond. Addressee and date not given.
[28] Ibid.

turned base, and three tapered, curved legs; and an Empire gateleg table. In addition are the secretary, the Heppelwhite bureau, and the unusual wine or dish cupboard discussed above (Figure 22).

Most of the rooms in the Great House were covered with printed wallpaper that was purchased in Philadelphia, whereas the rooms in the typical house were painted, usually a light blue. Another difference was in the stairs; those in the Great House are made of walnut and have side designs and a rose carving on the newel posts; the stairs in the Baker House, however, are unadorned oak. And at least one of the rooms in the Rapp House may have had a patterned carpet rather than the more common rag carpet made in the community.

****

Since there are no detailed descriptions of the furnishings at Harmony and New Harmony, and since there are few extant pieces from these towns, one cannot say definitely that the elegant furnishings of the Great House at Economy represent a pattern of increasing worldliness and a gradual, but by no means complete, dilution of the German rural elements in the material culture. But since there is such a pattern in the architecture of the Harmonist villages, one can speculate that at Harmony most of the furnishings were simple and essentially Germanic, reflecting their origins and their economic difficulties during their first few years in America. As they became wealthier and interacted with the outside world to a greater extent, their furnishings became more American, and certainly in the case of the furnishings in the Great House, more a part of the cultivated tradition.

What other conclusions can be drawn from an examination of Harmonist furnishings? For one thing, the differences in the quality and style of the furnishings indicate that the Harmonists, unlike the Shakers, were much more eclectic in their aesthetic practices, combining German and American vernacular forms, and various cultivated styles. The social and institutional freedom of the Harmonists, as compared with that of the Shakers, is indeed reflected in the absence of any one style that would characterize the Harmonists.

Second, just as there was a strong cultivated tradition of the architecture of a number of Harmonist structures, so was there in the furnishings of the Great House. For the Harmonist leaders a certain degree of indulgence in the finer things of life was not incompatible with the general insistence on simplicity in the life of the average member. The furnishings of the Great House, which were much more worldly than those of the typical dwelling, show that the Harmonists were a communal society but that not all were equal in terms of their material surroundings. This is not to say that the members of the Society lived in poverty while their leaders enjoyed the amenities of the cultured life, for the furnishings of the average home were comfortable and aesthetically pleasing if not striking. The elegant furnishings in the Great House, like the exterior size, served to honor George and Frederick Rapp as leaders of the community and to provide an impressive meeting place for those who visited the community.

It is possible, however, that some members of the Society took a more critical view of the worldly lifestyles of George and Frederick Rapp. Could the defections of almost 250 members in 1832 reflect some resentment about the disparity between the houses and belongings of the average members and those of the Rapps? A number of lawsuits were brought against the Society by former members who felt that they were owed money for what they had contributed to the community, but there are no written records that show dissatisfaction with the Rapps' belongings and houses.

Chapter 5
Arts and Artifacts

Certain pieces at Economy today reveal the communal nature of the Society. The simple side tables and kitchen tables with the exposed battens discussed above were more than likely found in every household. The Harmonist beds also reflect the philosophy of the community. Of the seven simple beds with rope springs used other than in the Great House and remaining in the collection at Old Economy, most are narrower than 45" and at least one is as narrow as 35". The beds extant at Economy are 42", 35", 43", 37", 50", and 44". [1] Since a full-size bed in the nineteenth century was usually about 45" wide,[2] the smaller beds at Economy show that they were sufficient for members who practiced celibacy.

One might expect that in a communal society all of the beds would be of an identical width. However, as in the case of much of the other furniture, pieces were made for households, and perhaps for individuals within the households, rather than for the community as a whole. Significantly, the two largest beds extant at Economy, measuring 64" and 59" respectively, were used by George and Frederick Rapp. One of the beds in the Rapp House, at approximately 50" wide, was used by a steward there, a person whose status was higher than a typical member of the Society.

Another group of objects reflecting the communal nature of the Society includes the numerous blanket chests with similar, although not identical, lines and dimensions. Even though there are a few chests which are larger and more

---

[1] Old Economy Archives. Accession Book. The widths given are those of the beds. Therefore the mattresses were at least 3" narrower.
[2] Earl F. Robacker, Touch of the Dutchland (New York: A. S. Barnes and Co., 1965), 155.

sophisticated in their execution than the typical chest, these are the exception, and more than likely were owned by the Rapps or by those who had positions of authority in the community. An example of the chest that was made for distribution to the members is a pine piece with overall dimensions of 43" x 19" x 22" high. This chest, like some of the others, is stained with red lead and lamp black and is nailed together rather than constructed with dovetails. It seems likely that community members kept their personal belongings in these chests and one can surmise that the chests extant at Economy were the ones used by the Harmonists when they moved from Indiana to Pennsylvania.

In addition to the household items, such as the beds, chests, and tables, which reflect the communal, egalitarian nature of the Society, there are other objects outside of the household that indicate the ways in which the Society maintained group solidarity. The various feasts held by the Harmonists during the year were a means of gathering together those who lived in households to remind them of the communal nature of Economy, to celebrate their success as a community, and to thank their God for their blessings.

Meals for the large gatherings were prepared in advance in the Feast Hall kitchen, a separate structure next to the Feast Hall. In this kitchen are four large brick stoves containing twelve cast iron kettles, each 29" wide and 20" deep. In these kettles food for over 700 members was prepared. A typical celebration meal there consisted of a thick rice soup, roast veal and roast beef cooked together in a stew, schnitz, sauerkraut, white bread made with milk, ginger cakes, wine, and beer.[3] These meals were prepared a day or two in advance, reheated on feast day and carried to the *saal* in large pots where they were placed on the tables.

A feast that took place late in the history of the Society was described by Christiana Knoedler:

---

[3] Christiana F. Knoedler, The Harmony Society (New York: Vantage Press, 1954) 127; and Karl Arndt, George Rapp's Harmony Society, 427.

At the front of the hall was a large platform on which stood two pianos. In front of the platform was a dias in the center of which was the table. The Board of Elders and the Trustees sat around the table on chairs, instead of the usual benches, so that they faced the entire assembly. From the platform to the rear of the hall was [sic] bisected by a wide aisle. On the right-hand side were tables for the men, with a special table for the boys near the wall. The women and girls sat at tables on the left-side of the aisle. Before the meal a blessing was asked by the trustee. After the meal a concert would be held, with both band and singers, children and adults, who sat on the platform, participating. This concert lasted until about two o'clock. Some of the ladies and a few men remained to wash the dishes and prepare for the evening meal, while the others went home to perform their usual chores. At about six o'clock the evening meal was served. This consisted of leftovers from the noon meal except for the soup. After it was over there was more music by the band and choirs, and the entire audience would sing from the community song-books.[4]

The number of members at a meal in the Feast Hall varied from time to time and some members, for one reason or another, did not attend. A notebook of one of the Harmonists stated that on July 19, 1829, there were thirty-three tables of men and thirty-nine tables of women in the *saal*. The following day's gathering, however, consisted of thirty-nine tables of men and forty-three tables of women.[5] If there were ten people at each table, the meal on July 19 was served to 720 members while that on the following day was served to 820.

The tables in the *saal* are simple pine pieces 31" x 13'6', although there are slight variations in these dimensions from table to table. The benches are the same lengths as the tables; except for a simple scroll outline on the front sides of the bench legs, there is no ornamentation (Figure 33).

Another group of objects both reflected the communal nature of the Society and functioned to reinforce group solidarity by giving the members an identification as a unique community separate from and better than the outside world. This is the Harmonist clothing. No visitors commented on the dress of the Harmonists at their first village, Harmony, but it is likely that during their first

---

[4] Knodler, 127.
[5] Arndt, George Rapp's Harmony Society, 427.

years in America the members wore clothing similar to what they had worn in Germany. By the New Harmony period a number of visitors described the dress of the women in the Society. William Hebert noted in 1823 that "These good people retain their German style of dress. There is nothing remarkable in that of the men. The women wear close and long-bodied jackets, or spencers, and gipsey bonnets."[6] In 1825 William MacDonald noted the clothing of those attending a church service: "The men dress in a plain blue, brown frock coat or surtout, trowsers & shoes; the females wear white caps, checked neck handkerchiefs, cloth gowns, and checked aprons."[7] An English visitor to Economy said that "the dress of the people in Economy is still exactly as it was in Swabia, only somewhat finer," [8] and another visitor described the dress in some detail:

> The men wear short jackets, or half-coats, and trousers, of grey cloth, with waistcoats of lilac or brown, and black hats and shoes of the ordinary kind. The women wear gowns with long sleeves, or a sort of light woolen cloth, like coarse merino, of a dark colour, with a near-handkerchief of silk or cotton over the shoulders, pinned down tight before, a plain white or checked apron, and a perpendicular German cap of black when in their laboring dress, and white in the evenings and on Sundays.[9]

These descriptions, as well as drawings and photographs of Society members and an examination of the clothing extant at Old Economy, give an accurate picture of Harmonist dress.

The clothing worn by the men for work usually consisted of short blue, brown or gray jackets, dark trousers, and tall, broad-brimmed hats. On Sundays, at least after the 1840s, the men wore long dark blue or black frocks, and gray vests.[10] It is likely that the leaders of the community wore the frock coats during the day and

---

[6] William Hebert, A Visit to the Colony of Harmony, In Indiana (London, 1824). Reprinted in Harlow Lindley, Indiana as Seen by Early Travelers (Indiana Historical Commission, 1916), 336.
[7] Donald MacDonald, "The Diaries of Donald MacDonald, 1824-1826," Indiana Historical Society Publications, XIV, 2 (1942), 249.
[8] Buckingham, 218.
[9] Arndt, George Rapp's Harmony Society, 218. Arndt quotes Wilhelm Weitling, who visited Economy in 1851. Karl Bernhard also said that the clothing was "Swabian."
[10] Buckingham's description in 1840 did not mention the long frock coats, while Nordhoff's 1874 description did.

certainly when they visited the outside world. A drawing of the Harmonists in 1874 in Nordhoff's The Communistic Societies of the United States shows a scene in which both sleeveless jackets and frocks were being worn by different members (Figure 26). Thus, by the 1870s the male Harmonist's wardrobe consisted of a sleeveless jacket (or vest), a long-sleeved jacket, and a frock coat, as well as his underclothing, shoes, and hat.

Although visitors do not mention them, blue silk smocks were also worn by the men of the community, probably during church services in the summer. Approximately fifty of these smocks are extant at Old Economy today. Since the production of silk did not begin until the Harmonists moved to Economy, these smocks probably were worn only at that village.

The leader of the community, George Rapp, was provided with at least one garment which was finer than the clothing of the average member. This was a floor length maroon velvet robe and a matching silk cap now in the collection at Old Economy Village. In 1840 William Passavant noted that during the church service Rapp "was dressed in the common garb of the society and wore a woolen night cap," yet a painting of Rapp shows him wearing the maroon silk cap. So Rapp may have worn the silk clothing in the Great House, perhaps when receiving visitors.

The Harmonist women wore three types of hats. The first was a large straw summer hat with a wide brim that was worn in the fields or gardens. This type is evident in the illustration in Nordhoff's book. The second, and most striking to visitors because of its uniqueness, was a stiff, perpendicular "Normandy cap" placed on the top of the hair and tied under the chin. A Harmonist woman working in the household might have worn a black cap for work and a white or blue cap for church. The third type was the winter hat. During the winter months the women wore knit hats which covered their ears. Today the collection at Old Economy contains fifteen winter hats (which were not described by visitors and which do not appear in any drawings), fifteen cotton Normandy caps, over two dozen silk Normandy caps, and a few summer hats.

The clothing of the women consisted of ankle length woolen, cotton, or silk dresses, a white or checked apron, and a shawl of silk or cotton). The heavier materials were worn during the winter months, and the more elegant ones for church and formal occasions. There are extant a number of black cotton shawls that were worn around the house and in the gardens, and also silk shawls with a rose pattern around the edges. The silk shawls, which are white, blue, and pink and which have similar but not identical patterns, were likely made in the 1830s when the Society was a leading manufacturer in the production of silk.[11]

The virtually identical dress of the Harmonists served two functions. First, since the style of dress was distinctive to the community, it was a factor in creating "insulating boundaries" between the community and the outside, and of giving a sense of uniqueness as a community to its members. Second, the uniform dress was a means of discouraging individual vanity and the importance of the self. For the Harmonist, as for a member of the military, the dress symbolized that one's identity was not to be developed as unique and self-serving, but as a subservient part of the larger and more important whole. According to Rosabeth Moss Kanter, eight of the nine "successful" communes in nineteenth-century America required that members wear uniform dress, what Kanter refers to as a "deindividuating mechanism." Conversely, only five of seventeen unsuccessful communes required a uniform.[12] Thus, the success of the Harmonist may have been partially due to their insistence on a uniform dress.

Finally, there was a practical reason for the use of identical clothing. It was both cheaper and more efficient to provide a common dress for the members than to make each piece according to the desires of the individual.

---

[11] In September, 1831, Frederick Rapp showed one of these silk shawls to the editor of Poulson's American Daily Advertiser. See Arndt, George Rapp's Harmony Society, 392.
[12] Kanter, 112.

Symbolic Motifs in the Material Culture

The Harmony Society had a strong element of mysticism in its religious philosophy, and a number of objects at the three villages have symbolic reference which reflects deeply held beliefs by the members. In using certain symbolic motifs the Harmonists were reinforcing their religious dedication and their sense of being a community both separate from and more holy than the outside world. However, since the Harmonists were breaking away from the established church, which they felt was corrupted and encumbered by an overabundance of religious artifacts having little or no relationship to true worship, the symbolic motifs that they used had a general rather than specific purpose in reminding the community of its special role. In addition, since the village as a whole was an exemplum of the true church, they had little need for specifically religious objects.

The most commonly used motif by the Harmonists was that of the rose, or, more specifically, the Golden Rose, which had long been associated with the beauty and majesty of Christ. One of the first uses of the rose on a Harmonist object may have been at Harmony on the grave stone of John Rapp, George's son, who died in a mill accident in 1812, although the date of the erection of this stone and of the building of the cemetery wall was not until 1815, for an inscription above the two massive stone doors at entrance to the cemetery reads "Here rest 100 members of the Harmony Society who died from 1805 to 1815." There are no records to show when the John Rapp stone was made,[13] but it is significant as being the only grave marker ever erected by the Harmonists (Figure 27) and perhaps as having one of the first displays of the Harmonist rose. At New Harmony the lintel of the 1822 Cruciform Church contained a carved rose and the inscription "Micah- 4:8" which in Luther's translation of the Old Testament reads "Unto thee shall come the golden rose, the first dominion." For the Harmonist the Golden Rose was the symbol of the risen Christ who would reign during the

---

[13] Correspondence with John Ruch, curator of Historic Harmony, May 10, 2008.

millennium. Since their community was built in preparation for this event, the rose was their inspiration. Other examples of the rose motif in the material culture are the carved flowers on the newel posts of the Great House (Figure 28), those on the flat-irons at Economy, and the rose patterns on a number of silk shawls. The fan window at the 1822 Church and that over the main door of the Great House have a pattern that may represent a flower, but this was also a common pattern in Georgian doorways.

Like most Christians, the Harmonists also saw the lily as a flower with religious connotations of longing or hope for redemption.[14] Such a motif (often with a heart also to represent Christ's heart) is common on some reformed churches in Pennsylvania. George Rapp was very much influenced by the philosophy of Jacob Boehme, a seventeenth century German mystic who saw the lily and the rose as interchangeable and symbolizing

> the pure divine principle which both dwells within and transcends substantial reality, being the dialectical counterpart of what he calls the *magna turba*, or the principle of radical evil which inhabits all reality. In this sense also the Lily is apocalyptic in that the "time of the Lily," as Joahim of Flora predicted, is that glorious age at the end of time when all evil shall have been overcome in the final victory of God.[15]

In his Thoughts on the Destiny of Man George Rapp compared the lily to Christ. "How extraordinary and astonishing that the Lily should make its appearance," he wrote, "just at the time when the moral faculties of the whole human mass were almost exhausted & decayed, and when the mind of degenerate man, was wholly transported with the pomp and arrogance of war and with the wild indulgence of unrestrained liberty."[16] An example of the lily motif is on the lintel of the store at Harmony where four carved lilies flank a carved head, which probably represented the Virgin Sophia (Figure 10).

---

[14] John Jacob Stoudt, Early Pennsylvania Arts and Crafts (Cranbury, N.Y.: A. S. Barnes and Co, 1964), 310.
[15] John Jacob Stoudt, Pennsylvania Folk Arts (Allentown: Schlechter's, 1948), 5
[16] [George Rapp], Thoughts on the Destiny of Man (Harmony, 1824; Reprint ed., (New York: Augustus M. Kelley, 1971), 9-10.

According to Harmonist belief, the original Adam was a dual being who contained both male and female elements in one person. This Adam, said Jacob Boehme in his Hirtin Brief, "was in general like the angels and blessed spirits, who neither marry nor are given in marriage for the propagation of their kind, but in the chase embrace of *Sophien* (wisdom), the general mother who is above, are prolific, and propagate themselves in a magical, supersensual way."[17] After the fall, the Hirtin Brief related, Adam "lost the heavenly indwelling of *Sophien* at the time God created for him a helper with whom he could gratify his false desire and propagate himself in an animal way."[18] By pursuing a course of spiritual wisdom the Harmonists believed that they would achieve their salvation; thus the Virgin Sophia that is carved in the lintel at Harmony is a personification of the wisdom that they as a community aspired to. In venerating Sophia, the Harmonists were saying that they were attempting to regain the wisdom that was a part of the original Adam and in so doing they would restore harmony to the world.[19]

At Economy the Harmonists commissioned Benjamin Rush to carve a life-sized statue of a woman and they placed it, during different periods, in the Grotto or in the Pavilion (Cover Figure). According to a newspaper report at the time, the statue was "emblematic of Harmonie," thus representing the harmonic balance within the community. The statue in the Pavilion could also be a representation of the Harmonist Sunwoman,

> who brought forth a manchild, who was to rule the world but who for a time was forced to flee into the wilderness 'where she hath a place prepared of God'.... This woman was another symbol of the Harmony Society, which had fled to America and which, like the woman of Revelation, would have to flee again.[20]

---

[17] The Hirtin Brief is reprinted in Aaron Williams, The Harmony Society (Pittsburgh, 1866 Reprint New York: Augustus M. Kelley, 1971). In 1855 the Harmonists reprinted the Hirtin Brief and placed copies in each household.
[18] Williams, 153.
[19] Ibid, 158.
[20] Arndt, George Rapp's Harmony Society, 101.

Two pieces at Economy reveal a religious symbol that was common in medieval and renaissance Europe as a representation of Christ. This was the pelican, which, when feeding its young presses its sack against its neck in such a way that it seems to open its breast with its bill. Since the breast plumage of the white pelican is a reddish tinge, a folkloristic notion was created that the pelican actually drew blood from its own breast, thus sacrificing itself as Christ did for mankind.[21] The persistence of this motif as well as its continental origins can be seen in numerous examples of the pelican on Pennsylvania-German pottery and *fraktur* (illuminated writings).[22]

At Old Economy the pelican is found on a slip-ware pie plate (Figure 40) and a cut glass tumbler, both in the museum. On one side of this tumbler is the monogram "R," suggesting that it was owned by one of the Rapps; on the other side is the figure of the pelican surrounded by what appear to be the symbolic roses and lilies. Since the Harmonists did not make glass, this piece was commissioned to a manufacturer in Pittsburgh.

In spite of these examples of religious motifs in the Harmonists' material culture, what is striking is the absence of icons in a community so completely dedicated to a religious way of life. Nowhere was the absence of religious objects more evident than in the Harmonist church at Economy, as described by James Silk Buckingham in 1842. The interior of the building, he observed, "was perfectly plain...in which respect it resembled the simple interior of a Quaker meeting-house."[23] On the platform for the preacher were a table and chair.

The table mentioned by Buckingham is a simple desk at which George Rapp sat when he gave his sermons to the assembled members. Even though this piece (now at Economy) has turned legs, it is no more elegant than the typical Harmonist kitchen table. In its simplicity, this preacher's table is representative of a Pietistic hostility towards any ornamentation that suggested the organized

---

[21] The New Catholic Encyclopedia (New York: McGraw Hill, 1967), XI, 60.
[22] See Stoudt, Early Pennsylvania Arts and Crafts, 305-313.
[23] Buckingham, 221.

church. The Harmonists were in basic agreement with the statement made by the Puritan Cotton Mather that "God's altar needs not man's polishing."

The difficulty in determining provenance of Harmonist objects is obvious in the current display of tables used by George Rapp at two historic sites. In the museum at Harmony is a small table, not much larger than a child's school desk, identified as being used by Rapp, and at the Workingmen's Institute at New Harmony is a U shaped desk that the display sign says was used by George Rapp. If so, then one has to ask why it was left behind when the Harmonists moved from New Harmony to Economy, although it is possible that at this point in history Rapp decided that it was an inappropriate shape for a desk.

Artifacts Reflecting Harmonist Education and Culture

The cultural and intellectual milieu of the Harmonists can be seen in descriptions of the community by visitors, in Harmonist correspondence, and in a number of extant objects at Economy. Many of the visitors to the Rapp house and to the museum in the Feast Hall commented on the number and variety of paintings and prints owned by the Harmonists. The existence of these works shows that the Harmonists had the opportunity to broaden their artistic sensibilities, although there is no evidence to indicate just how many took advantage of it. Most of the paintings and prints were of religious subjects, but the Harmonists also owned portraits of the community leaders, landscapes, and paintings relating to American history.

Correspondence between Frederick Rapp and T. Hillier, an art dealer, indicates that in 1830 the Society purchased the following paintings for either the Rapp House or the museum:

No. 1. Joseph and Mary & Child Jesus. Painted by Macheitti, a celebrated Italian Artist of 1646. Florence. ($50.00)

No. 2. Laban and Rachel at the Well. Painted by Diepenboech who studied under Rubens. Born in Antwerp and died in 1675. ($30.00)

No. 3. Roman Daughter. Painted Francis Leachin Beich. A painter of Swabia whose pieces are much admired. Died 1784. ($30.00)

No. 4. 2 Landscapes by Martin De Vos (who studied under Pintoret) Excelled in Landscape painting. A native of Antwerp. Born 1520. Died 1604. ($30.00 each)

No 5. 2 Cattle Landscapes. By John Hendrich Roos. A Dutch painter of Landscapes and cattle. Born at Ottenburgh 1631. Died 1685. ($20.00 each)

No. 6. A small picture. Abraham and Hagha. Supposed to be painted by Paul Veronese, a native of Verona (greatly distinguished and a historical painter). Died in Venice 1588. The above picture from the collection of the Louvre, Paris. ($15.00)

No 7. 2 Small pictures by David Teniers the younger. Born at Antwerp. Died 1694. Celebrated for his Low-Born Scenes. Interior of Alkemist Laboratory and Flemish Repast. Received instructions from Rubens. ($10.00) [24]

The dates given by Rapp are attributions and the paintings were actually done much later. Another painting purchased by Frederick and displayed in the museum was Anton Raphael Mengs' Adoration of the Shepherds (c1765). Although Frederick, perhaps the most cultivated of the Harmonists, attended concerts and visited museums when he was in Philadelphia, he was apparently not an art expert. Still, he enjoyed the pleasures afforded by the outside world; in an October 1832 letter to Gertrude Rapp, Mary Graff reported that when her father and Frederick were in Philadelphia they went to see a performance by the famous actress Fanny Kemble.[25]

Since there is no evidence that the typical Harmonist dwelling contained any paintings, it is probable that all of the paintings were in the Rapp House or the Museum. It is possible, however, that there were inexpensive religious prints in

---

[24] Old Economy Archives. Correspondence Books. Of these paintings, numbers 1, 2, 4, 5, and 6 are in the collection at Old Economy.
[25] Arndt, Karl, Economy on the Ohio, 817.

the households. Of the paintings in the Rapp House, the most impressive was the large copy of Benjamin West's Christ Healing the Sick, now in the Trustees Room. This painting and the Nativity that was mentioned by Agnes Gormley in the 1870s are still in the Rapp House. Perhaps the largest painting owned by the Harmonists was the 15'x 10' painting by a "Louis Cortambert" showing the assembly of the Israelites at the foot of Mount Sinai.[26] Cortambert, a French journalist who taught French at Economy for a year, later became the French vice-counsel in St. Louis. The original painting has been lost but there is a study of "The Great Assembly" at Old Economy. Evidence that it may have hung on the east wall of the museum are two large hooks some 5' apart which obviously held a heavy piece.

Of the non-religious paintings in the museum, Buckingham noted

> An extensive series of Chinese drawings of costume . . . and a series of American historical portraits, from Columbus and Americus Verpucius [sic], down to General Jackson and Mr. Van Buren. . . . Some better engravings of Colonel Trumbell's historical pictures, such as the Declaration of Independence, and others, follow; and some highly interesting religious subjects are appropriately mingled with them. But the effect of these is strangely marred, by their being found in close juxtaposition with some very inappropriate and unworthy associates; such as tawdry French prints, representing Venus and Cupid, one as "L'Amour supplicant" and the other as L'Amour triomphante" and a still more tawdry English caricature in the "Portrait of Tim Bobbin."[27]

It seems ironic that the mostly celibate Harmonists would display two paintings celebrating secular love, but they may have purchased a group of paintings and other objects from another collection and been loathe to discard works of art, regardless how "tawdry" they were. And since their museum was in the tradition of the *Wunderkommer*, a variety of objects and subjects in paintings and prints was desired. The historical paintings and prints are another indication

---

[26] Buckingham 226.
[27] Buckingham, 225.

of the Harmonists' ability to isolate themselves from the world and yet still be aware and proud of America's history.[28]

So the existence of the paintings at Economy is important in comprehending the cultural life of the Society. That a relatively small village in Western Pennsylvania in the 1830s should possess such a collection shows that the Harmonists had the means to educate themselves and opportunities for cultural experiences perhaps surpassing those of a large majority of Americans in the first half of the nineteenth century.

Books, Magazines, and Newspapers

Further evidence of the educational opportunities offered to the Harmonists are the books, magazines, and newspapers available to the typical member. In 1830 the Harmony Society had a library of 360 volumes of works on religion, literature, science, and mechanics.[29]

> This important list...documents the Harmonists' awareness of current religious and social thought in Europe and America. Jane Leade, Johann Heinrich Jung-Stilling, Johann Friedrich Oberlin, Gottfried Arnold, Jeanne Marie Guyon, and Christian Gotthilt Salzmann were all internationally famous writers [and] Oberlin College was named for Oberlin.[30]

The archives today contain a number of other works that were either purchased by the community after the 1830s or deposited there when the members died. These include medical and dental books that were probably used by the community physicians, patent office reports, surveying books, and such periodicals as The Water Cure Journal and The American Phrenological Journal.

At their store in Economy the Harmonists sold books that would appeal to a wide range of interests for outsiders. Among the books stocked in 1825 were the following:

---

[28] Like other patriotic American, the Harmonists celebrated the Fourth of July with music and food.
[29] Bole, 89. A complete list of the titles can be seen in this work.
[30] Arndt, Indiana Decade of the Harmony Society, II, 441.

The Bible	French Revolution
Plutarch's Lives	Memoirs of Napoleon
History of Religion	Webster's Grammars
Summer's Botany	Pilgrim's Progress
Researches in Asia	Thornton Abbey
Mose's Geography	Mississippi Navigation
Mercantile Arithmetic	Roman History
Goldsmith's Rome and England	Washington's Life
Vicar of Wakefield	Son of a Genius
Ready Reckoners	Mexico and American Pilots[31]

The Harmonists purchased their books from various booksellers, especially those familiar with German language texts. In a letter to Frederick Rapp in 1820 offering such books for sale, Jacob Hulick wrote:

> Since I received a very beautiful collection of German books directly from Hamburg a few months ago and hear from Maltz here that you, as a friend of German literature, wish to complete your German library, I hereby respectfully ask whether you which to have the same.... This collection contains about 250 volumes, which are very nicely bound and consist of the works of Kotzebue, Göethe, Schiller, Meissner, Wieland, Gleim, Pffel, Voss, etc. [32]

The school texts used in the Harmonist school were similar to those used in the outside world. A statewide study of textbooks by the superintendent of common schools listed the most common books use in Pennsylvania in 1838. Of the ten readers, spellers, and histories cited in the report, the Harmonists used five, including the Old and New Testaments, The English Reader, Cobb's Series, Cobb's Spellers, Webster's Spellers, and the United States Spellers. In addition the Harmonists used such traditional books as the McGuffy Readers, the Osgood Readers, and Ray's Arithmetic, and provided their students "with books, supplies, and equipment not found in the ordinary school of their day."[33]

The Harmonists also subscribed to magazines, periodicals, and newspapers that were made available to community members. As the list of periodicals makes

---

[31] Bole, 88-89.
[32] Arndt, Indiana Decade of the Harmony Society, II, 184-5
[33] Melvin R. Miller, "Education in the Harmony Society, 1805-1905," (Doctoral dissertation, University of Pittsburgh, 1972), 251.

clear (see Appendix), the Society subscribed to local and national, English and German, and secular and religious publications. Activities in the community during certain periods can be seen in some of the titles. For example, American Conchology was probably purchased for Frederick Rapp or Dr. Müller to use in setting up the displays of shells in the museum. The Culturist, a magazine devoted to the manufacture of silk in America, Ladies Garland, and Lady Book were likely used by Gertrude Rapp, who organized the silk industry for the community and as such may have been interested in particularly popular styles and patterns of clothing for manufacturing purposes. And the post-1841 subscriptions to such periodicals as Bicknell's Reporter, Counterfeit Detector and Prices Current, The Daily Commercial Journal, Kennedy's Bank Notes and Commercial Review, and the Commercial Bulletin of Boston reflect the Society's growing involvement in outside economic ventures as well as its increasing dependence on investments rather than on production. It seems likely that these periodicals were ordered for Frederick Rapp who was the financier of the Society.

The Harmonists printed a few books themselves on a press they bought in Indiana. These books included a volume of George Rapp's philosophy that was printed in both German (Gedanken uber die Bestimmung des Menschen-geschlechts) and English (Thoughts on the Destiny of Man) in 1824. In 1826 the Society printed a collection of prose pieces by the members entitled Feurige Kohlen der aufsteigenden Liebesflammen im Lustspiel der Weisheit (Fiery Coals of the Rising Flames in the Joyous Play of Wisdom); and in 1827 and 1829 the Society printed editions of the Harmonist hymnbook, Harmonisches Gesangbuch. A fifth book which was apparently printed at Economy was a German grammar by K.B. Krause, Lehrbuch Der Deutschen Sprache Fur Schulen.

Formal education was provided for all of the Harmonists. Children were required to attend school until age fourteen, and adults were given the opportunity to take classes on Sundays and evenings in such subjects as music, art, drawing, and handiwork. There were separate classes for old men, old women, young men, young women, and children.[34]

The archives at Old Economy contain a number of pictorial works created by the Harmonists. Nancy Kraybill's study has identified the following items: seventy-seven architectural drawings, three picture maps, two collections of ornithology illustrations, fifteen natural history drawings, and fifty-nine decorative drawings.[35]

Drawings of buildings and machinery were either exercises for students or working plans for the construction of particular buildings. An example of the former is a drawing of a large building in the Renaissance style, and of the latter an unsigned drawing probably illustrating the mechanical works in one of the Harmonist mills (Figure 39).

Although utilitarian draftsmanship was encouraged at Economy, one Harmonist, Wallrath Weingärtner, created a book of pen and ink drawings of birds. This book, titled Ornithology or the Natural History of the Birds of the United States, Illustrated With Plats [sic], Economy, 15 January 1829, Wallrath Weingärtner, included drawings of some sixty-seven birds. According to both Karl Arndt and Nancy Kraybill, however, these drawings are directly based on Alexander Wilson's book American Ornithology, issued from 1808 to 1825. Kraybill meticulously compared Wilson's and Weingärtner's drawings by placing one on top of the other and concluded that "Weingartner did not only copy but traced Wilson's birds."[36] There are also extant several works made by Gertrude Rapp, who "painted several watercolors that have survived. Two flowers grace the title page of her handwritten Keyboard Accompaniment Book of 1822. She

---

[34] Miller, 178.
[35] Nancy Kraybill, The Pictorial Arts of the Harmony Society, 1805-1834, (Masters thesis, University of Delaware, 1983), 5.
[36] Ibid, 5.

also painted an Austrialian lyrebird, a tryant fly-catcher (*Anius Tyrannus*), and her pet elk at New Harmony."[37]

Wallrath Weingärtner also made two of the four maps of Harmonist villages made by members of the Society. Weingärtner's first map was of New Harmony, Indiana, and was drawn in 1832. It stated: "Thus was situated New Harmony, on the Wabash, which was begun in the year 1814 and finished 1825." This map is in color and shows the structures in architectural perspective and identifies the functions of the buildings or the names of those who lived in the houses. Several buildings, such as the store, the hospital, the drugstore and a mill located over a mile from the center of the village on the Wabash River "cut off" are not seen because of minor damage to the map. This map shows approximately 190 structures in the 1820s and reveals that many of the log houses that were built when the town was first settled still exist on the plot of land where the more substantial brick or frame houses were built. While many of the travel narratives describe individual buildings, this remarkable record of what the town looked like during the last year in Indiana helps us to visualize the town as a whole.

Weingärtner's map of Harmony, Pennsylvania, drawn from memory in 1833 while he was living in Economy, shows Harmony as it was in 1815. An inscription on the map said: "So lay the town Harmonie in Butler County in the year 1815. It was laid out in the year 1805. In June 1814, the first transport left for the Wabash. Drawn by W. Weingärtner, February 22, 1833." As Kraybill has observed, Weingärtner "justaposed two distinct perspectives in his picture maps of the towns. Individual structures are shown in elevation while the streets and physical features of the land are presented from a bird's eye view."[38] This map shows that a number of the dwellings are still log structures, a type that was used at the two succeeding villages only while the more substantial brick buildings were being built. That there are forty-five more buildings at New Harmony

---

[37] Donald Pitzer, "Harmonist Folk Art Discovered," Historic Preservation, 29, No.4 (Oct-Dec. 1977), 12.
[38] 37.

indicates how the town became larger and more sophisticated by the time the Harmonists moved from Harmony to New Harmony.

The two other maps drawn by a Harmonist were those of Eusebius Böhm, the head gardener of the Harmony Society and during a period of time one of those who lived in the Great House of George Rapp. Böhm's undated map shows Harmony and in some ways is similar to that of Weingärtner. While Karl Arndt said that Böhm's map was a working model for Weingärtner, Nancy Kraybill argued that "with other artworks by Weingärtner in existence and references to him as a watercolorist, it seems more likely that his map is the original and that Böhm, a less talented artist with no other known works to his credit, copied it." [39] However, even though the maps of New Harmony by Weingärtner and Böhm are similar, Böhm's does include insets of some of the important buildings that are drawn with more detail than those of Weingärtner (Figure 38). Böhm gave his map to Simon Beiter of the Zoar commune in Ohio and eventually it was donated to the Ohio Historical Society, where it was eventually discovered by Karl Arndt.

The Harmonist interest in music is evidenced in a number of extant objects at Old Economy, including a French horn, two organs that were played in the Harmonist church by Gertrude Rapp and Jacob Henrici, four pianos, and numerous song books. Music was an important part of Harmonist life:

> Expressing themselves in song the Harmonists achieved a dual purpose, a respite from the sameness of their being and a call to worship. Song for them spelled charisma, whether it was a psalm or a song of their own composition. It not only drew them to it, but to each other, creating the unity and brotherhood of which they sang. They became one in spirit, synthesizing their beings for a state of harmony where the love of God reigns supreme.[40]

Music was sung or played by the Harmonists during many occasions.[41] They sang during their feasts in the *saal* and during church services; the Harmonist

---

[39] 39.
[40] Kring,104.
[41] The best work on Harmonist music is Richard Wetzel, "The Music of George Rapp's Harmony Society: 1806-1906" (doctoral dissertation, University of Pittsburgh, 1970).

band gave frequent concerts to the community and to outsiders who came to hear the Harmonist music; and visitors who came to the Great House, perhaps to talk religion with George or business with Frederick, were sometimes entertained by vocal and instrumental music written by Harmonists or by composers such Mozart, Meyerbeer, and Beethoven.[42] One of the visitors to a Harmonist factory was treated to several songs sung by the girls working in the factory. And frequently when a traveler met with George Rapp in the Great House he heard a piano performance by Gertrude Rapp.

In an 1816 letter Frederick Rapp, who had not quite mastered English spelling, wrote to David Shields, one of his outside business contacts, that he was interested in purchasing a piano: "Our Dr. miller says that he hath tried Mr. Rosenbaum's forte Piano, and found very good and if you can get them examined by some of your friend I am in no ways in a great haste but whish to get a good one." Rosenbaum, a Pittsburgh piano maker, responded that

> the veneer of the instrument is not of mahagony [sic] but of a beautiful nut brown wood which proves attractive to everyone. Above all, however, it is very well made and has a very strong tone. If you have not yet bought another instrument, and if you should like to have one from me; I can serve you with the above instrument or with another very soon, if you will write me about this soon. The price is $300.[43]

Frederick apparently expressed some interest but thought that it should not be shipped to New Harmony before the spring because of the weather.

There were also objects at the Society indicative of Harmonist interest in science. These include a 4' high static electricity machine that was used in science instruction classes for the children, or for the adults in the evening school; a celestial globe that was purchased by Frederick Rapp in 1820; and a microscope. The existence of two wooden heads from Fowler and Wells, as well as the 1852 copy of The American Phrenologist indicates that during the 1850s the Harmonists or one of the leaders who had authorization to purchase such

---

[42] Buckingham, 230.
[43] Arndt, Documentary History of the Indiana Decade, I, 258.

heads, may have been interested in the popular pseudo-science of phrenology. Another pseudo-science pursued at Economy was alchemy. As mentioned previously, a painting in the Great House by David Teniers the Younger (1610-1694) had as its subject an alchemist in his workshop; this would have appealed to both Frederick and George Rapp, both of whom practiced alchemy. A letter from outside business-agent David Shields to Frederick noted that "The chemical glasses and Barometer tubes are not forgotten. I have frequently called about them at the glass works [and]... they will be sent with your other goods."[44] There is some evidence that an attachment to the George Rapp House was used for alchemical experiment, and a serious breach in the relationship between George and Frederick was related to alchemy. As his laboratory assistant George had the attractive Hildegarde Mutschler whom he allowed to return to the Society even after she had left to marry Conrad Feucht. Frederick was incensed that George was so smitten with Hildegarde that he would give her preferential treatment.[45]

In 1823 the Society inquired of "Messrs. Dolland, Opticians" [in London or Philadelphia] about the purchase of an Achromatic telescope. And a letter to Frederick Rapp from Andrew Leibbrandt in 1813 indicates that the scientific-minded Frederick may have been interested in a perpetual motion machine. "I heard very little about Redhoeffer's machine since I wrote," says Leibbrandt, "except only once he had sold a patent right to an Englishman for $10,000 and that his complaints are before a court and that he is living happily as a Gentleman; I am eager to know how your experiment in this regard turned out."[46] There is no record of a reply from Frederick or any other evidence that he was working on such a machine.

Two large objects at Old Economy that reflect the practical concerns of the Harmonists are the fire engines and the water pump. The Society bought its first fire engine from the famous Philadelphia builder, Patrick Lyons, in 1814 and

---

[44] Ibid, 322.
[45] See Arndt, George Rapp's Harmony Society, 509-511, and "An American Alchemist," in Rosicrucian Digest, XXXII (March, 1954).
[46] Arndt, Harmony on the Connoquenessing, 669.

brought it to Indiana when they moved (Figure 29). They left this engine in New Harmony when they sold the town, but when Karl Bernhard visited Economy in 1826 he noted that they owned "a fire-engine of their own making."[47] This fire engine is a close copy of the Lyon engine at New Harmony. Harmonist correspondence reveals that in 1830 the Society bought another fire engine, this one from John McClure of Wheeling, West Virginia.[48] Both of these are at Old Economy today. The Harmonists provided additional fire protection by the establishment of a fire company and by the use of large iron tanks in the top stories of the mill and factory.[49]

Water was supplied to the Harmonists from two sources: flowing water for washing, cleaning, and the like was provided from the reservoir through wooden, and later ceramic, pipes. Drinking water was obtained from the community pumps. John Duss said that there were two such pumps, but there may have been more before the 1850s. These pumps, of which one is extant, had a wooden housing to cover the works and long, wrought-iron handles providing the leverage to pump water from the 85' wells at Economy. The first housings were square and later housings evolved into a hexagonal shape. There are similar pumps found in Pennsylvania in the eighteenth and nineteenth centuries[50] which may indicate Germanic origins. Although the original pump at Old Economy is not functioning, a reproduction has been made which pumps water efficiently (Figure 30).

Unfortunately there are no extant steam engines at the Harmonist villages to examine how the Society used them. The steam engines were used to power the factories for the Harmonist manufacturing enterprises as well as for more domestic purposes. In the 1860s the Harmonists built a three and a half story building that was used primarily as a laundry but which had other functions. The

---

[47] Bernhard, II, 164.
[48] Old Economy Archives. Correspondence Book 5, 274.
[49] Bernhard, II, 164.
[50] For photographs of similar pumps in Pennsylvania see Eleanor Raymond, Early Domestic Architecture of Pennsylvania (New York: William Helburn, 1931).

steam engine that was either inside or outside of the building was used to agitate the clothing in large tubs, to power the wine presses, and to provide steam heat for warmth and for the cooking of fruit and jellies.[51]

Other lost examples of the Harmonist use of steam power are the two steamboats built for the Society. The first, "William Penn," was built in Pittsburgh in 1825 for the purpose of transporting goods and members from New Harmony to Economy. According to John Livingston Hunter, the Harmonists used this boat to convey their oil to Pittsburgh. The other steamboat, the "Pittsburgh and Wheeling Packet," was constructed in 1827 and purchased by the Society because that was the only way that a debt owed them by the boat building company could be repaid. Poulson's Philadelphia American Advertiser described the boat in March 4, 1828, as

> a beautiful vessel, very handsomely finished, with two decks.... A number of ladies and gentlemen from Pittsburgh and Freeport came as passengers. Next morning a large party was got up in town who took an excursion of six or seven miles up the river.... It stemmed the current at the rate of 5 or 6 miles an hour, and came down at about 15. ... We returned about 11 o'clock; and in a few minutes the boat left the wharf for Pittsburgh, amid the united cheers of the people on the shore and on the boat. Both boats were disposed of after a short period of time because the operation and maintenance of a steamboat "involved certain things which interfered with their way of life."[52]

During the period in the last quarter of the nineteenth century when the Harmonists were changing from manufacturing to finance and investments in the outside world, they had two railroad steam engines, both named Economy, built by the Baldwin Locomotive Company so that products at their sites could be transported efficiently. Engine No. 513 was used for the Little Saw Mill Run Railroad and Engine No. 466 served the Darlington Canal Coal Railroad.

For a period of time the Harmonists experimented, somewhat successfully, with the manufacture of silk. Gertrude Rapp, the granddaughter of George Rapp

---

[51] Knoedler, 100-101.
[52] Arndt, George Rapp's Harmony Society, 398.

suggested the idea of producing silk in the 1820s, and it was she who oversaw the silk industry that was established at Economy. In the early 1830s the Harmonists produced five to six thousand pounds of cocoons annually, and between 1836 and 1839 between 90 and 150 pounds of silk were created each year, some of which won awards at such venues as the Franklin Institute in Philadelphia, the Boston Fair, and the American Institute in New York.

The dominance of the Harmony Society in Pennsylvania's silk industry is evident in newspaper notices giving the amounts that the State paid in premiums for silk production. In 1838 of the $518 paid to sixteen persons, Gertrude Rapp alone received $363, and a 1844 notice from the North American and Daily Advertiser in Philadelphia says that the "whole amount of the premiums on silk, paid in this State, for the year 1843 . . . is $3425.76. Of this amount, Miss Gertrude Rapp, of Economy, received $1248.67."[53]

Gideon Smith, the corresponding secretary of the National Silk Society in Baltimore, wrote to Frederick Rapp stating that the Harmonists had "'brought the art to a state of perfection equal to any establishment in Europe, and in some respects [had] gone beyond any thing of the kind in any other country."[54] In 1841 George Rapp, through his Philadelphia friend and merchant J. Solms, presented President Tyler with a piece of Harmonist silk for a suit of clothes, and Solms mentioned in a letter to Rapp that the financier and president of the Second Bank of the United States, Nicholas Biddle, had been dressed entirely in Harmonist silk when they met. The Harmonists abandoned the cultivation of silkworms by the early 1850s, perhaps reflecting the change in the Harmonist economy from an internal one where many of the products were produced within the community to a system where the community began to invest heavily in outside businesses. When Charles Nordhoff visited the community in 1874 he made no mention of the silk industry there.

---

[53] February 27, 1844, col B.
[54] Kristen B. Shutts, "The Harmonists and Their Silk Experiences," w.smith.edu/hsc/silk/papers/shutts.html, 3.

There are two striking silk scarves now in the collection at New Harmony (Figure 41). Each is approximately three feet square and displays the name of George or Frederick Rapp. A small fragment of a similar scarf (showing little more than the name "George Rapp") can be seen in a Harmonist display case that was shown at Chicago Exposition of 1893. Each has a vibrancy of color and pattern that is quite unlike the typically simple designs found on other Harmonist pieces.[55] Since the silk industry was begun only after the group moved to their third village, it is assumed that the pieces were made at Economy. The Harmonists made scarves to give to important people, such as congressmen, to promote the silk industry in America. In a photograph of a woman assumed to be Gertrude Rapp she is wearing what appears to be a scarf with a pattern similar to those at New Harmony.[56]

There are numerous objects at Old Economy today which reflect the growing interaction with the outside world in the 1850s. Among these are the maps of Harmony Society land investments in Huron County, Michigan, and in Beaver Falls, Pennsylvania; a map of Haifa, Palestine, where the Harmonists invested for religious, rather than economic, considerations; letterheads for the Economy Lumber Company and the Economy Oil Company; and printed checks of the Economy Savings Institution, which was largely owned by the Society. As the number of members who were able to work decreased after the 1850s, the Harmonists changed from an economy of "communal work to communal investments"; in this paradigm the group's money rather than its labor force insured continued prosperity. But there continued to be some attempts to create goods at the society during the last quarter of the nineteenth century. Throughout their history the Harmonists sold beer and whiskey to the outside world; while as good Germans they drank beer themselves, they did not drink whiskey but

---

[55] According to Joanne Ingersoll at the Rhode Island School of Design, "this pattern is a type that shows interest in botany, in general, almost on a cellular level. We start seeing much of this in the 1840 and it continues to some degree into the 1850s." Correspondence by email. July 17, 2008.
[56] Correspondence with Sarah Buffington, collections specialist at Old Economy, May 12, 2008.

realized that it could be readily sold to outsiders. In the 1880s, the leader of the Society, Jacob Henrici,

> inaugurated the brewing of boneset tea on a large scale. The Harmonists had always held the boneset herb in high esteem, using it for medicine. But Henrici now planned to secure a large amount of boneset extract to mix with crab-apple cider, whiskey, and sugar into a "bitters."[57]

But this internal business venture was the exception to the general pattern of the Society's investment practices in the outside.

Material evidence of the Society's activities in outside business ventures is a 15' pipe tong that was used at the Harmonist oil and gas drilling operations in Warren County where the group became pioneers in the American oil industry. They were so influential that they managed to have a bill passed in the Pennsylvania legislature granting them the rights to build their own pipeline across the Allegheny River.

The Harmonists invested $300,000 in the Pittsburgh and Lake Erie Railroad and in 1884 sold its shares to the Vanderbilt family for over $1.4 million. Just a few of the external investments after the 1850s were those in the Beaver Falls Cutlery Works, the Western File Works, the Economy Savings Institutions, the C.C. Modes and Company (a glass manufactory in Beaver Falls), the Valley Glass Works, the Beaver Falls Steel Company, the Meyers Company (manufacturing shovels), the Beaver Falls Car Works, The Beaver Falls Gas Company, the Beaver Falls Bridge Company, the Union Drawn Steel Company, and the Eclipse Bicycle Company. The Society also owned shares in the Rochester National Bank, the Bank of Pittsburgh, the Allegheny Bank, and the Merchants and Manufacturers National Bank.[58]

****

---

[57] Duss, 179.
[58] Ibid., 266-269.

As was true of the town planning and architecture of the Society, the artifacts of the Harmonists manifested some definite changes during the years between the settling of Harmony, New Harmony, and Economy. Unlike the buildings and town plans, however, the furnishings did not move so much towards classicism as towards a combination of several styles. The lack of a definite Harmonist style of furniture and the generally eclectic nature of the furnishing may have resulted from the fact that a number of craftsmen were responsible for the construction of furniture, whereas only one or two men, the leaders of the Society, were responsible for the architecture. In addition, perhaps the Society as a whole was too flexible, too eclectic, and insufficiently dogmatic to advance a total aesthetic philosophy as did the Shakers with their obligatory celibacy, segregated dormitory living, and elaborate codes of conduct for the two genders.

Although the absence of artifacts at Harmony, Pennsylvania, makes generalizations difficult, it is likely that at that village there were a number of German inspired objects that the Harmonists either brought with them from the fatherland or made here reflecting German styles. By the Economy period, however, many of these objects had undergone an Americanization as the Harmonists in their business dealings had increased their contact with the outside world.

Despite the adoption of such American styles as the Windsor ladderback chairs which, like the architecture, exhibit a general rather than a specific American influence, certain German forms persisted, notably the *stuhl* and the traditional kitchen table. Harmonist clothing, especially for the women, also retained many of its Swabian characteristics throughout the history of the Society, providing a strong element of group identification.

This community identity was also reflected in such communal elements at Economy as the similar chests, chairs, wardrobes, beds, and other household furniture, as well as by the institutions of feasts in the *saal* of the Feast Hall Building. Variations in size, style, and construction of Harmonist furniture reveal that pieces may have been made for the households and individuals rather than as identical pieces for the entire community. Like the dwellings with their small family groups and the community's Feast Hall Building with its cultural and educational facilities, the furnishings allowed for some degree of individualization within the group.

More marked than the individualization, however, was the distinction between the Harmonist members and their leaders. The Great House where George and Frederick Rapp lived had furnishings that were much finer than those in the members' dwellings and were greatly influenced by the cultivated tradition. As such, they provide a striking example of the Society's growing interaction with the outside world and of its leaders' control over the cultural interplay between the Society and the world. Frederick Rapp, who often traveled in the outside world on business matters, purchased fine pieces for the Great House and may have suggested particular styles to the Harmonist cabinetmakers who combined them with the German characteristics of mass and heaviness. At Economy the cultivated pieces complemented the position George Rapp held and provided an impressive environment for those who visited him at the Great House.

Although a few Harmonist images, including the Virgin Sophia, the rose, the lily, and the pelican, reflect an element of mysticism in the Society, such religious motifs were not pervasive, although in the case of the statue of Harmonie in the garden Pavilion, they were centrally located and visible. Indeed, Classical motifs seem to have been equally as important. Nor were there any purely religious objects to speak of. The Harmonists were Radical Pietists who had broken away from the established church and their material culture was indicative of their belief that religious icons were unnecessary in a community which was itself a church.

In such a community, the members' needs were conceived of as cultural and educational as well as domestic and spiritual. At Economy, the Feast Hall housed a library with an extensive collection of books and periodicals with various subjects; local and international newspapers; periodicals; a museum with objects of natural history and with paintings; and a school for children and adults. Although the opportunities at the school were of a practical rather than a philosophical or artistic nature – even Wallrath Weingärtner's bird drawings show limited creativity – the Harmonists were exposed to cultural advantages comparable to, if not greater than, those in towns in the outside world.

Chapter 6

The Harmony Society: Reflections on the Material Culture

The usual picture of the Harmony Society in the histories and descriptions of the community such as those by Nordhoff and Noyes in the nineteenth century is that of a group of Pietistic and celibate communists who were successful in their economic ventures and who built three comfortable but culturally isolated villages in America. These German Pietists, the histories relate, left Europe to escape social pressures, used their religious beliefs to justify economic communalism and celibacy as ways of meeting demands of the new land, and prospered as a result of the leadership of George Rapp. According to most histories, the Society was characterized by the following elements:

A religious intensity which caused them to emigrate to American where they could worship according to their belief;

A communitarian social organization that was, in its similarity to other communal societies outside of the main stream of American life;

A celibacy that was based on their religious principles and which led to their ultimate demise;

A prosperity which resulted from their communal system as well as from their manufacturing on a large scale;

A success that grew out of the strong spiritual leadership of George Rapp and the financial ability of Frederick Rapp; and

A degree of isolation that kept them from the outside world except in economic matters.

While this is an essentially accurate characterization of the Society, it is somewhat one-dimensional and can explain only partly why this communal society thrived for almost a century in a period of social mobility and economic expansion in America where there was opportunity for individual initiative. Any examination of the success of the Society must take into account the physical elements which satisfied the needs of the community members.

A study of the material culture of the Harmonists has shown that the group was neither isolated from the mainstream of European and American cultural traditions, nor was it rigid in its idea of what the physical form of the community should be. The Harmonist leaders were aware of and took from the best elements of cultures of the past and present in their creation of the perfect environment.

The Harmonist conception of the utopian village occupied a middle ground between the basically futuristic communities envisioned by Robert Owen and Charles Fourier, in which the social arrangements and material culture would be altered drastically from what the inhabitants had known in their previous communities, and the more conservative community of Ephrata in which some material culture was patterned after medieval forms and in which the social arrangements were similar to those in medieval cloisters.

Unlike the Fourierists, the Harmonists created a community in many ways similar to those that the members had known in Germany, including small houses, gardens, fields, a town hall, a church, and vineyards, as well as a few medieval German forms in architecture and furnishings. However, the Harmonists were not reactionary in their creation of the ideal community, for they included a number of elements in their material culture that reflected a Renaissance, rather than a medieval, aesthetic, and as such revealed the Harmonist imitation of the near, rather than the far, past. For a Harmonist such as Frederick Rapp, the Renaissance with its Classical elements represented what was stylistically sophisticated in its rejection of medievalism.

Thus, a major element that has been overlooked by historians depending mainly on written sources was the Classical influence on the Harmonist community and its expression in a number of aspects of the material culture. These include the rectilinear street plan, clearly distinguishable from the medieval pattern of the typical rural village in Germany and directly traceable to the Classical influence, whether from German new towns or from Philadelphia. Also there are the exterior and interior forms of many of their buildings: the Feast Hall with its German gambrel roof, its Georgian door, and its classical *trompe d'oeil* interior of the second floor *saal*; the churches with their Renaissance cupolas; and the Pavilion.

There are, it is true, certain symbolic motifs in the material culture of the Society. However, in their emphasis on the mystical elements within Harmony, some historians have overlooked the Classical, and therefore opposite, tendency in the community. For example, whereas they have seen the interior and exterior of the Grotto as strictly symbolic, I have shown that they were very much a part of the Classical tradition that a stone mason *cum* architect such as Frederick Rapp would have been aware of in Germany.

The material culture also demonstrates that the Harmonists were not primarily conservative peasants with a reactionary concept of an ideal community pegged at a certain place in time, but were instead progressive and experimental, capable of changing to meet the social, cultural, intellectual, physical, and spiritual needs of the members and of competing successfully with the outside world in economic matters.

The Harmonists not only moved twice in America to establish a firm economic base, but also changed their town plans and buildings to meet changing community needs and possibly eliminate certain weaknesses in the social structure of the Society. The Harmonists moved from an essentially agricultural economy stressing viniculture at Harmony, to a mixed agricultural-industrial base at New Harmony, to an industrial and then financial enterprise at Economy. This shift is apparent in the layout of their three villages: the very center of the town changed from a square, similar to what the Harmonists knew in Germany, where agricultural and other goods could be sold and where outsiders could be accommodated at the inn, to a tightly circumscribed commercial area at Economy that lacked a square. At Economy the Ohio River was a major route for receiving and shipping products and the village square was unnecessary for funneling business to the community.

Also in their attempts to meet community needs, the Harmonists experimented with living patterns and with the very buildings that accommodated the daily life of the members. Whereas the houses at Harmony were built for the families as they had come from Germany, consisting of the traditional unit of husband, wife, and children, dwellings at New Harmony and Economy were designed to de-emphasize the nuclear family and to emphasize the larger community. At New Harmony the Society tried the dormitory system as a means of providing housing for the growing numbers of celibate, unmarried members. Yet the experiment seems to have failed, for at Economy the dormitory system was abandoned and smaller dwellings for extended, non-nuclear families were built, allowing for some individualization while providing a mechanism for commitment to the larger community and forestalling the problems attendant on mass housing.

The use of common dress and of German as a common language also strengthened this commitment, as did the community's increasing use of the public buildings, culminating in the Feast Hall Building with its large hall for community gatherings.

Interestingly, the experimentation with living patterns did not come to the Society immediately. When the Harmonists first came to America and settled at Harmony, the wealthy and influential members had better homes than the average member. At New Harmony and Economy, however, the average members lived in houses of equal size, and only George Rapp, along with Frederick and several relatives, continued to enjoy the distinction of a larger dwelling. At Economy, of course, the dwelling was the spacious and elegantly furnished Rapp House, which functioned both as a place of receiving outsiders visiting the community, and a suitable dwelling for the spiritual and financial leaders of the Society. The Rapp House was also a kind of public relations effort that would impress outsiders with the success of the Society, and perhaps convince some investors or business contacts of the financial health of the community. Although its elegance would have been a source of pride rather than jealousy for most members, the discontent that emerged several times in the Society's history was quite possibly due to the growing power of George Rapp that the Rapp House signified.

That at Economy the average members lived in moderately furnished and equally sized households of fewer than a dozen members, however, did not indicate a complete presence of equality. Social status determined the location, if not the size, of the houses. Those who brought wealth into the community and those who held positions of authority in many instances lived nearer to the Rapp house at the center of the village. And those who continued to have children despite the community preference for celibacy had houses on the outskirts of town.

Yet the material culture demonstrates that the Harmonists attempted to shape their community through other means besides alternative living patterns. As the Society refined its notion of the group and its needs, it constructed different public buildings to meet those needs. At Harmony, for example, the church was the first public building raised for group gatherings; at New Harmony a large and architecturally elaborate Greek-cross Church with room for social-communal functions was built to replace the smaller and more traditional first church at that village. At Economy, however, construction of the first church followed that of the Feast Hall Building, which was designed solely for social, cultural, and intellectual purposes. Whereas the church served a purely religious function, the Feast Hall Building satisfied what may have been the growing cultural and intellectual needs of the members. In short, at Economy, with the construction of the Feast Hall there was a secularization of social-communal functions.

An examination of the town planning, artifacts, and buildings at the three Harmonist villages results in a view of the Society as much more sophisticated than historians and some travelers have stated. Not only did this Society of what some called an "ignorant and priest ridden set of people," or "well-fed, well-clothed, hard-working vassals" provide for the social needs of the members, but also for their educational, artistic, and practical needs. Elements such as the school and museum, the band, the pleasure and botanical gardens, the water system, the fire engine, and the laundry were comparable to those found in substantially larger cities in the first half of the nineteenth century.

Despite the condemnation made by some travelers that the Harmonists were ignorant and insensitive, members of the Society obviously had unusual opportunities for self improvement, as evidenced by the number of drawings made in the drafting classes and the variety of books and periodicals in the community library. One can speculate that since the Harmonists were aware of their image, the museum, which was open to the public, was set up with both visitors and members in mind. Like the Rapp House, it was a kind of public relations venture to convince outsiders of the superiority of the communal system.

Members at Economy had access to the art collection, for unlike many of the successful communitarian societies in nineteenth century America, the Harmonists did not eschew worldly art as evil. Paintings and prints on secular and religious subjects were displayed in their museum and in the Great House. The building also contained furniture in the cultivated tradition, including Sheraton benches, an unusual wine cupboard, and a Heppelwhite secretary. The Harmonists, then, showed their awareness of the world in the Rapp House and the museum. Although the elegance of the Rapp House may have been largely an expression of Frederick Rapp's tastes, worldliness was evident also in the Society's library of books and newspapers, open to all members. These were no simple peasants, living in a transplanted German village under a German lord, but instead were far more sophisticated than has been thought.

Still, much of their material culture reflects their German medieval heritage. Some elements, such as the German *stuhl* and *schrank*, the carved lintels, and the household building types were transmitted merely because they were what the Harmonist builders were familiar with. Other Germanic elements, such as the half-timber first floor of the Granary, and the Feast Hall Building, resembling a town hall in Germany, may have been adopted to provide a degree of stability in the community at a time when the original religious intensity of the members was waning.

By the 1850s, after the deaths of George and Frederick Rapp, who were the spiritual and financial glue holding the community together, the Harmonists began to lose their initial creativity and self reliance and began to depend on external investments to keep the community financially stable. A sense of the degree of this outside investment, as well as the difficulty of transferring some of the community's wealth and responding to the demands or compensation from former members during the last decade of the Society's existence can be seen in the comments of John Duss:

> A tabulation of the sale of our stocks and bonds between April 1892 and July 1895 cannot possibly record the drama of those years, the tremendous worries, the sharp thrusts of fate, the miraculous twists of circumstance, the endless hours of scheming, fretting, work, work, work. I confess that whenever I hark back to the accomplishments of those hectic years feelings of awe and wonderment overcome me. I marketed more than $766,000 worth of stocks and bonds, exclusive of the $175,000 gained from the sale of the Beaver Falls Steel Company and the Union Drawn Steel Company.[1]

This is certainly far from the immediate concerns of the Harmonists when they created their three villages: where to get money to survive? what products can be made and sold? how many houses should be built? how to provide for the spiritual and physical needs of the members? how to move our belongings and

---

[1] Duss, 272.

philosophy from one village to a new one? But what makes the Harmonists special is not their transformation into a kind of capitalist venture, but their creation of three comfortable villages that served their needs for a number of decades.

Ultimately, the Harmony Society is somewhat of a paradox. On the one hand it was alien to the mainstream of American life in its communism, its celibacy, its retentions of a German language, dress, and architecture, and its conscious attempt to isolate itself, to some degree, from mainstream American life. On the other hand, the Society had a number of things in common with other noncommunal American villages. In its financial dealings the Society adopted capitalist methods to compete successfully with the outside world; the members were celibate, but unlike the Shakers, who lived in dormitories, the Harmonists lived in small households not much different from the typical American home; they were aware of the happenings in the outside world, subscribing to a number of international, national and local newspapers; they educated their children with books used in many American schools; and they celebrated the Fourth of July.

It is erroneous to say that, in spite of the advantages of the Society, it was an ultimate failure in its inability to persist into the twentieth century. From the point of view of those Harmonists who lived out their lives while members, the community was a success, for even though the millennium did not arrive in their lifetime, they created and enjoyed a holy village.

APPENDIX

Periodicals subscribed to by the Harmonists between 1815 and 1893

1837	Western Democrat
1838	Ladies Garland
	The Aurora
1839	National Gazette
	Lady Book
	Brick's Reporter
1841	Bicknell's Reporter
	Western Review
	Beaver County Patriot
	National Gazette
	Culturist
	Beaver County Palladium
	Reading Adler
	Pittsburgh Intelligencer
	Western Argus
1842	Cincinnati Daily Gazette
	Philadelphia Courier
	Pittsburgh Gazette
	Philadelphia Inquirer
	American Magazine
	Counterfeit Detector and Prices Current
	National Intelligencer
1843	Pittsburgh Courier
	The Spirit of the Age
1844	Western Star
	New York Daily Times
1845	Evangelical Repository
1847	Der Pittsburger Courier
	Western Star
	The Pittsburgh Daily American
	National Intelligencer
	The Daily Commercial Journal
1849	Pittsburgh Daily Gazette
1853	Beaver Star
1854	Vaterland-Wachter
	Pennsylvania Inquirer

1855 Journal of Music
     Missionary Herald
1856 Freiheits-Freund
     Kennedy's Bank Notes and Commercial Review
1858 Daily Journal
     The Commercial Journal
1859 Missionary Herald
     Chicago Times
1860 Philadelphia Inquirer
     Pittsburgh Courier
     The Warren Mail
     Pittsburgh Daily Commercial Journal
     New Brighton Times
1862 Philadelphia Weekly Inquirer
     Pittsburgh Missionary Herald
1864 Pittsburgh Commercial
     Commercial Bulletin of Boston
1865 Kennedy's Bank Notes and Commercial Review
1866 Missionary Herald
1867 The Pittsburgh Commercial
     Christliche Botschafter
1868 American Messenger
     Freiheits-Freund and Courier
1869 Philadelphia Free Press
1871 Soddentsch Warl
1878 Prophetic Times and Watchtower
1882 Beaver Star
     Tribune
1888 Beaver Times
1893 Pittsburgh Leader

BIBLIOGRAPHY

Albers, Marjorie K. Old Amana Furniture. Shenandoah, Iowa: Locust House, 1970.
___. The Amana People and Their Furniture. Ames: Iowa State University Press, 1990.
Andelson, Jonathan G. "The Community of True Inspiration from Germany to The Amana Colonies." In America's Communal Utopias, edited by Donald Pitzer, 181-203. Chapel Hill, The Universityof North Carolina Press, 1997.
Andressohn, John C. "Twenty Additional Rappite Manuscripts," Indiana Magazine of History, LXIV, 1 (March, 1948), 83-108.
Andrews, Edward Deming. "Communal Architecture of the Shakers," Magazine of Art, XX (December, 1937), 710-715.
___. The People Called Shakers. New York: Dover, 1963.
Andrews, Edward Deming, and Faith Andrews. Religion in Wood. Bloomington, Indiana: Indiana University Press, 1955.
___. Shaker Furniture. New York: Dover, 1963.
Argan, Guilio C. The Renaissance City. New York: George Braziller, 1969.
Arndt, Karl J. R. A Documentary History of the Indiana Decade of the Harmony Society: 1814-1824. Vol 1. 1814-1819. Indianapolis: Indiana Historical Society, 1975.
___. A Documentary History of the Indiana Decade of the Harmony Society: 1814-1824. Vol 2. 1820-1824. Indianapolis: Indiana Historical Society, 1978.
___. Economy on the Ohio, 1826-1834. Worcester: The Harmony Society Press, 1984.
___. "The Genesis of Germantown, Louisiana," Louisiana Historical Quarterly, XXIV (April, 1941), 378-433.
___. "George Rapp Discovers the Wabash." Western Pennsylvania Historical Magazine XXVI, nos. 3 and 4 (Sept.Dec. 1943): 109-116.
___. George Rapp's Disciples, Pioneers and Heirs: A Register of Harmonists in America. Evansville: University of Southern Indiana Press, 1992.
___. "George Rapp's Harmony Society. In America's Communal Utopias, edited by Donald Pitzer, 57-87. Chapel Hill, The University of North Carolina Press.
___. George Rapp's Harmony Society, 1785-1847. Philadelphia: University of Pennsylvania Press, 1965.
___. George Rapp's Re-Established Harmony Society. New York: Peter Lang, 1993.

_____. George Rapp's Successors and Material Heirs, 1847-1916. Rutherford: Fairleigh Dickinson University Press, 1971.
_____. Harmony on the Connoquenessing, 1803-1815: A Documentary History. Worcester, MA: Harmony Society Press, 1980.
_____. Harmony on the Wabash in Transition, 1824-1826. Worcester: Harmony Society Press, 1982.
_____. "The Harmonists as Pioneers in America's Oil Industry." German-American Review XII, no 1 (October, 1945): 7-9; 25.
_____. "The Harmonists as Pioneers in America's Silk Industry." German-American Review XI, no. 6 (August, 1945): 27-29.
_____. "Three Hungarian Travelers Visit Economy." Pennsylvania Magazine of History and Biography LXXIX, no. 2 (1955): 197-216.
Arrington, Leonard J. "Early Mormon Communitarianism: The Law of Consecration and Stewardship." Western Humanities Review VII, no. 4 (Autumn, 1953): 341-369.
Bailey, Rosalie Fellows. Pre-Revolutionary Dutch Houses and Families in Northern New Jersey and Southern New York. New York: William Morrow and Co, 1936.
Baker, Romelius L. "Description of Economy, Beaver County, Pennsylvania." Memoirs of the Pennsylvania Historical Society IV, Part 2.
Batz, Bob Jr. "Discovering a Sense of Harmony North of the City." Pittsburgh Post Gazette November 5, 2006.
Bausman, Joseph H. History of Beaver County, Pennsylvania. New York: The Knickerbocker Press, 1904.
Bayard, M.T. "The Communistic Celibates of Economy." Canadian Magazine. XVII (July, 1896): 199-204.
Beecher, Jonathan, and Richard Bienvenu, eds. and trans. The Utopian Vision of Charles Fourier. Boston: Beacon Press, 1971.
Bell, John F. "Frederick List, Champion of Industrial Capitalism." Pennsylvania Magazine of History and Biography LXVI, no. 1 (January, 1942): 56-83.
Belschner, Christian. Ludwigsburg im Wechsel der Zeiten. Ludwigsburg: Ungeheuer & Ulmer, 1969.
Bennett, Ralph C. "An Architectural Analysis of Economy, Pennsylvania." B.A. thesis, Carnegie Institute of Technology, 1954.
Bernhard, Karl, Duke of Saxe-Weimar, Eisenach. Travels Through North America during the Years 1825 and 1826. 2 vols. Philadelphia: Carey, Lea & Carey, 1828.
Bernt, Adolf. Deutsch Bürgerhauser. Tübingen: Ernst Wasmuth, 1968.
Berrall, Julia S. The Garden: An Illustrated History. New York: Viking Press, 1966.
Bestor, Arthur. Backwoods Utopias. 2nd ed. Philadelphia: University of Pennsylvania Press, 1970.
Betjeman, John. "Nonconformist Architecture," Architectural Review, LXXXVIII, 529 (December, 1940), 160-174.

Bezold, Gustov von. Die Baukaunst der Renaissance in Deutschland, Holland, Belgien und Dänemark. Leipzig: Alfred Kroner, 1908.
Binford, Lewis R. "Archeology as Anthropology," American Antiquity, XXVIII (1962), 217-225.
Birkbeck, Morris. Notes on a Journey in America, from the Coast of Virginia to the Territory of Illinois. London: Ridgeway and Sons, 1818.
Bishop, Morris. The Horizon Book of the Middle Ages. New York: American Heritage, 1968.
Bivins, John Jr. The Moravian Potters in North Carolina. Chapel Hill: University of North Carolina Press, 1972.
Blair, Don. "Harmonist Construction." Indiana Historical Society Publications XXIII, no. 2 (1964).
Blake, Nelson Manfred. Water for the Cities. Syracuse, New York: Syracuse University Press, 1956.
Blane, William Newnham. An Excursion through the United States and Canada during the years 1822-23. London, 1824. Reprinted in Lindley, Indiana as Seen by Early Travelers, 276-290.
Blunt, Anthony. Francois Mansart and the Origins of French Classical Architecture. London: The Warburg Institute, 1941.
Boewe, Charles. Prairie Albion. Carbondale: Southern Illinois University Press, 1962.
Bole, John A. The Harmony Society: A Chapter in German American Cultural History. Philadelphia: Americana Germanica Press, 1904.
Bonnin, Raymond, ed. Le Württemberg. Tubingen, 1950.
Bowen, Eli. The Pictorial Sketch-Book of Pennsylvania. Philadelphia: Willis P. Hazard, 1852.
Brewer, Priscilla, "The Shakers of Mother Ann Lee." In America's Communal Utopias edited by Donald Pitzer, 37-56. Chapel Hill, The University of North Carolina Press, 1997.
Brown, Paul. Twelve Months in New Harmony. Cincinnati, 1827.
Bruford, Walter Horace. Germany in the 18th Century: The Social Background of the Literary Revival. Cambridge, 1935.
Brumbaugh, G. Edwin. "Colonial Architecture of the Pennsylvania Germans." The Pennsylvania-German Society Proceedings and Addresses, 1930 XLI (1933): 1-60.
Buckingham, James Silk. The Eastern and Western States of America 3 vols. London: Fisher, Son and Co., 1842.
Burns, Lee. "Early Architects and Builders of Indiana." Indiana Historical Society Publications XI, no. 3 (1935): 179-215.
Calverton, Victor Francis. Where Angels Fear to Tread. Indianapolis: Bobbs-Merrill, 1941.
Carey Matthew. Essays on Political Economy. Philadelphia: American Antiquarian Society, 1822.

Chaffee, Grace. "An Analysis of Sectarian Community Culture: With Especial Reference to the Amana Society" Antiques XVI, no 2 (August, 1929): 114-118.

Chamberlain, E. R. Everyday Life in Renaissance Times. New York: G. P. Putnam's Sons, 1965.

Clarke, David L. Analytical Archeology. London: Methuen and Co., 1968.

Clune, George. The Medieval Gild System. Dublin: Browne and Nolan, 1943.

Cobb, S. H. The Story of the Palatines: An Episode in Colonial History. New York, 1887.

Coolidge, John. Mill and Mansion. New York: Russell & Russell, 1942.

Cotter, John L. Handbook for Historical Archeology. Philadelphia, 1968.

Cramer, Z. Cramer's Pittsburgh Magazine Almanac. Pittsburgh, 1809 and 1811.

Crowe, Sylvia. Garden Design. New York: Hearthside Press, 1958.

Cuming, Fortescue. Sketches of a Tour to the Western Country, Pittsburgh, 1810.

Cummings, Abbott Lowell, ed. Rural Household Inventories. Boston: Society for the Preservation of New England Antiquities, 1964.

Cummings, John. "Slat Back Chairs." Antiques LXXXII, no. 1 (July, 1957): 60-63.

Daniels, George H. American Science in the Age of Jackson. New York: Columbia University Press, 1968.

Day, Sherman. Historical Collections of the State of Pennsylvania. Philadelphia, 1843.

Dickinson, Robert E. "Rural Settlement in German Lands." Annals of the Association of American Geographers XXXIX (1949): 239-263.

Doll, Eugene. "Social and Economic Organization in Two Pennsylvania German Religious Communities." American Journal of Sociology LVII (1951): 168-177.

Dornbush, Charles H., and John K. Heyl. "Pennsylvania German Barns." Pennsylvania-German Folklore Society XXI, Allentown: Schlechter's, 1956.

Douglas, Paul. "The Material Culture of the Communities of the Harmony Society." Ph.D. diss., George Washington University, 1975.

___. "The Material Culture of the Communities of the Harmony Society." Pennsylvania Folklife XXIV, no. 3 (Spring, 1975): 2-14.

Duclos, Victor Colin. Diary and Recollections, Reprinted in Lindley, New Harmony as Seen by Partipants and Travelers, 1975.

Dudley, Dorothy H., et al. Museum Registration Methods. Washington: American Association of Museums, 1958.

Duffy, John. "Smoke, Smog & Health in Early Pittsburgh.," Western Pennsylvania Historical Magazine XLV, no. 2 (June, 1962): 93-106.

Dunlop, Ian. Versailles. New York: Taplinger Publishing Company, 1970.

Durnbaugh, Donald F. "Communitarian Societies in Colonial America." In America's Communal Utopias, edited by Donald Pitzer, 14-36. Chapel Hill, The University of North Carolina Press, 1997.
Duss, John S. The Harmonists, A Personal History. Harrisburg, 1943. Reprint. Ambridge, Pennsylvania: The Harmonie Associates, 1970.
Egbert, Donald Drew. Socialism and American Art. Princeton: Princeton University Press, 1967.
Egbert, Donald Drew, and Stow Persons, eds. Socialism and American Life. 2 vols. Princeton: Princeton University Press, 1952.
Embury, Aymar, II. "Pennsylvania Farmhouses: Examples of Rural Dwellings of a Hundred Years Ago." The Architectural Record XXX, no. 5 (November, 1911): 475-485.
English, Eileen Aiken. "Easter, 1832: A Brief Interlude of Peace for Georg Rapp's Harmony Society." Communal Societies 26, no. 1 (2006): 37-45.
___. "The Road From Harmony." Amercian Communal Societies Quarterly I, no. 1 (January 2007): 3-16.
Erixon, Sigurd. "West European Connections and Culture Relations." Folkliv II (1938): 137-172.
Federal Writer's Projects. The Harmony Society in Pennsylvania. Philadelphia, 1937.
Flanders, Robert Bruce. Nauvoo, Kingdom on the Mississippi. Urbana: University of Illinois Press, 1965.
Flower, George. History of the English Settlements in Edwards County, Illinois. Chicago, 1882.
Flower, Richard. Letters from Lexington and the Illinois, Containing a Brief Account of the English Settlement in the Latter Territory and a Refutation Of the Misrepresentations of Mr. Cobbett. London, 1819. Reprinted in Reuben Thwaites, Early Western Travels, X (Cleveland, 1804), 88-169.
Fordham, Elias Pym. Personal Narrative of Travels in Virginia, Maryland, Pennsylvania, Ohio, Indiana, Kentucky, and of a Residence in the Illinois Territory: 1817-1818. Edited by Frederick Austin Ogg. Cleveland. 1806.
Forman, Benno. "German Influences in Pennsylvania Furniture." In Arts of the Pennsylvania Germans, edited by Scott Swank, 102-170. New York: W.W. Norton & Co.
___. American Seating Furniture: 1630-1730. New York: W.W. Norton & Co., 1988.
Foster, Augustus, J. Jeffersonian America: Notes on the United States of America Collected in the Years 1806-6-7 and 11-12. Edited by Richard Davis. San Marino,California: The Huntington Library, 1954.
Fretegot, Nora, and W. V. Mangrum. Historic New Harmony. New Harmony, Indiana, 1914.
Garvan, Anthony. Architecture and Town Planning in Colonial Connecticut. New Haven: Yale University Press, 1951.

___ "The Protestant Plain Style Before 1630." Journal of the Society of Architectural Historians IX, no. 3 (October 1950): 4-13.

Gilbert, Russell Wieder. "Blooming Grove, the Dunker Settlement of Central Pennsylvania." Pennsylvania History XX, no. 1 (Januray, 1953): 23-41.

Gilman, Roger. "Mansard Legacy." Parnassus XII (May, 1940): 30-33.

Glassie, Henry. Pattern in the Material Folk Culture of the Eastern United States. Philadelphia: University of Pennsylvania Press, 1971.

Goodman, Paul, ed. Essays in American Colonial History. New York: Holt, Rinehart and Winston, 1967.

Gormly, Agnes. "Economy—A Unique Community." Western Pennsylvania Historical Magazine I, no.3 (July, 1918): 113-131.

___. Old Economy, The Harmony Society. Sewickley, Pennsylvania, 1920.

Gowans, Alan. Images of American Living. Philadelphia: J. B. Lippincott and Co. 1964.

Griswold, Ralph E. "Early American Garden Houses." Antiques XCVIII, no. 1 (July, 1970): 82-87.

Gutkind, E. A. Urban Development in Central Europe. London: The Free Press of Glencoe, 1964.

Hall, Edward T. "The Language of Space." Landscape X, no. 1 (Fall, 1960): 41-45.

"The Harmonists." Atlantic Monthly XVII (May, 1866): 529-538.

Harrison, J. F. C. Quest For the New Moral Order: Robert Owen and the Owenites in Britain and America. New York, 1969.

Hayden, Dolores. Seven American Utopias: The Architecture of Communitarian Socialism, 1790-1975. Cambridge, MA: The MIT Press, 1975.

Hays, George A. The Grotto at Old Economy. Ambridge, Pa.: The Harmony Press, 1959.

Hebert, William. A Visit to the Colony of Harmony, In Indiana, in the United States of America, Recently Purchased by Mr. Owen. London, 1824. Reprinted in Lindley, Indiana as Seen by Early Travelers, 327-359.

Heuschele, Otto. Württemberg: Bilder eines deutschen Landes. Frankfurt, 1969.

Hinds, William Alfred. American Communities. New York: Corinth Press, 1961. Reprint of the 1878 edition.

Hiorns, Frederick. Town-Building in History. London: George G. Harrap and Company, 1956.

Hopping, D. M. C. and Gerald P. Watland. "The Architecture of the Shakers." Antiques LXXII, no. 4 (October, 1957): 335-339.

Howitt, William. Rural and Domestic Life of Germany. London: Longman, Brown, Green and Longmans, 1842.

Hulme, Thomas, Journal of a Tour in the Western Countries of America: September 30, 1818—August 7, 1819. London, 1828) Reprinted in Reuben G. Thwaites, Early Western Travels, X (Cleveland, 1904).

Johnson, Paul. A History of the American People. New York: Harper Collins, 1997.
Kallbrunner, Hermann. "Farms and Villages: The European Pattern." Landscape VI, no. 3 (Spring, 1957): 13-17.
Kanter, Rosabeth Moss. Commitment and Communit. Communes in Sociological Perspective. Cambridge: Harvard University Press, 1972.
Katz, Herbert and Marjorie Katz. Museum. U. S. A. Garden City, New York: Doubleday and Company, 1965.
Kaufman, Emil. Architecture in the Age of Reason. Archon Books, 1966.
Kauffman, Henry. Pennsylvania Dutch American Folk Art. New York: American Studio Books, 1946.
Kimball, Fiske. Domestic Architecture of the American Colonies and of the Early Republic. New York: Charles Scribner's Sons, 1922.
Kirkland, Kevin. "Restored Grotto Stands as Unique Symbol." Pittsburgh Post-Gazette. (August 27, 2005).
Klinkowström, Friherre Axel. Baron Klinkowström's America. 1818-1820. Evanston, Illinois: Northwestern University Press, 1952.
Knappett, Carl. Thinking Through Material Culture. Philadelphia: University of Pennsylvania Press, 2005.
Kniffen, Fred. "Folk Housing: Key to Diffusion." Annals of the Association of American Geographers LV, no. 4 (December, 1965): 547-577.
___. "To Know the Land and its People." Landscape IX, no. 3 (Spring, 1960): 20-23.
Knoedler, Christiana. The Harmony Society. A Nineteenth Century American Utopia. New York: Vantage Press, 1954.
Kouwenhoven, John. "American Studies: Words or Things?" In American Studies in Transition, edited by Marshall Fishwick, 15-35. Boston: Houghton Mifflin Company, 1964..
Kring, Hilda A. "The Harmonists: A Folk-Cultural Approach." Ph.D. diss., University of Pennsylvania, 1969.
Krueger, Nancy A. "The Woolen and Cotton Manufactory of the Harmony Society With Emphasis on the Indiana Years, 1814-1825." M.A. thesis, State University of New York College at Oneonta, 1983.
Kuhns, Oscar. The German and Swiss Settlements of Colonial Pennsylvania. New York: Henry Holt and Company, 1901. Reprinted by AMS Press, 1971.
Lapisardi, Emily. "Harmony Society Silk: A Celebration of Aesthetics, Craftsmanship, and Ideology." Communal Societies 26, no. 1 (2006): 26-35.
Lerner, John. "Nails and Sundry Medicines: Town Planning and Public Health in the Harmony Society 1805-1840" Western Pennsylvania Historical Magazine XL, no 2 (June, 1962): 115-138; and no 3, (September, 1962): 209-227.
Leslie's Weekly (April 25, 1895), 274.

Lichten, Frances. Folk Art of Rural Pennsylvania. New York: Charles Scribner's Sons, 1946.
Lindley, Harlow, ed. Indiana as Seen by Early Travelers. Indianapolis: Indiana Historical Commission, 1916.
Lipscomb, Andrew, ed. The Writings of Thomas Jefferson. 20 vols. Washington: The Thomas Jefferson Memorial Association, 1903.
List, Frederick. Outlines of American Political Economy. Philadelphia, 1827.
Lockridge, Ross F. The Old Fauntleroy Home. New Harmony: New Harmony Memorial Commission, 1939.
___. The Labyrinth. New Harmony: New Harmony Memorial Commission, 1941.
Lockwood, George Browning. New Harmony Communities. Marion, Indiana, 1902.
Lubar, Stephen and W. David Kingery. History from Things: Essays on Material Culture. Washington: Smithsonian Institution Press, 1993.
Ludwig, G. M. "The Influence of the Pennsylvania Dutch in the Middle West." Pennsylvania Folklore Society X (1945).
MacDonald, Donald. "The Diaries of Donald MacDonald, 1824-1826." Indiana Historical Society Publications XIV, no. 2 (1942): 143-379.
MacDonald, Robert R. "Toward a More Accessible Collection: Cataloging at the Mercer Museum." Museum News XLVIII, no, 6 (February, 1969): 23-26.
McMinn, Joseph H. Blooming Grove. A History of the Congregation of German Dunkers, etc. Williamsport, Pennsylvania, 1901.
Martineau, Harriet. Society in America. New York: Saunders and Otley, 1837.
Mason, Harrison Deming. Old Economy As I Knew It. Pittsburgh, 1926.
Matter, Evelyn P. The Baker House. Old Economy: Pennsylvania Historical and Museum Commission, 1972.
___. The Great House. Old Economy: Pennsylvania Historical and Museum Commission, 1970.
Mead, Sidney E. "Denominationalism: The Shape of Protestantism in America." In Essays in Colonial History edited by Paul Goodman. New York: Holt, Rinehart and Winston, 1967.
Melish, John. Travels in the United States of America in the Years 1806, 1807, 1809, 1810, and 1811. 2 vols. Philadelphia, 1812.
Merton, Robert K. "The Unanticipated Consequences of Purposive Social Action."American Sociological Review I (1936): 894-904.
Michaux, Francois A. Travels to the West of the Allegheny Mountains. London: B. Crosby andCo., 1805. Reprinted in Thwaites, III, 105-306.
Millar, Donald. "An Eighteenth Century German House in Pennsylvania." The Architectural Record LXIII, no. 2 (February, 1928): 161-168.
Miller, Melvin R. "Education in the Harmony Society, 1805-1905." Ph.D. diss., University of Pittsburgh, 1972.
Miller, Timothy. American Communes, 1860-1960: A Bibliography. New York: Garland Publishers, 1990.

___ The 60s Communes: Hippies and Beyond. Syracuse: Syracuse University Press, 1999.

Miller, Warren C. "Utopian Communities in Warren County, Pennsylvania." Western Pennsylvania Historical Magazine XLIX, no. 4 (October, 1966): 301-317.

Morley, Edith J., ed. Crabb Robinson in Germany, 1800-1805. London: Oxford University Press, 1929.

Morrison, Hugh. Early American Architecture. New York: Oxford University Press, 1952.

Mumford, Lewis. The City in History. New York: Harcourt, Brace & World, 1961.

Murdock, George. Outline of Cultural Materials. New Haven: Yale University Press, 1965.

Murray, Peter. Renaissance Architecture. New York: Harry Abrams, 1971.

Murtagh, William J. Moravian Architecture and Town Planning. Chapel Hill: University of North Carolina Press, 1967.

New Harmony as Seen by Participants and Travelers. Philadelphia: Porcupine Press, 1975.

Nordhoff, Charles. The Communistic Societies of the United States, from Personal Visit and Observation. New York: Harper & Bros., 1875. Reprint. New York: Dover Publications, 1966.

North, Douglass C. The Economic Growth of the United States, 1790-1860. New York: W. W. Norton, 1966.

Noyes, John Humphrey. History of American Socialisms. Philadelphia: J. P. Lippincott. Reprint. New York: Dover Publications, 1966.

Noyes, Pierrepont. My Father's House: An Oneida Boyhood. New York: Farrar & Rinehart, 1937.

Owen, Robert Dale. Threading My Way: Twenty Seven Years of Autobiography. New York: G. W. Carleton and Co., 1874.

Owen, William. "Diary of Wiliam Owen. November 10, 1824 –April 20, 1825." Indiana Historical Society Publications, IV, no. 1 (1906).

Passavant, William A. "A Visit to Economy in the Spring of 1840." Western Pennsylvania Historical Magazine IV, no. 3 (July, 1921): 144-149.

Pears, Thomas and Sarah Pears. New Harmony, An Adventure in Happiness. Papers of Thomas and Sarah Pears. Edited by Thomas Pears, Jr. Indianapolis, 1933.

Peat, Wilbur D. Indiana Houses of the Nineteenth Century. Indianapolis: Indiana Historical Society, 1962.

Pillsbury, Richard. "The Public or Market Square in Pennsylvania Before 1820." Proceedings of the Pennsylvania Academy of Science XLI (1967).

___. "The Street Names of Pennsylvania Before 1820" Proceedings of the Pennsylvania Academy of Science XVII, no. 3 (September, 1969): 214-222.

___. "The Urban Street Pattern as a Cultural Indicator: Pennsylvania, 1682-1815." Annals of the Association of AmericanGeographers LX (September, 1970): 428-446.

___. "The Urban Street Pattern of Pennsylvania Before 1815: A Study in Cultural Geography." Ph. D. diss., Pennsylvania State University, 1968.

Pillsbury, Richard and Andrew Kardos. A Field Guide to the Folk Architecture of the Northeastern United States. Dartmouth, New Hampshire: Geography Publications at Dartmouth, No. 8.

Pitzer, Donald E. ed. America's Communal Utopias. Chapel Hill, The University of North Carolina Press, 1997.

___. "The Harmonist Heritage of Three Towns." Historic Preservation 29, no. 4 (Oct.-Dec. 1977): 5-10.

___. "Harmonist Folk Art Discovered." Historic Preservation 29, no.4 (Oct-Dec. 1977): 11-12.

___. "The New Moral World of Robert Owen and New Harmony." In American Communal Utopias, edited by Donald Pitzer, 88-134. Chapel Hill, The University of North Carolina Press.

Pitzer, Donald E. and Connie A. Weinzapfel. "Utopia on the Wabash: The History of Preservation in New Harmony." Cultural Resource Management 24, no. 9 (2001): 18-20.

Popp, Herman. Die Architektur Der Barock und Rokokozeit. Stuttgart: Julias Hoffman, 1924.

Porter, Lisa Ann. The Joiners of the Harmony Society. M.A. thesis, University of Delaware, 1999.

Pounds, Norman. The Medieval City. Westport: The Greenwood Press, 2005.

Prown, Jules David. "The Truth of Material Culture: History or Fiction?" In History from Things, edited by Stephen Lubar and W. David Kingery, 1-19. Washington: Smithsonian Institution Press, 1993.

Pursell, Carroll. Early Stationary Steam Engines in America. Washington: Smithsonian Institution Press, 1969.

Quimby, Ian, ed. Winterthur Portfolio 8. Charlottesville: University Press of Virginia, 1973.

Ramsey, John. "Economy and its Crafts." Antiques LVII (May, 1950): 366-367.

Randall, Richard H. American Furniture in the Museum of Fine Arts, Boston. Boston: Museum of Fine Arts, 1965.

Rasmussen, Holger, ed. Dansk Folkemuseum and Frilandsmuseet: History and Activities. Axel Steensberg in Honour of His 60th Birthday. Copenhagen: Nationalmuseet, 1966.

Raymond, Eleanor. Early Domestic Architecture of Pennsylvania. New York: William Helburn, 1931.

Reibel, Daniel B. A Guide to Old Economy. Harrisburg: The Pennsylvania Historical and Museum Commission, 1972.

___. Bibliography of Items Related to the Harmony Society. Ambridge: Pennsylvania Historical and Museum Commission, 1972.

Reibel, Daniel B. and Patricia Black. A Manual for Guides, Docents, Hostesses and Volunteers of Old Economy. Ambridge, Pennsylvania: The Harmonie Associates, 1970.
Reichmann, Felix and Eugene Doll. "Ephrata as Seen by Contempories." The Pennsylvania German Folklore Society XVII (1952).
Reiser, Catherine. "Pittsburgh, The Hub of Western Commerce, 1800-1850." The Pennsylvania German Folklore Society XVII (1952).
Renard, Georges. Guilds in the Middle Ages. London: G. Bell and Sons, 1918.
Reps, John. The Making of Urban America. Princeton: Princeton University Press, 1965.
___. Town Planning in Frontier America. Princeton: Princeton University Press, 1969.
Riedl, Norbert F. "Folklore and the Study of Material Aspects of Folk Culture." Journal of American Folklore LXXIX, 314 (October—December, 1966): 557-563.
Robacker, Earl F. Touch of the Dutchland. New York: A. S. Barnes, 1965.
Rohde, Eleanor Sinclair. Garden-Craft in the Bible. Freeport, New York: Books for Libraries Press, 1967. Reprint of the 1917 edition.
Roos, Frank J. Writings on Early American Architecture. Urbana: University of Illinois Press, 1968.
Rosenberger, Homer T. "Migrations of Pennsylvania Germans to Western Pennsylvania." Western Pennsylvania Historical Magazine LIII, no. 4 (October 1970): 319-335; and LIV, no. 1 (January, 1971): 58-76.
Rosenberger, Jesse L. The Pennsylvania Germans. Chicago: University of Chicago Press, 1923.
___. In Pennsylvania German Land, 1928—1929. Chicago: University of Chicago Press, 1929
Ruch, John S. "A Visit to Iptingen." Communal Societies 26, no. 1 (2006): 79-91.
Russell, Robert W. America Compared with England. London, 1848.
Saalman, Howard. Medieval Cities. New York: George Braziller, 1968.
St. George, Robert Blair. ed. Material Life in America, 1600-1860. Boston: Northeastern University Press, 1988.
Schlereth, Thomas J. Material Culture Studies in America. Nashville: The American Association for State and Local History, 1982.
___. Material Culture: A Research Guide. Lawrence: University Press of Kansas, 1985.
Schönes, Schwabenland. Stuttgart, 1968.
Sellers, Charles L. "Early Mormon Community Planning," Journal of the American Institute of Planners, XXVII, 1 (February, 1962), 24-30.
Siegner, Otto. Württemberg. Munich, 1966.
Siener, Otto. Württemberg. Tubingin, 1950.
Smallwood, William. Natural History and the American Mind. New York: Columbia University Press, 1941.

Snyder, Karl H. "An Architectural Monogrph: Moravian Architecture of
 Bethlehem, Pennsylvania." The White Pine Series of Architectural
 Monographs XIII, no.4 (1927).
Stanislawski, Dan. "The Origin and Spread of the Grid-Pattern Town."
 Geographical Review XXXVI (July, 1946): 105-120.
Stotz, Charles M. The Architectural Heritage of Early Western Pennsylvnia.
 Pittsburgh: University of Pittsburgh Press, 1966. Reprint of The Early
 Architecture of WesternPennsylvania. Pittsburgh: The Buhl Foundation, 1936.
___. "Threshold of the Golden Kingdom: The Village of Econony
 and its Restoration." In Winterthur Portfolio 8, edited by Ian Quinby, 133-
 169. Charlottesville: University of Press of Virginia, 1973.
Stoudt, John Jacob. Pennsylvania Folk Arts. Allentown, Schlechter's, 1948.
Stoudt, John Joseph. Early Pennsylvania Arts and Crafts. Cranbury, New York:
 A. S. Barnes and Co., 1964.
___. "Pennsylvania German Folk Art: An Interpretation." The
 Pennsylvania German Folklore Society XVIII (1966).
Swan, Mabel Munson. "Moravian Cabinetmakers of a Piedmont Craft Center."
 Antiques LIX, no. 6 (June, 1951): 456-459.
Swank, Scott. Arts of the Pennsylvania Germans. New York: W.W. Norton & Co.
 1983.
Thoughts on the Destiny of Man. Harmony: Harmony Society, 1924. Reprinted
 in Aaron Williams, The Harmony Society at Economy, Pennsylvania. New
 York: Augustus M. Kelley, 1971.
Thwaites, Reuben Gold. Early Western Travels. 32 vols. Cleveland, 1904-1907.
Tunnard,Christopher and Henry Hope Read. American Skyline. New York: The
 New American Library, 1956.
Turner, George Augustus. "The Harmony Society in Indiana." M.A. thesis
 Eastern Illinois University, 1963.
Tyler, Alice Felt. Freedom's Ferment. Minneapolis: University of Minnesota
 Press, 1944.
Versluis, Arthur. "Western Esotericism and the Harmony Society." Esoterica I,
 no. 1(1999):20-47.
Wagner, Elise M. Economy of Old and Ambridge of Today. Centennial
 Souvenir Program, 1924.
Wade, Richard. The Urban Frontier. Chicago: University of Chicago Press,
 1964.
Waterman, Thomas. The Dwellinigs of Colonial America. Chapel Hill: The
 University of North Carolina Press, 1950.
Weller, Karl and Arnold Weller. Württembergische Geschichteim
 Südwestdeutschen Raum. Stuttgart: Conrad Theiss, 1971.
Wetzel, Richard. "The Music of George Rapp's Harmony Society, 1806-1906."
 Ph. D. diss., University of Pittsburgh, 1970.
Whitehall, Walter M. A Cabinet of Curiosities. Charlottesville: University Press
 of Virginia, 1967.

White, Joseph. "Harmony in History and Memory, 1805-2005." Communal Societies, 26, no.1 (2006): 93-103.
Williams, Aaron. The Harmony society at Economy, Pennsylvania. Pittsburgh, 1866. Reprint. New York: Augustus M. Kelley, 1971.
Williams, Henry Lionel. Country Furniture of Early America. New York: A. S. Barnes and Company, 1963.
Williams, Henry Lionel and Ottalie K. Williams. A Guide to Old American Homes, 1700-1900. New York: A. S. Barnes and Company, 1962.
___. Old American Houses and How to Restore Them. Garden City, New York: Doubleday and Company, 1946.
Wilson, John H. The Historic Town of Harmony, Butler County, Pennsylvania, 1937.
Wilson, William. The Angel and the Serpent. Bloomington: Indiana University Press, 1964.
___. Indiana, A History. Bloomington: Indiana University Press, 1966.
Wittkower, Rudolf. Architectural Principles in the Age of Humanism. New York: Random House, 1965.
Wertenbaker, Thomas J. The Founding of American Civilization: The Middle Colonies. New York: Charles Scribner's Sons, 1938.
Wilson, John. H. The Historic Town of Harmony. 1937.
Zucker, Paul. Town and Square. New York: Columbia University Press, 1959.

INDEX

African-Americans, Stag Family, 60
Alchemy, 97, painting in Great House, 156, 165, George and Frederick interested in, 165
Andreae, Johann Valentin, Christianopolis, 49-50
Amana Society 1,2, 4, 5, 42, 127, 130
  furniture, 127
Ambridge, Pennsylvania, 15.
Andrews, Edward Deming and Faith, 12
Arndt, Karl J R. 12, 26, 98, 99, 161, 163
Articles of Association 1805, 19-20
Aurich, Germany, 80

Baker, Romelius, 57
Baker House, 71, 75
  furnishings, 131, 139-140
Beaver Falls, Pa., 35-36
Beds, 128, 140-141, 145, 146, 171
Beiter, Simon, 163
Bernhard, Karl
  description of factories, 117-118
  fire engine, 166
Bestor, Arthur, 2, 3
Bethel, Missouri 35
Biessel, Johann Conrad, 3
Bishop Hill, Illinois, 1, 5
Blair, Don, 71
Blane, William Newnham, 6-7
Boehme, Jacob, Hirten Brief, 153
Böhm, Eusebius
  map of Harmony, 163
Books
  library at Economy, 59, 93,96, 123
  sold at Economy store, 158-159,
  offered for sale to Harmonists, 159,
  in Harmonist schools, 159,
  printed by Harmonists 160
Boneset tea, 170
Botanical garden, 53, 180
Breitenstein, Henry,
  non member cabinetmaker, 129
Brewer, Priscilla, 4

Brown, Matthew
  describes museum, 104
Buckingham, James Silk,
  describes church at Economy, 105, 154
  paintings in Economy museum, 157
Buildings,
  Locations, 56-61
Burns, Ken, 13

Carey, Matthew, 15-16
Celibacy, 2, 7, 10, 23-25, 34, 38, 60, 71-72, 82, 89, 118, 121, 124, 140, 145, 171, 175, 179, 182
Cemetery at New Harmony, 98
Chaffee, Grace,
  on Amana furniture, 124
Chairs, 131-133
  purchased, 133
Chests, 127, 133-135, 140, 141. 146, 171
Churches, 98-106
  at Harmony (1808), 98-99
  at New Harmony (1815), 100-102
  cruciform (1822) 102-103
  "Door of Promise," 103
  at Economy (1824 and 1831), 103-105
Clothing,, 120, 147-149,
  George Rapp's, 149
Commonwealth of Pennsylvania, 11,13
Commager, Henry Steele, 8
Commercial buildings , 113-116
Commonwealth of Pennsylvania, 11, 12, 13
Connoquenessing Creek, 19, 28, 42, 43, 45, 58
Copeland, Aaron, 12
Cortambert, Louis,
  painting, 157
Cummings, John, 132
Cupboard, dish or wine, 138

Daut, John, joiner, 128-129
Dickens, Charles, 1, 30
Dormitories, at New Harmony, 11, 56, 65, 70, 75, 76-82, 91, 119, 121, 123, 124, 182

199

Dormitories, Shaker, 78, 79
Drawings,
 by members, 96, 148, 161, 173, 180
Duclos, Victor Colin, describes greenhouse
 at New Harmony, 54, houses, 72
 dormitories at New Harmony, 79
 church at New Harmony, 101
Duss, John, 13, 24 36, 96, 104, 129, 166, 181
Duss, Susie 13, 127

Economy, Pennsylvania,
 described by Nordhoff, 36, 39-40
Eberman, John, clockmaker, 100, 104
Education, 96, 97, 98, 99, 155, 160
Egbert, Donald Drew, 9, 88
Ephrata 3, 17, 26, 67, 80, 176
 Saal, 67
 Sisters' house, 80
Ernst, Ferdinand,
 describes New Harmony inn, 119

Factories and Mills, 116-119
Feast Hall, 33, 50, 56, 88-98
 style similar to dormitories, 89
 celebrations in *saal* 89-90,
 gambrel roof, 90-91,
 trompe l'oeil interior wall, 92,
 museum in, 94-96,
 kitchen kettles, 81,
 events in, 89-90
Fire engine,
 purchased from Patrick Lyons, 165-166
 made by Harmonists, 166
Flaharty, David, 109
Fordham, Elias Pym, 71
Flower, George 15
 Describes cruciform church, 101
Flower, Richard, 32
Fourier, Charles, 40, 67, 68, 176

Gallatin, Albert, 16
Glassie, Henry, 74
Gormley, Agnes,
 describes Great House furnishings, 141, 142
Graff, Mary, 150
Granaries, 111-113
Griffin, W.R., proposal for gas lighting, 142
Grotto 106-109,
 interior symbolism, 108,
 plasterer's bill for, 108-109,
 restored, 109

Haller, Dr. P.F. C., 19
Harmony, Pennsylvania,
 annual report, 25,
 described by Melish, 39

Harmony Society,
 Articles of agreement, 19-20,
 investments, 162-163
Hebert, William 94,
 describes 1822 church, 97,
 describes clothing, 141-142
Hinds, William, 15
Historic American Buildings Survey, 71
Hotel (Inn), 55-57,-114
Houses, 54, 67-76,
 prefabricated parts purchased, 70,
 floor plans, 73-74
Households, 68
Hulick, Jacob,
 offers books for purchase, 152
Hulme, Thomas, 6, 29-30
Hunter, John Livingston, 159

Inns, 119-120
Investments, external, 36, 37, 92, 125, 160, 167, 169, 170, 181
Iptingen, Germany, 18, 41, 46, 47, 48, 49, 54, 62, 73, 105, 128

Jefferson, Thomas, 16-17, 25, 41, 95, 104
Jenkins, William,
 grotto plasterer, 103
Johnson, Paul, 9
Jung, Georg, joiner, 122-123

Kanter, Rosabeth Moss, 144
Kauffman, Peter, requests belongings, 128
Kelly, Robert, 8-9
Kemble, Fanny,
 performance seen by Frederick Rapp, 150
Koch, Albert, 91
König, David
 joiner, 122
Knoedel, Johan,
 name on chest 128
Knoedler, Christiana, describes feast at Economy, 140-141
Kraybill, Nancy, 161-163
Kring, Hilda, 85, 108

Labyrinth, 106-107

201

Landis, Mary Ann, 107
Lee, Mother Ann, 3,
Leon, Count, 25, 34-36, 78, 128
Leibbrandt, Andrew, perpetual motion machine, 165
List, Friedrich, 15,
  describes gardem at Economy, 53
Lowell, Massachusetts, 113-114
Ludwig, Duke Eberhard, 48
Ludwigsburg, Germany, 49, 54

Magazine subscriptions, 159-160
Mansard roof, 79
MacDonald, William, clothing at Economy, 142
Mather, Cotton, 148
McLain, J. and furniture being moved, 121
McClure, John, 158
Mechanics' Building, 108-109
Melish, John, 39, 54. 105-106, 119
Mengs, Anton,
  Adoration of the Shepherds, 149
Miller, Timothy, 3
Monticello, 17
Mormons, 35, 84, 77
Morris, Dr. B.W., 92
Morison, Samuel Eliot, 8
Müeller, Dr. J. Christoph, 54, 60, 70, 94, 96, 160, 164
Müller House, Milbach, Pennsylvania, 77
Museum, 93-96
Music, 110, 147, 160, 163, 164,
  piano purchased by Frederick. Rapp, 164
Mutschler, Hildegarde, 165

Neff, Joseph, 60
Nevins, Allan, 8
New Harmony, Indiana,
  described by Blane, 7, Woods, 7, Hulme, 8, 30
  Duclos, 54, 72
  Scheel inscription on stair, 10,
  dormitories, 78-82
Niles, Hezekiah, 15
Non-Intercourse Acts, 27
Nordhoff, Charles 5, 15, 37, 39-40, 149, 168, 175
North, Douglas, 27
Noyes, John Humphrey 5, 15, 44

Ohio River, 15, 27, 36, 39, 43, 45, 52-53, 58, 61
Oil and gas interests, 162
Oneida Perfectionists 5-6,
  complex marriage, 5, 69
  stirpiculture, 5
Owen, Robert, 12, 30, 32, 40, 54, 67, 79, 76, 97, 103, 176
Owen, Robert Dale,
  describes grotto at New Harmony, 107

Paintings,
  in museum, 95, 157
  in Rapp House, 122, 142, 155-156
  purchased, 155-156
  non-religious, 157
Passavant, William,
  describes George Rapp's house, 59-60,
  describes trees at Economy, 62
  describes George Rapp's clothing, 149
Patterson, Samuel, 31
Pavilion, 54, 90, 92, 109-111,
  statue *Harmonie* 153
Pennsylvania Historical Commission,
  Duss collection donated to, 128
  Stirpiculture, 4
Periodicals, 158, 183-184
Perpetual motion machine, 165
Philadelphia American Advertiser, 167
Philadelphia National Gazette and Literary Register, 7
Phrenology, 165
Pillsbury, Richard, 51
Pittsburgh Gazette, 35
Pitzer, Donald, 2, 4,
Plato's Republic, 22
Port Royal House, Frankford, Pennsylvania, 85
Porter, Lisa Ann, on joiners, 129, 132,
Pounds, Norman 47
Prown, Jules, 10-11
Puritans, 22

Railroad engines, 167
Rapp House, 83-88
  furnishings described, 141
Rapp, Frederick,
  on celibacy, 24
  financial leader. 29
  death of 36,
  classical influence on 48-49,
  and Lombardy poplars, 61,
  community architect, 29, 68, 77, 86,

105, 177
  in house adjoinng George Rapp's, 83,
  remove kettles from dormitory, 81
  purchased paintings, 95, 156-157
  sees performance by Fanny Kemble, 150
  practiced alchemy, 165
  perpetual motion machine, 165
Rapp, George,
  in Iptingen, 18
  withdraws from church, 18
  citizenship, 18
  Articles of Association. 19-20
  meets Thomas Jefferson, 16-17
  on celibacy, 23-24
  location of main road, 52
  on dormitories, 80-81
  problems with young, 81
  destroy letters, 81
  Thoughts on the Destiny of Man, 55
  House 83-88,
  plans for dormitory, 80
  size of bed, 145
  velvet robe, 149
  influenced by Jacob Boehme, 153
  practiced alchemy, 165
Rapp, Gertrude,
  granddaughter of George Rapp, 44,
  stayed with Shakers, 44,
  and silk industry, 62, 124, 160,
  receives premium for silk production, 168,
  paintings, 161-162,
  played organ and piano, 156-157
Rapp, John, 21
  only Harmonist gravestone, 103
  rose motif on gravestone, 151
Rectilinear plan 46-51, 64
Roebling, J. A.
  on George Rapp, 8
Rose motif, 85, 152
Rush, Benjamin 110
Ruskin, John, 10

Saxe-Weimar, Duke of describes Owen "invention" 97
Say, Thomas, 96
Scheel, Lorenz Ludwig, inscription on dormitory stair, 11
Schism, 25, 36, 82, 96, 104, 118, 128
Schrank, 135-136
Shakers 1-6,
  Mother Ann Lee, 3,
  Eldress Gertrude Soule, 13,

West Union, Indiana, 43,
  chairs, 131, 132
Silk Industry, 62, 168, 169
  and Gertrude Rapp, 161,
  awards, 168,
  abandoned industry, 168,
  pieces made for George and Frederick Rapp, 169
Slater, Philip, 21
Soule, Eldress Gertrude, 13
Static electricity machine, 95, 164
Steamboat "William Penn" 53, 167
  "Pittsburgh and Wheeling Packet," described 167
Steam engines, 10, 43, 58, 64, 116, 117, 166
Street patterns, 46-51
Stanislawski, Dan, 47
Static electricity machine, 95, 164
Stotz, Charles, on grotto, 105
Stuhl, 130, 132
Sturm, J.W., sells museum items, 95
Stuttgart, 18, 48, 49, 91
Symbolic motifs,
  Virgin Sophia, 85, 152, 153, 172
  Golden Rose, 103, 151
  Lily, 85, 152, 172
  Pelican, 154, 172

Tables, kitchen, 133-134,
  side, 136, 148,
  in Feast Hall, 93, 141
Telescope, achromatic, 157
Teniers, David the Younger
  painting of alchemist, 156, 165
Thoreau, Henry, 33
Thoughts on the Destiny of Man, 55, 152, 160
Thurmond, Lawrence, 142
Town square, 51
Tyler, Alice Felt, 1

Ulrich, Karl, cabinetmaker, 123

Versailles, 109
Vincennes Western Sun,
  on Rush statue, 110
Village Square and Garden 51-56
Vitruvius, De Architectura, 48

Wabash River, 28, 31, 43, 58, 162
War of 1812, 27

Water system, 63-64,
    pumps, 63, 112, 117, 166
Way, Abishai 72
Weingartner, Wallrath,
    drawings of birds, 161,
    maps, 162-163
West, Benjamin,
    Christ Healing the Sick, 157
West Union, Indiana, Shakers, 4, 43, 44, 78, 124
Williams, Aaron, on grotto, 109
Williamsport, Pennsylvania, 19
Whitwell, Stedman 40, 50
Whittaker, James, 3
Wilson, Alexander,
    American Ornithology, 161
Wunderkammer, 94
Woods, John, 7

Württemberg, Germany, 7, 46, 48, 50, 74, 93, 123

Zinn, Howard, 8
Zoar, Ohio, 1, 21, 42, 163
Zoarites 6

Paul Douglas

Dr. Paul Douglas received his Ph.D. in American Studies at George Washington University and is currently a Professor of American Studies at Towson University in Baltimore. Dr. Douglas has published in the areas of communal studies, American inventors, and the works of publisher Charles Carrington. Most recently, Douglas has edited a 19th century travel narrative, Louis Jacolliot's *Voyage to the Country of Liberty*. Dr. Douglas has been a Fulbright lecturer in Turkey and an exchange professor in China.